THE FAMILY AND ITS FUTURE

The Family and its Future

A Ciba Foundation Symposium

Edited by
KATHERINE ELLIOTT

 J. & A. CHURCHILL
104 GLOUCESTER PLACE, LONDON
1970

First published 1970

With illustrations

International Standard Book Number 0.7000.1462.4

Printed in Great Britain

Contents

Membership

Symposium on The Family and its Future
held 10th–12th March 1970

Alex Comfort (Chairman)	Department of Zoology, University College, Gower Street, London, W.C.1, England
Jane Abercrombie	University College Environmental Research Group, Bartlett School of Architecture, University College, Gower Street, London, W.C.1, England
James L. Adams	Andover Newton Theological School, Newton Centre, Massachusetts 02159, U.S.A.
Tara Ali Baig	An Noor, R-8 Hauz Khas, New Delhi-16, India
Mario Borrelli	Oratory of St. Philip, Via Duomo 142, Naples, Italy
Nan Fairbrother	27 Weymouth Mews, London, W.1, England
Ronald Fletcher	Cranmere, Halesworth Road, Reydon, Southwold, Suffolk, England
Robin Fox	Department of Anthropology, Rutgers University, New Brunswick, New Jersey 08903, U.S.A.
Ralph G. Hendrickse	The Liverpool School of Tropical Medicine, Pembroke Place, Liverpool 3, England
Fernando Henriques	Centre for Multi-racial Studies, University of Sussex, Brighton, BN1 9QN, England
Hilde Himmelweit	Department of Psychology, The London School of Economics and Political Science, Houghton Street, Aldwych, London, W.C.2, England
Edmund Leach	The Provost's Lodge, King's College, Cambridge, England
Anne McLaren	Institute of Animal Genetics, University of Edinburgh, West Mains Road, Edinburgh, EH9 3JN, Scotland

Derek Miller	Department of Psychiatry, The University of Michigan Medical Centre, Ann Arbor, Michigan 48104, U.S.A.
John Newson	Child Development Research Unit, Department of Psychology, University of Nottingham, Nottingham, MG7 2RD, England
Norman W. Pirie	Biochemistry Department, Rothamsted Experimental Station, Harpenden, Hertfordshire, England
Rhona Rapoport	The Tavistock Institute of Human Relations, Human Resources Centre, Tavistock Centre, Belsize Lane, London, N.W.3, England
François H. M. Raveau	École Pratique des Hautes Études, Centre Charles Richet, 8 Boulevard des Invalides, Paris 7, France
Vernon Reynolds	Department of Sociology, University of Bristol, 91 Woodland Road, Bristol, BS8 1US, England
Su Rogers	Richard and Su Rogers Architects, 32 Aybrook Street, London, W1M 4BB, England
Ettore Rossi	Klinik für Kinderkrankheiten, Universität Bern, Freiburgstrasse 23, 3000 Bern, Switzerland
Thorsten Sjövall	Settervallsväg 15, Nacka, Stockholm, Sweden
Olive M. Stone	The London School of Economics and Political Science, Houghton Street, Aldwych, London, W.C.2, England
Nicholas Tavuchis	Department of Sociology, University of Cornell, McGraw Hall, Ithaca, N.Y. 14850, U.S.A.
Robert S. Weiss	Department of Psychiatry, Harvard Medical School, 58 Fenwood Road, Boston, Massachusetts 02115, U.S.A.

The Ciba Foundation

The Ciba Foundation was opened in 1949 to promote international cooperation in medical and chemical research. It owes its existence to the generosity of CIBA Ltd, Basle, who, recognizing the obstacles to scientific communication created by war, man's natural secretiveness, disciplinary divisions, academic prejudices, distance, and differences of language, decided to set up a philanthropic institution whose aim would be to overcome such barriers. London was chosen as its site for reasons dictated by the special advantages of English charitable trust law (ensuring the independence of its actions), as well as those of language and geography.

The Foundation's house at 41 Portland Place, London, has become well known to workers in many fields of science. Every year the Foundation organizes six to ten three-day symposia and three to four shorter study groups, all of which are published in book form. Many other scientific meetings are held, organized either by the Foundation or by other groups in need of a meeting place. Accommodation is also provided for scientists visiting London, whether or not they are attending a meeting in the house.

The Foundation's many activities are controlled by a small group of distinguished trustees. Within the general framework of biological science, interpreted in its broadest sense, these activities are well summed up by the motto of the Ciba Foundation: *Consocient Gentes*—let the peoples come together.

Preface

'Man and his Future' was the subject of an unusual Ciba Foundation symposium in 1963, and the controversy it aroused continues. It seemed appropriate in 1970 to look again at the impact of further scientific development, especially in the field of human reproduction, from the viewpoint of those immediately affected. For the first time in history woman is mistress of her fecundity; the implications for the world are profound and their foreshadowing still faint. Everywhere institutions are under scrutiny and criticism, and the oldest institution devised by mankind is the family. Its future concerns us all.

Among the diverse group assembled to discuss 'The Family and its Future' women were worthily represented. But sex antagonism has no place when, as Professor Derek Miller said in one of the discussions, "Behind each family now there is the blast of Hiroshima" and, in the face of increasing secularization, an estranged and turbulent youth is searching for a new ethic.

Apart from some illuminating sallies into Asian, African, Peruvian and West Indian experience, the group concerned itself with the family in the Western world. The range of the discussions proved to be as wide as that of the contributing disciplines, and often highly subjective. If it achieved nothing more, the conference emphasized the need to bring hidden fears to light and to remedy our defects in communication, which showed up the more clearly perhaps because the subject was one striking so close to home.

From the beginning, Dr Alex Comfort gave encouragement, inspiration, advice and support; as expected, he was a most skilful Chairman and threaded together the differing topics, interests and backgrounds throughout the meeting.

Sympathetic help came from Professor David Riesman, Professor Jerome Bruner, Dr Martha Wolfenstein, Professor M. Nagai, Dr John Bowlby, Professor W. J. Goode and Professor J. M. Tanner, and the members of the symposium contributed greatly by being, from the outset, warmly interested in the whole idea and open-minded in their participation.

Making the symposium proceedings into a book has been very much a family undertaking; all the Ciba Foundation editorial staff have enjoyed having a hand in it.

'Man and his Future' arose out of a suggestion first made by Dr Gregory Pincus and this book should again recall the debt owed to his work by millions of families at this time and in time to come.

KATHERINE ELLIOTT

1: Comparative Family Patterns

ROBIN FOX

I HAVE been asked to put the family into some kind of broad perspective and, to a general anthropologist like myself, this can roughly be described as comparative. The comparison is of two kinds: firstly it uses facts from various cultures to illustrate the range of variations within the species; secondly it uses facts about the evolution of the species to compare different stages of social development. The species as it stands today is the end product of a complex evolutionary process which has produced a creature, on the one hand moved to form certain bonds and pursue certain ends, and on the other hand intelligent and flexible enough to seek a variety of means to those ends. The range of variations cannot be understood without first understanding the themes on which the variations are played. These in turn can only be understood if we know what the creature is about in the first place, and this can only be understood from the knowledge of how it got to be that way. This species orientation, both comparative and evolutionary, is the one I shall adopt here.

As a preliminary, I must try to jeopardize the entire argument by asking whether or not we have a subject matter. Clearly in dealing with, say, contemporary industrial societies, we have a distinguishable social unit called the family consisting of parents and dependent children. For us this is so clearly a basic social, legal, domestic and economic unit that we tend to regard it as in some way inevitable. Sociologists and laymen both treat this unit as the basic building block of social systems, and, when they are being moralistic, of social order and stability. Sophisticated social scientists, recognizing that other arrangements are possible, nevertheless insist that extended families are based on nuclear family units by combining these cells into various patterns. (Note how the very term 'nuclear family' begs the question.) Some observers, realizing that such a position needs justification, have claimed that the nuclear family is universal because it is a basic biological unit; somehow the forming of nuclear families is in the beast. (It is ironic that many of those who claim this position in one breath, deny in the next that man has any biological propensities to social behaviour, and insist that all his institutions are cultural.)

It seems to me that we should be more open-minded about this issue, and ask ourselves, like good zoologists, just what the species does about matters such as the raising of children, and observe the patterns that

1

occur. After all the family is a complex arrangement with at least four basic dyads—father–child; mother–child; sibling–sibling; husband–wife; and it develops through time. Failure to see the family as essentially a dynamic unit composed of sub-units has vitiated, for example, discussions of incest and the incest taboo. Incest involves three other dyads—father–daughter, mother–son and brother–sister. Each of these represents a totally different kind of sexual relationship, and blanket remarks about the incest taboo miss the point, directed as they are to the family.

On the whole, it seems to me wise to consider the family less as an institution or unit and more as a field of action. In this field, various bonds operate for various purposes and it is the purposes that determine which bonds will be forged, which strengthened, which ignored. The biology of the species gives us not the family unit, but the potentiality for bonding which can be the basis of a nuclear family. It is quite possible that the bonds between family members are simply intensifications of more general bonds. Thus the father could be simply a special kind of older dominant male, the mother a special category of older nurturant female, and so on. This is important since many psychologists see the personality of the adult essentially as the playing out of family roles. The difficulties of young males with the older males are often put down to an *unresolved Oedipus complex*, in which all older males become the disliked father. This may well be putting the cart before the horse as the father may simply be the first adult male with whom the growing boy tries his combination of threat and bonding which he will try with all adult males anyway. In other words, the young male–old male bond shows up most strongly in the nuclear family but the problems inherent in it do not originate there.

This is a hypothetical example, but I think it is true. Equally I think that the relationship between a mother and her children is different; a mother is not simply an available older female to whom we react as such—she is essential to the mental and physical well-being of the child. The accumulation of facts on this issue is overwhelming. It is a basic ground-rule for any primate species that, if we want healthy and effective adults, we have to associate mother and child safely and securely through the critical period of birth at least to the point where the children become independently mobile. In humans, with their extremely long dependency period, this is even more important, so that in a very real sense the mother–child tie is the basic bond in our system of social relationships and one that is really taken over from nature (Diagram 1).* Thus, whatever else happens, any society needs to protect and provision its mother–child units. The impregnation of the mother is a relatively simple and brief

---

Key for Diagrams: o = Female; ∆ = male; ▅▅▅ = siblings; < --> = mating tie; '=' = institutionalized marriage tie; 1, 2, 3, . . ., n = indefinite number of possible other partners; (∆) = and (o) = peripheral member of group.

matter. There is no logical reason—although there may be many practical ones—for the putative genitor to pay any further attention to his sex partner. Why he so often does so must be explained, not just taken for granted. This approach treats the institution of marriage and the family as problematic rather than given.

One obvious way of protecting and provisioning the mother–child unit is to attach to it the mother's mate (Diagram 2). To attach one male to one female for these purposes can have advantages. For one thing, with equal sex ratios and simultaneous maturity in the sexes, this is statistically the most convenient. In many primates where females in the group exceed males (on average 4:1), the rates of maturity are different, with

females maturing twice as fast. Thus there are always more fertile females than males. To achieve such an imbalance in man, we have to falsify the position by, for example, raising the marriage age of males and lowering that of females. Other reasons for the one-to-one attachment are the sexual division of labour which requires contributions from both sexes, and the bonding effects of repeated sexual activity. None of these, however, requires a one-to-one assignment of mates, and even such an assignment does not necessarily lead to the setting up of family units in our sense. We must distinguish here between the existence of rights over females and the existence of actual domestic units. One thing that is clear is that in all human societies there is a regular assignment of mates— regulated sexual access. Random mating is rare or non-existent. But this simply establishes that all people have recognized spouses; it says nothing about the social units that emerge. Those who argue for the basicness or universality of the nuclear family are often saying only that most societies recognize and name the roles of husband–father, wife–mother. The point of this seems to be that if the woman's contribution to the economy is important (80 per cent of the food of hunters is vegetable) then rights over this are important. Equally, the mother–child unit's claim on animal protein is important. We still have not got a family in the popular magazine sense. We have moved up one stage from the primate pattern where the defence and coherence of the troop was in the hands of the males, but where food-sharing did not exist. Once hunting and food-sharing come on the scene the assignment of mates becomes more important and since women at this point become objects of exchange, rights over female offspring take on a previously non-existent importance.

Even so, this can work out in various non-familial ways. In some primitive hunters the total group pattern is still very like that of primates—the

4

females and young stay very much together as a group; the adult (initiated) males follow their own pursuits, while the adolescent (uninitiated) males form a peripheral set. Here the unit is the total group divided into these sub-units. Ecological pressures can force a different kind of organization. Sparse resources and large territory can force the group to split up. It may split into units of mother–child plus an adult male, or several mother–child units plus an adult male (Diagram 3). To call the

latter *nuclear families with a husband–father in common* is an almost ludicrous caricature. The advent of agriculture may settle these various types of units, thus perpetuating them; it also gives rise to other possibilities.

One is that the males attached to the mother–child unit can be consanguine rather than affinal (thus anthropologists sometimes distinguish consanguine families from conjugal families). The commonest of these schemes makes the brother(s) of a woman her protector and provisioner (Diagram 4). The incest taboo prevents him from becoming the father of

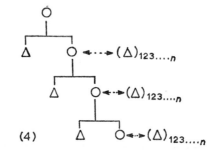

her children, but this can easily be taken care of by using other women's brothers for the task. This relatively logical solution is adopted in varying degrees and the reasons for the variation are not clear. At one extreme the brother–sister unit is the domestic commensal and legal unit, and the sisters are impregnated by males having no legal and certainly no domestic status in the household. The classic example of this scheme is that of the Nayar of Malabar. Here the bond that is activated for protection and provision is the brother–sister bond. The husband is reduced to genitor, with some rights of sexual access to a woman shared among several men. The brother–sister bond, in other systems, can remain the dominant legal tie, while domestic rights are granted to the genitor. Thus the other classic case, the Trobriand Islanders, has as its domestic unit the nuclear family, while the legal unit is the brother, sister and

sister's children (Diagram 5). Provisioning here again is partly the brother's responsibility. Among the Nayar the sisters are totally retained in
the consanguine family; the Trobriand woman is lent to a husband, but
rights over her children are retained by consanguines. Also, in the latter
case, her children are claimed back at puberty, making the nuclear family
a phase in the dynamics of the domestic cycle.

It is possible to work out other solutions which only minimally activate
the husband–wife tie. In the Western Pueblos, for example, the traditional domestic unit was the group of consanguine women with their
dependent offspring (Diagram 5). To this group (a grandmother, her

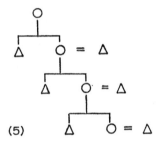

daughter and daughter's daughter, for example) two lots of males were
attached: sons/brothers and husbands/fathers, i.e. consanguine males
and affinal males. The economic provision of the household was primarily the business of the affinal males, the ritual provisioning that of
the consanguine males. Some affinal males became permanently attached
but it was very common for men to bring an affinal relationship to an end
and move on to another household. This has been described as a high
divorce rate, which begs the question. I prefer to describe it as a high
turnover of husbands. The female unit stays intact and does not need any
permanent males so long as some male help is provided from time to time.
The picture then is of the female households with males circulating
amongst them. Here the mother–daughter tie is activated and others
ignored. This is similar to patterns described for some ex-slave societies
and urban industrial populations where constellations of related
mother–child units form a domestic group, with both consanguine and
other males as a very variable quantity (Diagram 6). Interestingly, in
these circumstances the men seem to form their own all-male groups
(Damon Runyon's permanent floating crap game) and the adolescents
theirs. This corresponds, for example, to the Pueblo situation where the
men traditionally congregated in the *Kivas* and society houses. A tendency of all societies to strain towards this hunting pattern of adult-males
together, relatively separate from females-with-young, with adolescent
males as a third unit, seems universal. The problem of the females,
roughly speaking, seems to be to divert the attention of the males to

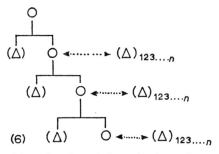

themselves; the problem for the adult males is to detach the young males from their mothers. Many institutions such as initiation ceremonies, for example, seem geared to the problems inherent in this basic division of the sexes.

A really firm attachment of the male to the mother–child group seems most likely when it is in his interest. Some socio-ecological situations demand the cooperative efforts of closely attached males, and in these instances fathers want to keep their sons with them (Diagram 7). This

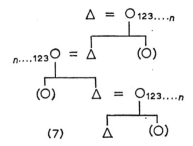

arrangement is more convenient in many ways than that of uncles trying to recover nephews at puberty. The father–son tie is thus made the spinal-cord of this system—but usually, as in China and Japan, it results in a strong mother–son attachment since the mother gives up her place in a consanguine group and attaches herself to her husband's unit. For various reasons she often sees her security as lying with her sons. The brother–sister tie here is ignored at the expense of the husband–wife, father–son and mother–daughter ties. Polygamy is common under such circumstances for obvious reasons, and so several mother–child units may be incorporated in the male groups by attachments to individual males. Such patriarchal extended families are very common (China, Africa, Indo-European, etc.).

In so far as the total group (e.g. the nation in welfare states like Sweden) can support the mother–child groups, no males need be attached to it. Societies, however, are rarely that generous. In most sub-human primate societies, the group as a whole is, in some sense, responsible for its members, and individual responsibilities are not assigned. The latter is part of the humanization breakthrough following hunting and food sharing.

What I am stressing here is that in all these arrangements the basic unit is that of mother–child and the basic problem that of its provisioning and protection in the context of the socio-ecological conditions of the society. Various other bonds—brother–sister, father–son, husband–wife —will be either exclusively or partially activated to meet the problem. The nuclear family is simply one of these solutions and one of the more common. Here the husband–wife tie is utilized to the exclusion of others, with all the attendant problems of a bond formed, not during socialization, but later in life between relative strangers who have to make a new and often difficult adjustment.

Also, it illustrates how we have to see as independent variables, for example, such seemingly related factors as marriage, household, domestic services, sexual access and legal authority. An example nearer home and from my own work might serve to make this point. A common custom in a small Irish island (of about 300 people) was for a couple who married to stay in their natal homes, sometimes for a period, sometimes for life. Children stayed with the mother and the father–husband had visiting rights and contributed to the wife's support. Typically a household consisted of a widow, her married and unmarried sons and daughters, and the children of the daughters (legitimate and illegitimate). Even in 1965, despite modern influences, 20 per cent of marriages adhered to this plan. Here again the consanguine ties of mother–child and brother–sister are emphasized at the expense of a reduced husband–wife tie, and the household is basically consanguineal.

Our own system (and those like it) makes all the above-mentioned variables coincide. Why this has happened must be explained by social historians—but in a sense it is for much the same reason as some very primitive systems make the same adaptation: there is a premium on mobility, and domestic units larger than the nuclear family are cumbersome; consanguine units are impractical.

The consequence, however, of dumping all the factors involved on to the nuclear family can be disastrous and this is why we should try to see it simply as one kind of solution rather than as a basic biological premise. Perhaps then we will not ask too much of it. So much is written about the breakdown of the family, about family failures and conflicts, neuroses and the like, that is inspired by a kind of mystical functionalism which sees the nuclear family as a God-given system that would work if only things didn't happen to spoil it. On the contrary, what is remarkable about so fragile an institution is that it works at all. The failures are probably simply those families which refuse to ignore the natural conflicts inherent in the situation, while the successes are the families with the greatest capacity for collective self-delusion.

As regards the future of the family in industrial society, our comparative and evolutionary approach suggests that instead of trying to prop up an institution of a supposedly given kind, we should explore the possibility of other combinations and permutations. If the family were indeed a given, we might rightly be perturbed if it were threatened. But since the mother–child tie is our only given, then we are free to ring a number of changes around the security of this unit: rotating spouses, consanguineal households, temporary unions, communal establishments and even legalized (as opposed to informal) polygamy for those able to afford it, may all be possible in the automated, affluent world of the future. Rather than trying to preserve the family we should perhaps be thinking of how we might transform it. All that is given in human nature is the mother–child bond and considerable imagination.

Bibliographical note
Readers can consult my *Kinship and Marriage* (Penguin Books, 1967) for further development of the argument and sources. On the mother–child tie, however, they should see John Bowlby, *Attachment and Loss, Vol. 1: Attachment* (London: Hogarth Press and Institute of Psychoanalysis, 1969).

DISCUSSION

Miller: What is missing from Dr Fox's presentation is any concept of personality development. The mother–child unit is certainly the basic unit but if no father figure is present the child, particularly a male child, apparently has great difficulty in establishing any sense of its own identity. Dr Fox wondered how societies persuade fathers to stay around. In the nuclear family the accent is on mothering, so males inevitably develop a strong identification with their mothers. They stay with the mother and infant to act as a mother as well as a father. In Poland for example, a whole generation of males grew up after the 1939–1945 war who had little concept of a father's role; they knew how mothers behaved but not fathers. As a society perhaps we 'hook' fathers into staying with the family by mothering the male for too long.

Fairbrother: During the war I brought up two children in a country community which was based on the mother-child unit alone—with the State as the providing male. At the clinic in the local town the many young mothers with their children all seemed to me most alarmingly self-sufficient and happy, wheeling their babies out together in flocks. A few still had their husbands at home and the ones without husbands rather pitied them, because they had these males upsetting their nice tidy mother–baby households. I felt very sorry for the husbands; I often wonder what happened when the families were reunited after the war and how the fathers adapted.

Fox: Groups of mothers and children often form very cohesive and supportive units amongst themselves, to which males are peripheral.

Fletcher: Dr Fox, it seems to me that it is one thing to say that the family, including the institution of marriage, which distributes rights and allocates duties, is universal; and another thing to say that the nuclear family is *always* monogamous. Nobody has claimed the latter.

Fox: I was not equating the nuclear family with monogamy; Murdock for example insists that polygynous families are really just a group of nuclear families with one husband in common, because he thinks that the nuclear family is universal[2]. I maintain they are not combinations of nuclear families, but combinations of mother–child units to which males are attached in one way or another.

Fletcher: I do not think you have said anything to justify the idea that one biological relationship, namely that between mother and child, is any more basic than any other. You have said there is no logical reason why a man should stay around; but—equally—there is no logical reason why a woman should stay around. You assume the existence of bio-psychological ties which link mothers with children. If these exist and if, as you also say, there are distinctive relationships between the children, there are probably other ties as well. It seems to me you have simply washed over the question of whether there are not similar bio-psychological elements in pair bonding, sexuality and the like. From your argument it is just as possible for human society ingeniously to mess about with substitute mothers, as it is with substitute fathers. I myself don't believe this, but you have not demonstrated the opposite to my satisfaction.

Fox: In some senses it is logically possible to do anything, but you must have a premise to start any logical system from and my premise is that to have viable communities you must have a mother–child association during a certain period. Certainly there are deep instinctive things to do with repeated sexual interaction that set up bonding relationships between males and females, and all I am saying is that these sometimes just do not get activated, whereas the mother–child relationship cannot be deactivated.

Fletcher: Yes, but my point is that you haven't given good reasons why that relationship cannot be deactivated.

Fox: I could go on for great lengths about the experimental evidence for this and the whole field of Bowlbyism, which suggests that if you do not have a very intensive and particular kind of relationship between mother and child you fail to get the right kind of imprinting, you fail to get the right kind of social learning, and you fail to get the right kind of emotional learning[1]. I don't mean necessarily the actual mother who gave birth. They could be adopted or foster children. I am talking about social roles and not necessarily biological ones.

Rapoport: Surely the only irreducible unit is an adult–child unit? There has to be somebody older than the child to look after it, and that adult could be a man or a woman. We can look at history to get the possible range of patterns but we are here concerned with the future of the family. In technological fields it is a truism that the future is based on the past but equally that it may take new forms. The present form of the nuclear family has evolved from the past but in the future it may be the framework for new variations each of which may be functional for different purposes. We must begin to think about alternative forms in addition to all those Dr Fox has discussed. There are many current social movements which are thinking up new organizational forms for different kinds of child care and child–adult arrangements where the mother–child unit is not the necessary irreducible unit.

Comfort: But if you don't have the mother, you must at least have a lactating female.

Rapoport: Not necessarily. You can bottle-feed babies, and some males may be as good as some females at doing so.

Miller: I think Dr Rapoport means you must have a mother figure. I take it you are not suggesting you can bring up a child by having 19 different mother figures in one year.

Rapoport: No, but I am saying that this doesn't have to be a woman. What is needed is a close, stable nurturing relationship.

Miller: It might lead to a little sexual confusion later.

Rapoport: I agree there may be a whole series of problems later; this will depend on how society structures particular sex roles. The child is likely to be confused if the adult is confused. If society changes its basic early units and there are relatively clear and viable alternative models, there need not necessarily be any confusion in the child.

Comfort: I think there is a fair amount of evidence that it does have to be a woman. There is a great deal on the question of texture and softness which is important, and even perhaps odour.

Leach: Despite what Professor Fox has said, there are many societies which organize fostering quite systematically so that it becomes the norm rather than the exception to find children being reared in households other than that of their natural parents. In other words, the question whether the difference between the 'real' mother and the 'false' mother is socially significant is not something we can answer *a priori*. It will vary from one society to another.

Comfort: But it is usually a woman!

Leach: I do hope we won't get ourselves too much involved in whether or not 'the family' is a universal institution. The nuclear family of father, mother and children is an easy enough category to understand but it does not exist everywhere as the normal unit of domestic organization. Once we try to use the term 'family' in any more elaborate extended sense we will land ourselves in all kinds of difficulty. But in this connexion Professor Fox has made a very important contribution. He has pointed out that we have no need to suppose that all human societies can be broken down into simple nuclear bricks of the same kind which we can call families. On the contrary, empirical ethnography suggests that there are at least two kinds of basic brick. There are nuclear units which consist of mothers and their young children and there are other nuclear units which consist of groups of adult males. It only leads to confusion if we try to incorporate these two very different types of unit within a single verbal category labelled 'the family'.

Reynolds: I would like to make a case for at least a third kind of brick, which has received hardly any attention so far: this is the male–female brick. I think it follows from the way we have been arguing that whereas a prolonged mother–child bond is basic, fundamental and biological, a prolonged adult male–adult female bond is much less basic. In the nuclear family as a bit of social structure you have the basic mother–child unit and the not quite so basic male–female unit. The nuclear family thus constituted usually remains the structural unit, even if the male–female unit runs into difficulties and there is a change of partners. Thus marital breakdown does not imply that the nuclear family as such is in any trouble. What is in trouble is the idea that one male and one female should stick together with their particular children, but that is a problem for individuals and not for the nuclear family as a structural entity.

Stone: The basic problem is whether we should now turn to one of the older systems, or some other new system, instead of the nuclear family. To what kind of systems might we in our kind of society look now? In Great Britain we have had much trouble about the *Children and Young Persons Act, 1969,* much thinking and rethinking, and nobody seems to have very much idea of an alternative for looking after young children. What are the most likely alternatives?

Fox: I don't know; but we ought to be thinking about this and we may end up with a whole variety rather than just one alternative.

Stone: Another point: male rights over the females arose when men were few and there was more land than people to occupy it. We now have a completely different situation where the world is over-populated. Doesn't this make a complete break?

Fox: It does. Most of our existence is predicated on one set of assumptions about relations between males and females and children; we have now a vastly different situation to which we are neither emotionally, intellectually nor physically adapted.

Comfort: We shall return to this point when we consider how the control of fertility will lead to a relative shortage of sibs to participate in family relationships.

Fox: The important thing here being that we are playing around with a very ancient system. For 99 per cent of our existence as a species we have not lived as we live now. We are basically what we are—upper paleolithic hunters.

Raveau: Professor Fox said that the family is a field of action. I feel he is considering it as a micro-society with its own dynamics and isolated from interactions with global society. For example, other factors can be taken into consideration to explain the brother–sister relationship amongst the people in the west of Ireland, such as the fact that they are isolated—the same pattern happens in high valleys cut off from other cultures.

Fox: I was treating as problematical the whole question of why the males should bother to control or attach themselves to female groups at all. At some point there was a very important breakthrough in human evolution, and women became objects of value and exchange; therefore they became property to males. This is no longer true in our own society, in this very technical sense, but it is the context of our evolution. You can't consider this in isolation from the global society and this is why I was talking about treating males as a group and females and young as a group, each with its own interests.

Comfort: In Ireland it is still a question of land tenure, I think!

Weiss: There are really two points at issue. One is the definition of particular bonds and the emphasis that society gives to a particular bond, and the other is whether the society confines the male–female bond to one household or separates it between households. It is both interesting and useful to speculate about the advantages and disadvantages of various organizations for the adult and also for the children. What kinds of lives result from these different ways of siting particular bonds?

2: The Analysis of Family Roles*

NICHOLAS TAVUCHIS

THERE are many ways in which one could discuss such primordial, universal and complicated subjects as the part played by generation and sex roles within the family.[6, 21] Here I have chosen to focus on some general methodological difficulties in the study of such family role relationships. I am especially concerned with the methods of study and the theoretical assumptions commonly used and accepted in studies of contemporary family patterns, and with the kinds of conclusions and products (both the empirical findings and theoretical insights) that result from a commitment to these techniques and premises by social scientists. Any attempt to forecast changes in sex, age and kinship roles must take into account existing knowledge of the culture, society, or sub-group being studied, but I believe that our present knowledge relating to the family is founded on research methods and theoretical assumptions that are less valid than is generally thought, and that this affects the validity of the images of the family that we project and call 'reality'. Moreover, these distorted images shape the kinds of solutions and programmes viewed as sociologically feasible when policies which seek to alter, or preserve, existing structures and patterns are being made.

In the past two decades there has been an enormous growth in both the scholarly and the popular literature on marriage and the family which has sought to chart, analyse, exhort, deplore, and—on rare occasions—predict and implement changes in this durable and flexible institution. Much of this work has been concerned with the tortuous relations between family patterns and the global, elusive processes of modernization and urbanization. The issues and problems raised include population control (and less often, its composition and distribution); freedom of mate selection; primary and secondary socialization; sexual norms and behaviour; generation 'gaps'; the position of the aged; the functions of extended kin networks; family disorganization; and sexual equality and inequality. However, most of the empirical inquiries made into family patterns and processes suffer, in varying degrees, from inadequate research designs and samples and a lack of historical perspective. These defects are mainly due to the relatively low priority given to such studies of families and kinship except during periods of crisis or rapid social change, or at the urging of articulate interest groups. Only when the full

* I would like to thank my colleagues, Professors Rose Goldsen, Carolyn Sherif, William Lambert, and Donald Hayes, for their criticism and helpful suggestions.

impact of a depression is felt, or when urban ghettos explode, rural slums are discovered, occupational discrimination against women and others is revealed, illegitimacy starts to cost society money, population pressure and pollution become defined as social problems, or the drug culture invades the middle-class suburbs—only then do policy makers turn to family researchers for definitive answers to their over-simplified questions. It is precisely then that knowledge about the family is found wanting or dated. Evidently it is only during periods of stress and up- heaval that social scientists are consulted, in spite of the fact that the family is an active institution capable of exerting an independent force of its own and that the social sciences can often pinpoint the sources of future developments.

A major deficiency is that except for population analyses drawn mainly from census data and a few area studies,[9] no large-scale, representative, longitudinal studies of family and kinship have been made by teams that include the necessary skills of anthropologists, sociologists, psycholo- gists, demographers and home economists; and even the most basic demographic data, crucial for establishing family patterns—such as marriage, divorce, migration and illegitimacy statistics—are of vary- ing quality. Moreover, there have been few systematic attempts to sample specific racial, ethnic, religious, regional, generational, or class variations and similarities using a standard method that would allow results to be compared.[27] Yet texts on *The American Family* continue to appear!

The complexities of a heterogeneous population such as that of the United States, combined with its political/judicial sensitivities, would suggest that efforts should be concentrated on limited programmes of investigation. We might, for example, systematically sample the family life styles of ethnic groups of different generations in order to assess differences in the way sex roles are defined and patterns of authority are perceived. This would obviously be at the expense of making generaliza- tions about the kinship system as a whole, but it would be a useful start- ing point for a series of *related* investigations.

In fact, many of the studies that have been made claim a wider applica- tion than is justifiable. A typical defect that is basic, obvious, and yet frequently overlooked is that in sociological studies of family and kin- ship patterns in Western countries the informants are usually women. Unfortunately, this is also true of one of the fastest growing bodies of literature in the social sciences—family planning and fertility control.

In studies on non-Western and primitive societies, it is my impression that the opposite is generally true and that men are both the questioners and the informants. This impression is partially confirmed by Professor D. Paulme, introducing a collection of essays by women ethnologists on the role of women in certain tropical African cultures. She writes:

"Avoiding the usual preconceptions about the inferior position of women in a traditional African setting, each essay deals with woman in her everyday life and with the problems that particularly concern her. *This is a new approach, for, since ethnographic research has almost always been exclusively carried out with the help of, and among, the male part of the population, the picture that has emerged has to a large extent been the image which the men, and men alone, have of their society.* It is well known that travelers in a foreign land, whether men or women, find difficulty in making contact with the womenfolk and in getting into conversation with them; and when, to the barriers of language and custom, are added those arising in a colonial situation between rulers and subjects, the difficulty becomes almost insuperable".[26] (Italics mine.)

In sharp contrast, a recent survey of studies made in the United States on child-rearing practices, conjugal relations and sex roles led the writer to conclude: "Most of the behavioral and social scientists have simply ignored husbands and fathers in their empirical studies . . .".[19] I would add that brothers, sisters and in-laws have been ignored as well. Two widely quoted studies on child-rearing, by Sears and co-workers[34] and by Miller and Swanson,[23] relied exclusively on mothers for their data. Goode's classical monograph on the adjustment to divorce also ignores the problems and adaptations of divorced males and relies solely on female informants.[12] Similarly, there are 25 studies of unmarried mothers to one of unmarried fathers.[40] In assessing research in an area that is at the centre of debates about sexual equality—the employment of women and its impact on their marriages and children—Orden and Bradburn find that "There are several important gaps in previous research. First, the husband has been completely neglected. Earlier studies have been based exclusively on interviews with women. The impact of a woman's participation in the labor market may be significantly different for the husband than it is for the wife".[25] The attitudes and sentiments of husbands have rarely been tapped. According to LeMasters,[19] the one major study where fathers were asked about child-rearing values and practices (revealing significant differences between spouses on several points) was the work of Seeley and co-workers in *Crestwood Heights*.[35]

A number of factors seem to account for the decided female bias in the American literature. In the first place, earlier workers concerned with marital adjustment found that there was a relatively good agreement between what husbands and wives reported about the quality of their marriages.[17] Sociologists have therefore tended to confine their interviews to one spouse. More recent national and cross-cultural studies on the marital bond and decision-making within the family cast strong doubts on the validity of answers elicited from one spouse or by joint interviews.[32] Nor has much attention been paid to the influence of features of the interview itself, such as the characteristics of the interviewer, the place where the interview is given, and the presence or absence of other relatives.

In projects dealing with the larger kin network, women are also the major source of information, simply because they are more accessible for interviews than men. In addition, several studies in the United States and Great Britain indicate that women are more likely than men to be involved with their kin and knowledgeable about extra-conjugal family matters.[3, 7, 28, 29, 31, 41] The extent to which these findings reflect a systematic bias stemming from the exclusion of male informants requires further investigation; but in the few studies that do bother to question men, their involvement with their kin, both positively and negatively, appears to be far from marginal.

My own research on a small sample of highly mobile middle-class Greek-American families in New York City using male respondents showed that strong affective and instrumental family ties were maintained by the men, despite wide disparities between their own values and experiences and those of their parents, siblings and in-laws.[38] Bell, in his study of middle-class families in Wales, found that male linkages in the extended family (father-in-law/father–son/son-in-law) were at least as important as the more usually stressed mother–daughter link and were, in fact, the channels through which aid flowed between the units in the extended family.[1] In a study of blue-collar (working-class) marriage, Mirra Komarovsky found that although husbands were not as close to their parents as were wives, they were not uninvolved or unconcerned with them. She also noted that while most studies of in-law problems in the United States show these to be predominantly 'women's problems', blue-collar husbands experience difficulties with their in-laws as often as do their wives.[18] In contrast with previous studies of working-class marriage, Mirra Komarovsky interviewed both husbands and wives. Finally, three recent imaginative studies of urban lower-class black by Hannerz,[16] Liebow[20] and Schulz[33] stress the variety of family forms and role relationships (real and fictional) in this subculture, and the strong socio-psychological needs (if not their realization) of ghetto males, which are too often ignored in discussions of the mother as the dominant figure in lower-class families.

Such gaps and imbalances are not limited to studies of the contemporary family; they also plague historical analyses. Goode comments on some of these problems:

"We know something about the public family values, and to some extent the private values, of *men*, who were literate, and who were members of the middle or higher social classes. Few *women* have left their observations about how the family system operated (more in England and the United States than in other countries); almost no Negroes; and perhaps no children at all. It is not only difficult now to reconstruct a trend in their family role definitions as they saw them; we also lack their versions of the family role definitions accepted by their betters".[13] (Italics in the original.)

I have noted a parallel tendency in analyses of mobility and the family: few efforts have been made to ferret out the consequences of various types of mobility for specific role relationships within the nuclear family and between more extended kin; yet it is the men who are moving, while the women are talking.[39] Although it could be argued that the mobility of husbands has been over-emphasized compared with that of wives or with their joint mobility experiences (social and geographical), it is nevertheless clear that the importance of a wide range of kinship relations for men in contemporary Western societies has not been accurately gauged. With increases in the lifespan and the amount of leisure already accomplished facts for large proportions of the population, kin may loom larger in the lives of males than most studies suggest.

In a standard treatise on marriage, Blood and Wolfe succinctly summarize the points I have raised, at the same time revealing a feeling of uneasiness that husbands had been excluded:

> "The selection of wives instead of husbands was largely a question of productivity. Wives are more easily located at home so that more interviews could be obtained from them. In addition, to the extent that wives invest more time and effort in family matters, they may provide more complete and careful data. Although unavailable at present, a comparable study based on the interviews with husbands would nevertheless add valuable detail".[2]

As far as I know, no one has taken the time or trouble to repeat this study with husbands.

One important consequence of the subtle and explicit focus on women in most studies has been that an incomplete and asymmetrical picture of family structures and processes has been painted. Whatever aspect of the family one chooses to explore, it simply cannot be *assumed* that males (or females) will be uniformly less involved with kin than females (or males) or that extra-nuclear family links are unimportant in the functioning of that unit. Even if we accept that their kinship roles are relatively less significant than their occupational roles for males in contemporary society, we are not released from the obligation to assess which aspects of these roles are subjectively significant for individuals, if any.

My concern is not simply a matter of methodological sophistication or a quixotic quest for completeness. If it can be shown that the studies and theories on family, kinship, and sex roles are coloured by a sexual bias on the part of investigators and their subjects in different cultural areas, such bias immediately raises crucial questions about the validity of the images claimed to be 'reality'. These images, in turn, shape the kinds of solutions that we view as sociologically possible in our attempts to cope with change. Moreover, issues of ethics and responsibility are at stake and cannot be ignored. The cultivated diffidence and 'irrelevance' of academics do not alter the fact that people do seek authoritative guidance in solving or coping with family problems such as child-rearing, mental illness, divorce or homosexuality, and that they act upon the primary and secondary information available to them.

I am not suggesting that studies of selected aspects of kinship and the family are bound to be misleading, but I would argue that the interlocking, complementary, highly affective, and primary (in the sense of not being easily delegated) quality of family and sex roles requires methodological sensitivity as well as sophistication.

A further approach that has helped to perpetuate myths and dubious generalizations in the sociology of the family has been the almost universal reliance upon survey analysis in gathering data, to the exclusion of alternative or supplementary methods. Lack of communication within and between academic disciplines has tended to foster rigidity and ignorance of alternatives. I would add that if my own university is representative, sociologists neither are familiar with the anthropological literature (or that of other social sciences), nor have they incorporated into their methods the observational skills and intensive analyses that anthropologists routinely use in their researches. Yet such skills and analyses may illuminate and explain the role of kinship in urban industrial societies. Fortunately, this situation appears to be changing, as witnessed by the generally good reception by sociologists of works that combine the survey with other methods or rely primarily on participant observation—including the studies of Hannerz,[16] Schulz[33] and Liebow,[20] already mentioned, and those by Goffman[10] and Firth[7] and the Institute of Community Studies in Great Britain'.[41]

A fourth consideration that has influenced the direction and substance of family studies turns more on the concepts held than the methods used. Most research in the United States has concentrated on ties between husband and wife and on child-rearing. Research on extended kin networks is a relatively recent phenomenon and there is virtually no sociological concern with bonds between siblings or relations with parents and siblings-in-law. This apparent lack of concern is especially puzzling when one considers the ubiquitous nature and duration of such ties. One could consult a host of texts on marriage and the family and come away with the notion that people do not have brothers and sisters (except for purposes of rivalry) or any ties with relatives by marriage.

Family sociologists have only recently shown interest in the problems surrounding relationships between adult children and their parents. In general, when research workers have examined ties between the different generations, they have tended to focus on such disjunctive aspects as the parent–youth conflict, the 'generation gap', and adolescent rebellion. For example, Mannheim's otherwise brilliant theoretical essay on relations between generations and processes of social change has little to say about post-adolescent ties between children and their parents.[22]

The motifs of conflict, tension and isolation are also characteristic of much of the psychodynamic literature on inter-generation relations and in research on social gerontology, with relatively less emphasis being put on the integrative and affective aspects of generation ties between parents and their adult children. The belated interest shown by social scientists in the number and quality of links between generations can be traced to a number of sources. First, the interaction of such demographic variables as an earlier age at marriage, fertility, and a dramatic increase in lifespan has increased the proportion of three and even four-generation families. Coupled with this development has been the growing concern of the United States and other nations with social welfare policies associated with a large population of elderly persons.

Despite these two developments, the tendency to view the aged as a problem and within a context of infirmity, disability and dependence has been shown to be at odds with their actual situation.[27] This clarification has led to some utilization of the skills and needs of the older age group. As reported by Streib and Orbach, a federal programme was instituted in the United States that employs people of sixty years of age and over, whose income is low, to work closely with institutionalized children under five years of age. They conclude:

"The program gives the older person a definite social role in the community, because he is paid for doing an important, humane public service. Furthermore, the child receives the kind of love, warmth, and attention which has been shown to be essential by a large body of research on human growth and development. Although the initiators of the idea had some reservations as to whether old people would respond positively to this kind of parent surrogate role, there have been more applicants for the program than could be accommodated".[37]

There is little question that many other issues could be cited that seriously compromise any claims for the depth, extent and validity of our present knowledge of the family. Few studies have attempted to locate or interpret family changes within a broad theoretical orientation or to delve deeply into reciprocal relations and influences between the family and other institutional spheres.[5, 11] The methodological and substantive problems are painfully familiar to serious students of family and kinship.

There is, however, one particularly insidious consequence arising from the current state of affairs that is not immediately evident and is often overlooked. This is the extreme circumspection of social scientists and their inability to propose or evaluate experimental or alternative social structures that might serve as competing models for conventional marital and family patterns. It is true that the study of change is probably the most difficult and least developed area of sociology, but the rapid and potentially disastrous pace of change that we are witnessing (if not experiencing) calls urgently for new formulas and interpretations and for informed speculation.

In short, there has been a reluctance to suggest, endorse or validate new family forms and arrangements that may be sharply at odds with the *status quo*, even when our own research findings support such innovations. With few exceptions (such as the programme described by Streib and Orbach[37]), we have abdicated this role to philosophers, novelists, science-fiction writers, young and old militants of both sexes, and social commentators. For example, apart from impressionistic and journalistic accounts, we have few systematic appraisals of experimental communes, past and present, that have attempted to alter sex and age role distinctions in a radical way. The kinds of studies I have in mind include Geiger's work on the family in Soviet Russia,[8] Spiro's account of an Israeli kibbutz,[36] and Carden's excellent study of the Oneida Community.[4]

The literature on the changing role of women is growing rapidly but is uneven in quality and fails to take into account or to anticipate structural and institutional linkages that promote or inhibit changes in roles. One of the most thoughtful and cogent attempts to grapple with the question of institutional alterations and sex equality is Alice Rossi's essay where she discusses the consequences of the changes in child care, residence and educational patterns that must, at a minimum, occur if the goals of sex equality are to be realized.[30] Such attempts are critical, for, as the work of Geiger and Spiro and more recent reports on the position of Finnish women by Haavio-Mannila[14, 15] suggest, increasing the number of roles available to women in political, economic, legal, medical and educational spheres does not necessarily lead to a reduction of their other role obligations, to increased prestige, or to an increase in familial and non-familial power.

A recent study on the effects of a woman's work status on marital happiness in the United States that takes both husband and wife into account found that a woman's freedom to choose among alternative life styles is an important predictor of happiness in marriage. After taking into account different educational levels and stages in the life cycle, and part-time and full-time employment, the researchers found that when wives worked out of economic necessity rather than by choice, there was less happiness for both partners. They conclude that where there is freedom of choice and the woman opts for the labour market rather than the home market there are generally good effects on the marriage.[25]

The tendency to equate social changes with problems and social pathology, rather than with tactical and strategic opportunities for new ways of meeting human needs is seen in the highly charged and sensitive areas of marriage, sex and reproduction. For example, outside the pages of *Playboy* one rarely finds serious arguments in support of the benefits of extra-marital relations or of the extent to which such activities preserve and revitalize failing marriages, serve as useful outlets for tensions and anxieties in cases where dissolution is impossible, or lead to new attachments and satisfactions.[24] In studies on intermarriage or on unmarried mothers who choose to remain in that status, one also finds a marked tendency to dwell upon the number of marriages that fail or the problems of adjustment for both parents and children, with little or no emphasis on mixed unions that have been successful over time, or on unmarried women who cope. What hindsight often reveals as the initial and temporary strains inherent in any new social form become defined as insuperable obstacles.

Finally, the pressure of increasing population, together with the prospects of increased longevity and leisure, contraceptives, radical changes in the occupational structure, and increased articulation and legitimation of alternative life styles, based on personal choice, for all sexes and ages, provide us with an unprecedented opportunity for transforming and enriching human experience within the context of the family. To proceed with such an ambitious programme without critically evaluating what is known and possible would, I have tried to suggest, defeat these purposes.

DISCUSSION

Pirie: You pointed out that surveys among primitive people are as a rule made by men, and those in Britain and the U.S.A. are almost always made by women. Has anyone made a proper survey to compare the answers given to men and to women interviewers? You would probably get the same answers on purely factual issues, but you might get totally different answers when asking for opinions.

Tavuchis: I can't answer that point, but not only the sex and age but the race of both interviewer and informant also seem to count. When blacks are interviewed by whites, at least in the United States, they tend to give much more conventional answers to questions about race problems.

Comfort: People will not take the chain off the door so readily for men with a clipboard.

Newson: I would agree intuitively with Dr Tavuchis that men feel a need for involvement with children, but have you any actual information on this point, relating to the question of whether men need families as much as the families need the men?

Tavuchis: Because of the nature of most studies on child-rearing you never get the father's impression of what he feels his role should be. I don't know of any studies that have focused on the male response with regard to the need for kinship. I am arguing that we cannot assume *a priori* that males are uniformly less involved with kinship than females. My own research suggested that males wanted their success to be recognized by their kinsmen as well as by their peers.

Weiss: We have done some studies at the Harvard Laboratory of Community Psychiatry which bear on these issues. One was a study of parents without partners, in which we got to know a good many divorced men who had lost custody of their children. In discussion groups many expressed great distress at the feeling of distance from their children. After taking the children out on Sunday and then having to return them to the mother's home, many of the men reported that they experienced a feeling of great loss—and this was repeated weekly.[2] In another study we were unsuccessful in an attempt to build up a sample of men who were no longer married, whom we could interview over a period of time. Their lives were just too incoherent: they really couldn't make appointments because they didn't know where they would be next Saturday.[3] Having a family may be stabilizing for men.

Miller: There are also differences among males from puberty onwards. Many boys at mid-adolescence may wish to fertilize a female to prove their masculine potency, but they do not wish to occupy the role of a father. The adult wish to father children is quite different.

Comfort: Do they wish to fertilize her or do they merely want to have intercourse?

Miller: They want to fertilize. Studies in the United States of lower social class adolescents show a clear relationship between an assessment of their own masculine potency and getting a girl pregnant. The boys say quite openly that for example they "like to ride bare-back and get a girl pregnant".

Newson: It may be a false biological premise to assume that the attraction is always a sexual one. In future men will perhaps deliberately marry in order to have children, not just to have sex.

Fletcher: I strongly support this emphasis on the father. A picture had been building up of the fastnesses of fixed social institutions which regulate women and their children, but of men as casual chaps who impregnate women within five seconds. It is a fair sociological comment that it takes a lot longer than that for boys and pubertal youths and men to come to the position of impregnating women in any society— geared, as they are, responsibly and definitely, to the institutional fabric of family relationships. Men have their psychological and social needs, constraints and obligations, just as women and children do. The role of the father—both sociologically and bio-psychologically—in relation to these fundamental needs is a highly important thing to bear in mind.

Sjövall. Another point about the so-called need of the male for children is that in a secularized world this is frequently the only way of obtaining some diluted kind of immortality. In the field of sexology, non-reproductive sexual activities are considered essentially suspect and even pathological. Although this word pathological is certainly abused, it is also meaningful here, because non-reproductive sexual activities all have the drawback of not guaranteeing this measure of 'immortality' which appears to be very important to both sexes.

Leach: The notion of the nature of descent must be distinguished from the notion of fatherhood, however. It is very widespread among human beings to want a kind of immortality in the sense of having descendants, but if as a male you grow up in a matrilineal social environment your descendants are your sister's children, not your own. You will then be greatly concerned that your sister should have children but this has nothing at all to do with the question of whether you yourself do or do not impregnate a girl. It is quite compatible with a matrilineal principle of *descent* that male prestige should be felt to depend on whether or not a man can demonstrate his sexual potency by making a girl pregnant. The valuation of masculine dominance, the Latin-American *machismo*, is quite distinct from the valuation of fatherhood.

Fox: In all primates the adult males take great interest in the young. Male baboons are protective towards the young of the troop and give them their constant attention. They allow young infant males all sorts of privileges in terms of being close to them, that they would never grant to other mature males. This strong concern goes deep in all primate species and obviously has tremendous evolutionary implications. Children set off very powerful ethological signals to all males. If a house is burning down and someone says there is a grown able-bodied man inside, you say good luck to him, but if someone says there is a baby still inside, in you go. Because we have nuclear families and because these are our children, all these feelings are directed towards our own children, but in societies which are much more communal, for example the Pueblo Indians and even the Irish, there is a much more diffuse attraction and protectiveness towards children as such.

Newson: Men are apparently looking for a secure haven of warm intimate relationships which I do not believe exists in the male hobnobbing groups in our society to the extent some people think.

Tavuchis: If this is true, one might argue that as society becomes more industrialized kinship ties become more significant, and given the high degree of geographical mobility that exists, kin can be defined on personal rather than strictly consanguineal lines. You can activate certain kinship ties or deactivate others and have special bonds both with your kin and with your friends.

3: Parental Responsibility for Adolescent Maturity

DEREK MILLER

EMOTIONAL growth in children is possible only if they can form attachments[2] to people of significance to them. The first such relationship is the nurturing one with the mother; the next is with the father or father substitute; and later ones are with other children, brothers and sisters or substitutes for them. Men, like higher primates, live in social groups which provide a protected existence for the immature members of the species while they develop emotionally and learn the skills necessary for adult life.

The work of Freud and other nineteenth-century psychologists seemed to confirm the idea that, for human development through to adult life, the only significant social group necessary was the nuclear family unit of father, mother and siblings. Modern psychiatry continues to act as if this were true. Most case studies of psychologically disturbed people make only marginal comments about their environment and even less about the existence of any emotionally significant extra-parental adults. Yet anthropologically, ethologically and historically the nuclear family in itself does not appear to be a satisfactory child-rearing unit. The earliest emotional base for a child's growth is not the only one necessary for maturation.

Anthropologists[4] have even argued that the nuclear family is not the basic and elementary social unit of mankind. In primitive tribes the male accompanying a mother and an infant is not necessarily the child's father, and in some such groups the concept of individual biological fatherhood does not exist. Nevertheless no one denies the significance of the mother–child bond or the necessity for a father figure in a child's life.

In adolescence the behaviour of humans and primates is very similar. Prepubertal boys and girls form important peer group attachments and these groups often make significant relationships with one or other of the mothers.[6] Similarly, preadolescent chimpanzees form a nursery group of up to a dozen juveniles and adolescents who move about with one or two mature females.[5] Adolescent boys need significant attachments to extra-parental male adults[6]; adolescent chimpanzees between the ages of seven and eleven associate with groups of mature males. So during adolescence in man, chimpanzees and gorillas there are obvious changes in the figures with whom significant emotional relationships are made.

Before the nineteenth century the family was not the only significant unit for emotional growth and development in western society. During the Middle Ages the aristocracy sent adolescent children to other noble houses to be educated and the burgeoning middle classes farmed their children out to be trained by others as soon as they reached puberty.[8] The life expectation of the poor was particularly short, and in no social classes were childhood or adolescence understood in the same way as they are today.[7] The movement from childhood to adulthood was sufficiently rapid for there to be time only for puberty, not for a prolonged psychosocial reaction to this physiological event.

The recognition that bonds other than those of the nuclear family occur in development is not new. Bowlby[2] writes: "A child's tie to his mother is a product of a number of behavioural systems that have proximity to mother as a predictable outcome . . . during adolescent and adult life further changes occur, including a change of the figures to whom the behaviour is directed . . . During adolescence a child's attachment to his parents grows weaker. Other adults *may* come to assume an importance equal to, or greater than that of the parents and sexual attraction to age mates begins to extend the picture." However this concept does not give sufficient importance to the necessity for extra-parental attachments.

For psychological maturation during and after puberty to take place in any individual, there must be a dynamic balance of meaningful emotional relationships between the individual and his parents, the peer group, and extra-parental adults. The importance of any one of these social groups varies to some extent with the sex of the individual and with the values of the social system within which the individual lives. In western urban society a significant bond remains between mother and daughter into adulthood and old age.[9] The weaker the structure of the social system the more significant are the attachments to individuals, and without the latter the former cannot be used in the service of emotional development.

There is no clinical or other evidence to support the theory[9] that the development of attachment to groups is mediated, at least initially, by attachment to a person holding a prominent position within that group. It is probably not true that "for many a citizen attachment to his State is a derivative of, and initially dependent on, his attachment to his sovereign or president", particularly if attachment to smaller groups is a measure of strength of attachment to larger. In gangs, for example, most newcomers do not enter because of attachment to a gang leader, who keeps his leadership role because among other things he symbolizes the conflicts and strivings of the groups. Newcomers enter gangs usually through attachment to gang members who do not occupy a leadership role, and they then undergo a more or less formal initiation ceremony. Identification,[3] the development of the concept of *this is who and what I am*, is not finally possible in adolescence unless the individual has arrived at this stage with the capacity already developed of making emotional ties with others. There is no denying the significance of the nuclear family and of parental bonds in making this possible. At puberty the situation dramatically changes. Parents, extra-parental adults and a peer group are then all of so much significance that absence or premature separation from one or other of them may give rise to the classical triad associated with premature separation of the infant from its mother: protest, despair and detachment.

If parents are not available to adolescents, the individual can nevertheless develop a sense of autonomy if he still has relationships with a peer group and with extra-parental adults who are not expected to occupy a substitute parental role. Only early adolescents seek in addition parent substitutes, and then only tenuously. This is because the imprint of a child's relationship to his parents has become internalized by the time puberty is reached, so the individual can then identify with and gain support from the world of adults and other adolescents with whom he has relationships.

If there are no extra-parental adults with meaning in his life, an adolescent who is striving for autonomy must, of necessity, try to weaken the existing bonds with his parents. This is because an adolescent who identifies directly with his parents, and incorporates his perception of their personality directly into his own, cannot have a sense of autonomy. Apart from weakened bonds with parents, adolescents who lack contact with extra-parental adults also need stronger than usual attachments to their peer group. The basic struggle is a conflict between dependent and independent strivings. In order to free themselves from parental bonds and infantile attachments, adolescents must have relationships outside the nuclear family which will provide support while allowing them to develop a sense of personal autonomy. The generation gap, whatever its other causes, is thus an inevitable result of the failure of society to provide the opportunity of forming attachment bonds to extra-parental adults.

Without such adults, dependence on the peer group, not on the parents, intensifies. The peer group has a fluctuating value system and is of necessity unstable; it fails to provide easy mediation with the value systems of the parents which the individual has been incorporating since infancy. Therefore attachment to the peer group lasts longer in the absence of emotionally significant extra-parental adults. Adolescents are driven to retain intense peer group attachments into young adulthood and the transient gang structures of early adolescence, in which leaders become appointed for specific social or asocial tasks, continue. The organizational groups of young people who attack the educational system are similar to those of early adolescents who commit petty crimes together. Adolescents who are over-attached to their peers often become vulnerable to a group contagion, which reinforces peer group bonds by projecting the hostility produced by the group's anxiety onto the outside world either of adults or other adolescents. The widespread use of a forbidden drug, marijuana, by middle-class American and British adolescents, of stimulants by British working class youngsters, the development of the 'greaser' cult in the U.S.A. and 'skinheads' in Britain, are examples of this process.

If neither a peer group nor extra-parental adults are available for attachment bonds, then despair and detachment are the common adolescent emotional responses. Attempts at individual autonomy appear doomed to failure. The lack of a peer group is usually not so much due to the unavailability of a potential group as to the difficulty adolescents encounter in making peer relationships. Even potentially healthy adolescents need consistent access to a peer group and time to attempt tentative relationships with others before they are able to make any significant emotional attachments.

In the United States part of the Junior High School system is conducting an unwilling social experiment which renders it inordinately difficult for pubertal adolescents to make either peer group or extra-parental adult relationships. In order to provide a wide choice of subject, pubertal adolescents are exposed to eight daily classes, with only five minutes to move from room to room; they have eight different teachers; they have to line up and wait twenty to thirty minutes for lunch; and they have no recess periods. And these are schools with a thousand or more pupils. Early adolescents with a personality structure which makes them intensely shy are then extremely vulnerable. They detach themselves emotionally from others and may withdraw to the nuclear family. Alternatively they may become involved in behaviour which leads to a further failure of personality development; when drugs are available, they tend to use hallucinogens such as LSD or mescaline, drugs which are rarely if ever used by those early adolescents able to make peer group attachments.

It is difficult to envisage a situation in which parents and extra-parental adults are available, but not a peer group. However, it is not uncommon for psychologically disturbed adolescents to appear unable to make relationships with anyone but their parents. In successful psychotherapy with these youngsters who previously lacked extra-parental attachments, when they receive help from other adults, a first common sign of maturation is that they begin to develop peer group relationships. Even without this stage, emotional maturation is still possible and the adolescent moves straight back into making relationships on a more adult level.

In the conurbations of the western world, with increasing social mobility (which may be vertical, from one social class group to another, or horizontal, because of movement from place to place) adolescents have less natural chance of tribal attachments to other adults and to a peer group. Clinical observation indicates that children are more likely to continue relationships with the parents of childhood friends made before the age of ten if they remain in the same neighbourhood. After the age age of ten new peer group attachments do not automatically lead to new adult connexions, except for those rare adults who possess the capacity of making easy relationships with adolescents. Apart from the probable dearth of emotionally significant extra-parental adults within neighbourhoods, the extended family has also become less available through a number of factors: a decrease in family size, horizontal mobility and increasingly passive isolation within the nuclear family because of media such as television. The necessity for population control and the problem of pollution must make a large extended family group increasingly rare.

The disintegration of tribal society is not new in human history, but whenever this has occurred, there have been many signs of widespread psychological disintegration. A typical example of this was at the beginning of the industrial revolution in Britain. The poor, who moved rapidly from the country to the town, showed much evidence of psychosocial disintegration, interestingly manifested by the widespread use of drugs, in this case alcohol. This process ended only when a tribal society of the street was created. In England, especially in the industrial cities of the north and in the east end of London, the street culture became extremely strong and to some extent still survives.[9] Social policy, so far as rehousing is concerned, appears to take little heed of the necessity to maintain tribal life and so fragmentation of social groups increasingly occurs. The British middle and upper classes have similarly to deal with the disintegration of extended family groups, but they often attempt, even if unconsciously, to provide the equivalent of tribal support by sending their adolescent children away to school.

In the United States before the depression, the extended family group was typical of both the white protestant immigrants who came to the U.S.A. before the twentieth century and the newer immigrant groups who either set up subcultures equivalent to those found in the large European cities, or, failing this, showed severe social pathology. The depression years in the United States increased the tendency to horizontal mobility already present among some middle and lower class social groups. In recent decades severe pathology has manifested itself in middle class adolescents in the widespread use of soft drugs, and in the ghetto through increasing violence. The movement to the city of the black American reproduces a similar migration of European peasantry in the eighteenth and nineteenth centuries.

Apart from the effects of the breakdown of the tribe on adolescent development, the nuclear family itself becomes more vulnerable. Parents cannot find social validation for their child-rearing practices; as a result, with great anxiety, they seek constant support from experts who will instruct them as to how to relate to their young. Psychological studies of adolescents sufficiently disturbed to warrant referral for help indicate that, with only a nuclear family and a peer group, maturation in adolescence is not possible. Those adolescents who show spontaneous recovery appear to do so because by chance they develop a special attachment to an adult whose relationship with them appears to act as a catalyst for the process of maturation. There is no doubt that the relationship with a therapist also has within it aspects of a positive relationship with an extra-parental adult.

Perhaps with an unconscious awareness that adolescents cannot mature in isolation, various attempts have been made by various groups of society to reconstitute extrafamilial networks of adults and provide the potentiality for peer group attachments. In Israel, the kibbutz[1] is a conscious effort to rear children without intense parental involvement. It is quite clear, however, that if the actual parents are not available to occupy the role of mother and father, some extra-parental adult is chosen for this position, and others occupy the role of the significant 'other' adult. In the U.S.A. and in Britain an unknown number of late adolescents and young adults have set up communes. When children are born in the commune they are clearly members of a large tribal group, but of special interest is the relationship that adolescents who enter these communes as runaways create with the adults within them.

John, a 14-year-old boy, was admitted to a university hospital's Adolescent Service because his behaviour had become increasingly bizarre. He had run away from home and joined a commune which consisted of some ten late adolescents and young adults and two babies. The commune had attempted to integrate the boy into their way of life. Its value systems were basically derived from the assumption that everyone could 'do their own thing', that all goods should be shared, and no one member of the commune should have authority over another. John had however insisted on manipulating a young man of 23 into a paternal role; he would behave badly in front of this man and so irritate him that he would begin to act in a controlling manner, telling John to stop. John disintegrated because he provocatively imported more and more drugs into the commune, apparently hoping the young adult would stop him. When he would not do this John began to take his imports in quantity. Hospitalization was precipitated not so much by John's bizarre behaviour as through John's driving the young adult to violence by declaring he would turn the commune over to the police for harbouring a runaway, if he could not do as he wished. John also suggested bringing a group of 14-year-olds to the house to 'drop acid' together, an action which would have threatened the life of the commune because of the danger of police intervention. Other young adults in the commune were not manoeuvred into the same paternal role and so did not feel as intensely angry with John. Within the commune John was creating his own tribal group, with a father figure and extra-parental adults, and he was attempting to import a peer group.

It is a hypothesis as yet unsupported by hard facts that the extra-parental adult is of such prime importance in adolescent development. If the hypothesis is confirmed, the implications for what has unhappily come to be called 'social engineering' would seem significant. The hypo-thesis was deduced from clinical observation, and evidence to support it is being sought in a current study of drug-taking adolescents, to be under-taken by the author and others in the U.S.A. The specific hypothesis being studied is that, if drugs are available, adolescents with only parental and peer group attachments are more likely to use drugs in toxic amounts than those adolescents who have parental, extra-parental and peer group involvements.

Adolescents who cannot develop a firm sense of their own identity often fail to make satisfactory sexual relationships. The excessive use of marijuana decreases the sexual drive of the recipient. Stimulants such as amphetamines in large dosage lead to temporary inhibition of male potency; LSD and other hallucinogens generally lead more to mastur-batory than heterosexual activities. Drug usage thus provides a way of studying the failure of personality development.

CONCLUSION

All adolescents seen in psychiatric clinics represent a biased sample of the population at large. Nevertheless, the intensive study of individual patients and the fact that there is often not much difference between the disturbed and the non-disturbed make the study of hypotheses derived from clinical observation justified. The essential hypothesis of this paper is that for psychological maturation in adolescence to occur, a varying balance must exist between the individual, the nuclear family, extra-parental adults and the peer group. The most significant actual relation-ships in adolescence which assist in the development of identity are attachments firstly to extra-parental adults, secondly within the peer group, and thirdly to the nuclear family. In preadolescent childhood the hierarchy of attachments is to the nuclear family, the peer groups and extra-parental adults. The varying significance of each of these social groups for individual development depends on the maturational age of the individual, the quality of the relationships available within these

2*

three groups, and the strength of cultural norms. All are necessary and if one is absent maturation is to a greater or lesser extent impeded.

If man is to survive without grossly polluting his environment and destroying himself, population growth must be brought under control and a small family unit with less than two children on average becomes inevitable. Such a small family unit, living in emotional isolation with no significant attachment to other families, is even less satisfactory as a child-rearing unit than a large family in the equivalent situation.

Society will probably make conscious and unconscious attempts to re-create tribal society at the same time as psychological disintegration increases. Tribal linkages can be re-created in many ways. One possible change point in western society is the school system, but the provision of a climate which meets the emotional needs of children will necessitate the revision of some current educational theories and goals. Another change point could be in the attitude of industry to its employees. Personnel policies need to take conscious note of the developmental needs of employees' families if industrial mental health is to become truly preventive. It is highly improbable that planned social change will occur except in a few systems of society. In the twenty-first century extended networks of people with relationships not necessarily based on blood ties are likely to exist alongside subgroups of drug-taking and violent individuals who have been unable to make such relationships.

DISCUSSION

Weiss: One of the things often missing in planned communities such as new towns is a place for teenagers to get together, as in Levittown which Herbert Gans[2] described as having absolutely no facilities for teenagers. Adults there were in fact greatly concerned that such facilities would be a source of disturbance.

Miller: Youth leaders are often extremely diffident about involving themselves directly with adolescents. Our experience is that adolescents very much want adults to do things with them, provided that at the same time they are allowed their peer group privacy when it is needed.

Pirie: How exactly was the commune organized from which the unfortunate John got slung out? Had it any official status?

Miller: I don't know how this particular one grew, but what usually happens is that a group of adolescents who sleep in the summer on the streets collect in the winter in a house, usually broken-down property which is about to be demolished. These communes seem to vary enormously in their quality; in a university town they collect many runaways, as do equivalent groups in, say, New York. The commune seems to be a sort of self-chosen group of late adolescents who decide they will live together.

Pirie: If children use adults as father substitutes, about how many can share one potential pseudo-father in a practical way? Is it a dozen, a hundred, or how many?

Miller: It depends on the quality of the adult.

Pirie: Isn't this a rather inefficient method of making use of a rather rare sort of adult?

Miller: The problem is that adolescents who look for father substitutes are often very angry with their own fathers. Perhaps the father died, left home or was inadequate. Because of these and other feelings about their natural father, such adolescents do not easily create a benign relationship with some good-hearted adult who can see himself as a substitute father. Even though he chooses the parent figure himself, the adolescent can become extremely demanding on that adult.

Borrelli: As you know, I have dealt with street urchins and I lived their vagabond life with them for several months, trying to understand them better. I can confirm that this mechanism really exists among the street urchins. In some cases the youngster tries to revenge himself on the adult, operating a sort of identification of the adult with the father; it is a tremendous contradiction because he loves the adult and hates him at the same time.

Miller: Another important point is the need for more than one other 'adult'. One adult gets elected to a substitute father role and may get most of the brunt of an adolescent's hostility, but this will not stop a youngster using a positive relationship with other adults.

Borrelli: Poor children are in some respects more like those in your communes since they are obliged to leave school and go to work. We then get this phenomenon of the so-called street-corner societies, which are sometimes considered pathological.

Miller: I would agree that they are not always pathological.

Ali Baig: Dr Miller, are you implying that the nuclear family as a child and adolescent rearing unit is not a suitable instrument?

Miller: I mean that once adolescence is reached the nuclear family is not a suitable instrument, but without it in early life the stage is not reached when other attachments can be used.

Ali Baig: But is it still a valid instrument in normal society? The extended family system is still widespread in India, but as economic circumstances improve the extended families are beginning to break up into nuclear ones. With fewer children and greater prosperity there will be a change. How will this affect the Indian society of the future?

Miller: If the adolescents can no longer make satisfactory identifications and know who they are, they will probably then be forced to behave in the same way as adolescents behave in many parts of Western society, particularly in the big cities. There may be a prolonged attachment to an adolescent peer group in a way which does not occur with an available extended family. Protest behaviour and detachment from others will be common. A substitute has to be found for the extended family, because the mistake has been to assume that the only really significant child-rearing unit is parental and that relationships with other adults can be left to chance.

Tavuchis: Before industrialization, the family worked as a unit and solidarity was maintained. When conditions changed to the employment of young children or individual labour away from the home, the family patterns changed.

Miller: I was talking about the migration which took place in Great Britain in the 18th century from the country to the town, which is when the family broke up.

Tavuchis: In the United States we have an ideology of a nuclear family, but in fact studies show a great deal of extended kin interaction. This doesn't vitiate your argument, but I wonder how much actually does depend on this extended family.

Miller: The point I am making is that if an adolescent can't find significant extra-parental grown-ups he cannot mature, and that is the crucial thing.

Reynolds: Your way of putting this seems to indicate a fundamental problem in your whole analysis. You began by talking about animals and then you went on to talk about human maturation. You were using a psychological or psychiatric frame of reference and the terminology applicable to such a frame of reference, but you wanted to answer the kinds of problems you set yourself in terms of sociological changes: changes in the social system. I think this is an inadmissible approach, because social systems actually create needs, like the need for significant other grown-ups; the idea that there are basic needs and a basic maturation process which society may or may not satisfy is completely incompatible with this kind of sociological frame of reference. The whole argument seems to me to be fraught with the difficulties raised by this fundamental fact—that we are dealing with two separate and barely related frames of reference.

Miller: If I have been so obscure, I'm sorry! My strong feeling is that the answer is not just to be found in one discipline. Psychiatrists can perhaps deduce answers from a close study of individuals; they may by chance discover techniques of manipulating the social environment which help some people. We may go on to discover that society seems to be failing to meet emotional needs; then we might seek to find out whether sociological, anthropological and historical data help to confirm or deny our hypotheses.

Sjövall: From my clinical experience I think your emphasis on the importance of extra-parental figures in adolescence is very pertinent. In 'very good' families, particularly very intellectual families, there is a tendency towards inbreeding and over-protection that isolates the adolescent. The youngsters tend to idealize their parents to quite an unrealistic extent and some of us here may have personal experience of this. This idealism frustrates their need to express their aggressive tendencies, which might explain why it sometimes appears to be insidiously traumatic to have psychoanalysts or other experts on human relations as parents!

Rapoport: What Dr Miller said about adolescents from nuclear families is a special case of a much more general issue. Can we in fact have a whole range of varying family and household patterns in our society in the future? If we assume that we can—and I, for one, would feel we can—then we must think about the range of functional substitutes that will be needed by parents and children at different stages of the family life cycle, for elements formerly provided by the extended family and other kinds of traditional relationships. Children living alone with either mothers or fathers, for instance, are going to need different kinds of outside groups.

Miller: I agree entirely.

Adams: In the nuclear family there is a good deal more tension between the adolescent and his parents than in the extended family. This tension is aggravated by the elaborate organization of contemporary youth culture, with its stylized behaviour patterns and its variety of rather sharply defined personality types. Thus the youth culture provides models that represent functional equivalents to models previously available in the extended family.

There is a paradox here, however. On the one hand, the youth culture offers the adolescent the opportunity to achieve a certain independence and autonomy *vis-à-vis* the nuclear family. On the other hand, the youth culture can bring the adolescent into a conformism that often approaches tyranny. In exaggerated form we see this when the adolescent explains his taking of drugs by saying that he does not want to be thought 'different'.

Doesn't the youth culture in its imposing of models and patterns of behaviour provide a certain competition with the adult culture and its models? And more specifically, doesn't the youth culture serve in some measure to prevent or impede the adolescent in his search for a surrogate father outside the nuclear family?

Miller: If extra-familial adults are not available, adolescents in puberty quite clearly make intense peer group attachments. These are often very rigid and certainly the pubertal group is often intensely conformist. This is probably related to the turbulence which is going on inside youngsters, associated with the attempt they are making to try to free themselves from dependent relationships on their parents or parent surrogates. If one security has to be abandoned, a transitional external security is created. If all goes well, after the three-year turmoil of puberty adolescents are able to look at the world and find the people who, at a conscious and unconscious level, they wish to be like. These people may be their own peers or adults. Sometimes adults with whom they identify are astonishingly like parents and the adolescent is unaware of this. Sometimes identification models are unlike parents. If identification proceeds smoothly, heterosexual relationships then become significant. Peer group attachments matter and may be intense, but they often do not continue after early adolescence. If adolescents cannot find emotionally significant other adults, they then remain tightly involved with their own peer group, which becomes intensely vulnerable both to the rigidity and to the peer group contagion you mentioned.

Stone: Would you say that it matters less that a nuclear family is a one-parent family, than that the nuclear family may be so isolated that there are no other adults available? I think you were touching on the idea that a mother-dominated young man tends to become a homosexual.

Miller: I think there is a link between mother domination and absence of male figures and homosexuality in young men. I believe that if the mother and child are isolated the mother cannot possibly bring up a healthy child, girl or boy. The teenage mothers of illegitimate babies can bring up their children, providing society can offer them social support and father figures. But a father and a mother in isolation, however good they are at meeting a child's needs, cannot bring up a healthy child. It is unfortunate that we project our anxiety about adolescent disturbance only on to parents, and blame only them.

Fletcher: I disagree enormously with this whole perspective; there is no historical evidence for it at all. This talk of a tribal society in Britain being disrupted by great migrations during the early onset of industrial civilization is totally false. There was no such thing as tribal society; there was a very impoverished feudal society. People were involved in peasant-like labour for up to 19 hours a day, not only in agriculture, but in domestic industry, and it was they who were drinking the gin. Gin drinking was itself connected with the keeping up of prices of wheat on the part of aristocracy. Pre-industrial families in Britain suffered deprivation on every count—biological, psychological and social.

The idea that the middle classes sent their children to school to get a wider *tribal* experience is surely much oversimplified. They sent them there because there was no public education. They were the new rulers of society, and they wanted to train their children for the competitive opportunities which were opening up towards the end of the 19th century —when, in fact, the largest development of the public schools took place. And surely it is totally false to say that town planning is not sensitive to human relationships beyond the family. People seem to have a fixation on Michael Young and Peter Willmott's book, *Family and Kinship in East London*,[5] rather than on what all the town planners have said since: namely that once these families have broken away from Bethnal Green and lived for some years in Harlow or Welwyn Garden City, they manage to get over their earlier attachments and make new relationships. The planners deliberately develop neighbourhood shopping centres, community halls, sports stadiums for young people—which they never had in Bethnal Green until people started altering it in recognition of these sorts of needs.

I find no evidence for the idea that the modern family shows more anxiety and less stability than earlier families, or for the idea that the modern family is emotionally isolated. Studies of even middle-class families in Woodford and elsewhere[1,6] show that the motor car and the telephone allow families not only to live separately from each other, but also to remain in close touch with each other. There is probably a closer but a *chosen* (a very important thing!) continuity of relationships between families than earlier. At least the historical perspectives need looking at carefully!

It seems to me that a good many behavioural problems—like drug taking and the difficulties that the young find in accommodating themselves to modern society—may have very little to do with the lack of an extended family network. They may have much more to do with the enormous complexity of the society young people now have to face, and the lengthy and often directionless education to which they are subjected. The explanation for all this may be much broader than the one we have had so far.

Weiss: In a survey comparing American and Danish adolescents done by the Harvard Laboratory of Human Development[4], the adolescents were asked to whom they went for advice about certain issues. Among the alternatives in the list were teachers, parents, other adults and guidance counsellors. None of these adults were chosen by more than 40 per cent of either American or Danish adolescents except in connexion with the choice of books, school work, career decisions, and clothing; fewer than 40 per cent consulted any of these adults about personal problems or morals and values (although the mother was noted by a minority of adolescents as a resource in connexion with moral issues). Most adolescents have few relationships other than slight ones with adults outside the family, or at any rate few which are elicited by a question asking to whom they go for advice.

Miller: We are hoping to repeat a rather similar study in some rural and city schools in the United States. We are trying to assess whether adolescents do relate to adults and if so to whom do they relate, and what they see themselves as needing. We are finding it difficult because adolescents try to decide the expected answer, then either give it or not, depending on how they feel. Survey techniques in adolescence are difficult.

Himmelweit: At an East–West experimental social psychology meeting last year a Czechoslovakian study with similar findings to the American one was described.[3] This study aimed to find out who was important for adolescents in a whole variety of settings. The list included teachers, parents, brothers and sisters, and friends. None of the adults featured at all significantly.

Miller: We propose to ask "Do you know any grown-ups" and "Do you like any grown-ups"? We then want them to describe the perceived qualities of any grown-ups they like, what sort of people they themselves would like to be like, and the qualities of their parents. We are trying to discover what they are acquiring from grown-ups without asking the direct question "Do you talk to them"?

Commonly, in therapy, adolescents will talk of grown-ups whom they like, and describe qualities in them which are similar to qualities they have previously described and rejected in their parents.

Himmelweit: Why in the States do the children with problems often run away? In this country they may have the same problems but they don't necessarily physically run away from home.

Miller: I really don't know, but adolescent running away is very much more frequent in the United States than when I was there 15 years ago and the threat of running away is being used by adolescents as a technique of controlling their parents. But American society has always been highly mobile; movement has been in the culture for a long time.

Fox: There is also somewhere to go now; there are all these centres which accept runaways.

Miller: This may be a kind of safety valve. The places adolescents run to may telephone the parents. A centre for drug taking adolescents in New York has a large telephone bill because of this.

Stone: To run away you need not only somewhere to go to but also the means of running away. The typical American adolescent goes outside and drives off in his own or somebody else's car. This is also what happens with matrimonial disputes. English reports of these resound with doors being slammed and locked, American ones with cars being driven furiously a thousand miles or so.

4: Future Family Patterns and Society

FRANÇOIS H. M. RAVEAU

I AM not an expert on family patterns, but as an anthropologist it is part of my work to take a special interest in such an important element in cultural patterns. Nor am I an expert on the future, but as a psychiatrist I am sometimes drawn into making prognoses and I then try to do this on the basis of observations and data furnished by the present. In neither profession can one neglect history, and a diachronic approach to social phenomena is always necessary.

At l'École Pratique des Hautes Études in Paris a team consisting of an anthropologist, a sociologist, a psychologist, a biologist and a clinician has been studying the normal and abnormal or pathological processes of intercultural modification (acculturation). From the different population samples being surveyed we have picked out certain elements which may help us to understand how the family is rooted in societies, what its role is, and how it will develop in the future.

Here I shall first try to describe the breaking-down process that the family undergoes in a well-defined and circumscribed primitive society which has changed so rapidly during its contact with another society that in a few years it has been possible to observe a complete change of structure. Of course a society's internal evolution modifies it without the action of external forces, but the processes are slower and more difficult to grasp.

Secondly I shall try to show how people from traditional cultures with classical extended family patterns cope when they move to our western society. The study of this process of family restructuring may help us to see our own society in a more relative and therefore less ethnocentric way.

Finally, in the light of the factors determining these changes, I shall try to imagine the family in the future.

FAMILY CHANGES IN A PRIMITIVE SOCIETY

The Shipibos are a South American Indian race living in the Amazonian forest of Peru, near the Brazilian border. They number 5000 to 8000 and are scattered over a territory the size of Scotland. They belong to the linguistic group of the Panos. Hunters, fishermen and food-gatherers, they were long protected from the outside world by the extreme difficulty of penetrating their wild territory. They therefore preserved their complex society and a highly sophisticated family pattern, patrilinear, matrilocal and polygamous. Missionaries reached them early

39

in the 17th century. The least harmful were the Catholics, since they just baptised the people and left. Almost 300 years later the white Anglo-Saxon Protestants arrived and, faced with the pagan outlook of the family, tried to modify it without success. Later still the Peruvian Government, because of a population explosion on the Pacific coast and in the Andes, decided to open up the forest as a territory for internal colonization. After 1950, a great effort was made and roads were built. The *mestizos*, of mixed Indian and European ancestry, began to invade the hunting grounds, to pollute and devastate the rivers (oil was discovered at the same time) and to import disease, producing epidemics of tuberculosis, chickenpox, smallpox, measles and influenza that soon decimated the population. The family was the first social institution to crumble and throughout the whole process of destruction it remained the clearest example of this process.

An ecological illustration of this was given by the successive changes in types of houses used. Traditionally the clan used to cohabit in a big house (60 to 80 yards long) which sheltered from three to five extended families. They then switched to living in smaller houses, one for each extended family, grouped together in a kind of village. This phase was a most disruptive one; the exchange of women between clans was confused by their dispersion and what had previously been regarded as incest in their system began to develop. The last stage was reached with the use of smaller houses surrounded by bamboo walls (the two previous types had no bamboo walls) in which lived monogamous families that had abandoned the matrilocal system.

Erratic attempts to resist the pressure were also observed. The Shipibos tried to modify their economic conditions by acquiring new ways of getting food and goods. As part of the dissolution of the traditional family, marriages and temporary unions occurred between brothers and sisters. New myths appeared, like Messianism—often the last hope of a crushed culture.[1,3] Incapable of offering an effective opposition to the pressure of the *mestizos*, the Shipibos are now disappearing, either dying or vanishing in the shabby suburbs of the pioneer towns of the forest.

Without going into details, we may conclude that when the pressure from outside was merely ideological (through the missionaries), the family pattern remained untouched. It may be that it offered a coherent alternative to other patterns, being well adapted to the conditions of living in this particular *milieu*. But as soon as variations appeared at the economic level through ecological disturbance, or in inter-group relations through the disappearance of many Indians by disease, the family became highly vulnerable. This allows us to understand the function of this institution as a privileged channel of communication where interaction takes place between adults.

The family thus has a number of functions besides the biological ones of the conception, gestation, and rearing of children, and the subsequent socialization of the child and the building of his superego. Mature personality is acquired only through the psychosocial interrelations of adolescents and adults.

We shall leave the Shipibos here. We cannot use this sample to study the process of restructuring a new family type, since this ethnic group has now been virtually destroyed.[5]

IMMIGRANT GROUPS IN FRANCE

Let us now consider a sample made up of black Africans coming to live in France from Senegal, Mauritania, the Ivory Coast, Mali, Camerroon, Tchad, Gabon and the Central African Republic. This apparently heterogeneous collection of nationalities all have in common an extended family pattern, modified perhaps by the influence first of Islam and later of European colonization, but still much in evidence.

At the beginning of our studies of these immigrant populations in France, we took great care to differentiate between tribal origins.[6] Later we realized that during the acculturation which they undergo the only consistent variable is that of class, and up to a certain point this holds good when these people go back to their own countries. As Klineberg has recently shown,[2] with the growth of nationhood the tribal society of Africa has been replaced by a society of class. Of all the different ethnic groups that have settled in France, only the black African working class has created communes (50 to 100 people living in the same place, on a tribal model).

We found that because of an initial shortage of African women among the immigrants (there was one woman for every three or four men), a kind of extended family without wives or children, and without the blood ties of the traditional extended family, was created to fulfil a need for interpersonal communication. Up to now this has appeared to be a highly successful means of getting rid of tensions. When the men later have their own women (and thus child-rearing units are established), they do not enclose themselves in their new family units but continue to frequent the group. If they live with French girls, they use this fraternity group as a means of Africanization for their wife or companion (the latter description is usually more correct: very few are married according to French law).

When we asked what was important to the members of the commune in their daily life, as measured objectively in time (time schedule) and space (the urban distance to be covered), and subjectively as expressed in their own accounts of their activities, we found that half their time-budget is devoted to professional activities, next comes the time spent in the commune, and the child-rearing unit gets the smallest share.

The commune system as we have seen it, then, appears to be a means of continual social exchange. Within it one can discern groups concentrating on their professional or leisure activities. The wife–children entity is not the first choice but is subordinated to a specific, chosen collectivity. This is an inversion of what we are accustomed to finding in our own societies. We may here be observing the emergence of a new social type of family integration, hitherto concealed among the rest of our customs.

The other Africans whom we can classify as lower middle class, middle class and upper middle class, also revealed very interesting behaviour, along the same lines,

Studies of French families in Paris made by Chombart de Lauwe some 15 to 20 years ago showed that social class (indicated by whether they lived in the western residential section or in the eastern working class area) determines how open the French family is to the outside world.[4] The higher the family is in the class hierarchy, the more tenuous is its contact with the neighbourhood. We have made similar observations ourselves. Our method of study was to assess the quality and intensity of exchanges taking place outside the family, taking the term in its narrowest meaning.

We have found that for African and mixed couples, although the influence of class is still pertinent, it is much less so than for the French families. It is so much attenuated that the child-rearing unit is never dominant. Both wife and husband give most of their available time to community activities, whether para-professional, leisure, cultural, sport, political or religious. As soon as the child seems old enough to be 'minded' collectively, the parents spend even less time in the family unit. Compared with the French families there is a definite loss of interest in the family nucleus and increased receptivity to outside activities. This of course has its corollary in a different view of sexual fidelity and conjugal morality.

Here we must note that among the Africans there are some ultra-conformists who try to imitate at all costs the outward behaviour of the milieu into which they want to be assimilated. It is noteworthy that this group has the largest amount of psychopathology related to family breakdown. The social causes for this could be summed up as an inability to identify with the model given which is already being devalued by an evolving society. These people are conservative, maladjusted outsiders battling for a system they had never made their own.

Can we say that the changes observed in our main sample of Africans accustomed to an extended family life and re-creating a communal life in France correspond to the changes in a western society in the process of deserting a nuclear family pattern for a system in which exchanges outside the family are the principal means of education and expression? In both, the system of reference to values centred in the family unit tends to disappear. Paternal authority gives way to the collective authority of teachers and of abstract leaders synthesized by the mass media. The centre of interest shifts and post-industrial leisure society then appears to offer, according to age or taste, multiple channels of socialization which used to be the prerogative of the family unit.

THE FAMILY IN THE FUTURE

The Shipibos have shown us the important influence of economic changes on the dynamics of family modification. The ideologies produced by the new systems in fact represent a rationalization of choice (for instance, the acceptance by polygamous Islam of monogamy, imposed by the cost of keeping a wife in a new economy, is justified by new religious and up-dated philosophical theories). So if present economic changes lead to hypercollectivization in urban surroundings and ever-increasing dependence on community services, people in future may tend to free themselves from the family unit in favour of new patterns of multiple community exchanges, corresponding for example to centres of leisure or professional interest. The child-rearing unit would then become a temporary one and be rapidly taken over by the specialized services (education, dietetics, etc.) of the community. In People's China, for example, strong family ties have given way to a highly collectivized society.

But so far there still remains the procreating unit. Instead of considering sociological expressions of economic determinants, one can evisage a drastic modification of the system of procreation. The advent of the oral contraceptive and its success show that our societies are prepared to manipulate the laws of conception. Contraception may also lead to certain forms of selection through voluntary genetic modification. However, so far the contraceptive pill and other techniques do not seem to have altered the nature of the child-rearing unit. The pill may have displaced a certain number of interpersonal relations but it has not disposed of them. Sometimes it has brought up new problems without solving all the old ones connected with conception. But the next step will be fertilization and procreation outside the parental unit—'the test-tube baby'. We may then revert to the type of family instituted by the Africans in France, but without any blood ties. This may sound like science fiction, but we have to realize that such developments are not impossible. Population pressures and their consequences are forcing on western society a radical transformation which in its turn is made possible by the development of technology. The family cannot escape the general change. If its nucleus (gestation, procreation, early rearing) disappears entirely, other activities which are now subordinated to it will attach themselves to other centres of interest—whether sexual, leisure, professional or ideological; one may be prevalent for a time, another later. We shall then reach the commune system illustrated by the African groups—the family without blood ties. The age group may be the new factor which will determine this new type of polynuclear family.

DISCUSSION

Henriques: In Peru, ideological factors such as a new religion seemed to have very little effect on the indigenous family structure. In the Caribbean tourism has developed tremendously in the last 25 years and this has introduced a very powerful economic factor through opportunities for work and the earning of incomes which did not exist before. A very important disturbance of relations inside the family unit is happening there now, because young men and women working in hotels and so forth are presented with a way of life totally alien from their previous experience. This changes their view of things, and since they also have a powerful economic advantage, compared to the normal family income, situations of severe conflict can arise. A similar pattern can be observed in England among immigrants from the Caribbean. The earning of wages which cannot normally be earned in the Caribbean today has altered their family structure to such an extent that it now conforms much more to the British model. This, I think, has an important bearing on the whole problem of integration in this country, and I would even say that the changing economic conditions may in time change the ideology which is presented to people.

Fletcher: How much does the different degree of industrialization in the two examples enter into your findings, Dr Raveau? You say in your abstract that these traditional societies "avoid the nuclear family model occurring in the Western world", yet they accept the patterns proposed by 'post-industrial' society, and this puzzles me.

Raveau: Post-industrial society is the society of leisure and easy outside contacts. The leisure factor helped the Africans most because they worked for only about four days a week, especially the middle-class people, and were able to use the three other days for interpersonal contacts. But they were not at all ready to modify their family structure to the so-called nuclear family pattern as they saw it among the bourgeois families of Paris or Strasbourg.

Fletcher: So they did fit into an industrial society, but because of the degree of leisure they enjoyed they were able to retain their own traditions.

Miller: Don't children in Paris play with each other, Dr Raveau? And if they do, doesn't this create contacts between the parents in the locality? You have given a picture of a family with its contacts scattered all over Paris.

Raveau: This applies only to the higher middle class, and their children don't play in the staircase or in the street.

Miller: I mean that children who go to the same school become friendly because of arrangements like car pools; whole networks of neighbourhood friendship are created around children in London and other cities.

Henriques: The business of car pools etc. is surely vestigial. What really happens is that parents make a definite decision that these are the children's friends, and actual choice of adult friendships doesn't come into it at all. The adults may happen to like each other, but this may be an exception.

Reynolds: In *Childhood in Contemporary Cultures*, Margaret Mead and Martha Wolfenstein wrote about the relationships between children in French and German parks.[10] These children were sometimes accompanied by their mothers and sometimes by their nannies, so they must have been upper middle class. The odd thing was that in French parks strange children were not allowed to play very much together or share toys, whereas in German parks they were allowed to borrow and if necessary fight over possession of toys.

Weiss: There have been only a few studies of friendship networks, but in more or less settled upper middle class communities the friendship network tends to be very much based on a husband's occupation and may extend over some geographical distance.[1] But in very new communities, among individuals from more or less the same background, friendship networks do develop around children's contacts.

Newson: The two factors are obviously linked for the upper middle class through the business of choosing the right sort of school, because the parents of other children who go to the same school are also professional people whom one would wish to know. I think that the child contact sometimes facilitates getting to know someone you want to know.

Henriques: I agree it can be used.

Rapoport: At the Tavistock Institute (in conjunction with Political and Economic Planning) we have studied university-educated women and their families and university-educated men and their families. Although a range of different family and household structures already exists in our society, there has been very little research on what those forms are, what their implications are, and what the effects on children are. Just looking at the combination of work and family of the highly qualified women, we find there are multiple forms, each of which creates a new kind of family structure. In our study[4] we assessed the orientation of men and women to their family and their work, in relation to the amount of time they planned to work during the life cycle. We identified at least eight types. Only about 22 per cent of highly qualified women are 'conventional' in that they do not intend to work at any time during the life cycle, and one third of these are ambivalent in that they feel a conflict at having to make this kind of choice. A second group of about 43 per cent are 'non-continuous workers', who fall into three sub-types; the largest, which we call the 'new-conventional', plan to work again, when the youngest child reaches secondary school age, and the other two are variations of this. The third main group consists of three types of 'continuous workers', intending to work more or less continuously throughout the life cycle. But their orientation to work and to the family is affected by whether they are really committed workers in the career sense or not. Some women will work throughout the life cycle, for instance, even with very young children, but they don't regard a career as a salient part of their lives and so are not tremendously taken away from their family needs through working. They are working for sociability, for money or for whatever it is, but they don't have a twin saliency. About 20 per cent of the highly educated women in our study have this dual saliency where work and family are both of major importance to them.

The orientation of the husband to his work and family, and the satisfaction he gets from them, greatly affect the kind of life pattern his wife is likely to have. It is not profitable to talk about the role of women or their problems except in relation to the significant men in their lives, if they are married. One has to take account, not only of the husband's orientation to women generally, but also of his way of integrating the spheres of his own life. Most highly qualified men accept and get their greatest satisfaction from career, not family. Family is always a close second, whereas with most women it is the other way round. But there are some men, and the fact that these are a minority shouldn't mean that they are forgotten, who prefer family activities to career activities and who would be very much happier if they could legitimately perform more family and fewer career activities. Similarly there are some women who would like to put much more effort into work and less effort into family activities.

The main plea I would like to make, apart from the need for more committed research on these things, is that we as social scientists should not set self-fulfilling prophecies going; that we at least should document the possible variations. To some extent documenting them makes it possible to legitimize them. If not, the problems that occur—and all structures inevitably have problems—are aggravated by the sense of deviance or illegitimacy that may come from functioning in a covert or unrecognized pattern.

Pirie: Most of the contributions to this symposium depend on certain assumptions and prejudices. Unlike the others, I will state what my assumptions and prejudices are! I assume that the mental capacities of women are equivalent to those of men, though not necessarily identical. Evidence for that assumption comes from personal experience and from the past existence of matriarchies such as that in pre-Homeric Greece and among the Dravidians. There is no evidence that these communities functioned any less smoothly than the male-dominated communities that replaced them. Some people argue that they worked better.

My prejudice is that educated women, playing an equal part with men in running society, are very much better company than women whose interests and opportunities are restricted to domesticity. I do not find the company of women who are solely housewives or who regard themselves, as Hindu women do, as "the ground on which men flourish" congenial. The latter role is unpleasantly like the role assigned to women by Hitler: "Kirche, Kinder, Küche".

Discrimination prevents most women from achieving equal status. But discrimination depends on the cooperation of the women themselves. Most of them seem to accept a second-class status, and for as long as this is so it will be very hard for the women who do not accept it to gain equal status. The primary reason for the widespread acceptance of such a status is failure of imagination. From infancy women are confronted with a man-dominated society and most of them find it impossible to envisage any other state of affairs. That is no doubt the primary reason for inequality. People do not struggle actively for what they do not think of as attainable. The other important reason is laziness. In a moderately affluent world, mismanaged by men, it is made extremely easy for women to avoid mental and physical exertion. Little is expected of many of them except that they should be decorative and agreeable. I see no reason to think that this is an innate or unalterable attitude of mind. Men would be every bit as lazy if they could get away with it. Perhaps in matriarchies they did and a group of them were maintained more or less as pets.

At present I doubt whether most women, in Britain at any rate, genuinely seek equal status if that would involve losing the privileges that they now enjoy. But I hope I am wrong.

Himmelweit: We have been talking about the significance of one activity or another but we have not discussed whether there are any biological differences in wanting to look after children. I personally think, until you prove me wrong, that there may be not only a culturally assigned role, but a greater biological preparedness among women for wishing to look after children. After all, most women who have a responsible job, if it comes to the crunch, always dispose of the job to look after the children.

McLaren: I would like to emphasize this point about the importance and difficulty of getting any scientific evidence of biological differences. Earlier, in talking about foster mothers or surrogate mothers, we stressed the absolute necessity, for emotional development, of having one individual on whom the small child could feel dependent, to provide continuity. Mrs Rapoport raised the question of whether this foster mother could be a male. You, Mr Chairman, said there was evidence that this would not be satisfactory, that the female had tactile properties —and you also mentioned smell—that made her more suitable as a foster-mother. Have you any evidence on that, or were you in fact airing your own prejudices as to the sort of foster-mother you would like to have if you were a baby?

Comfort: I was airing my prejudices, but a lot of work was done on olfactory stimuli by Brill[2] and Kalogerakis,[7] and a number of other people have made pyschoanalytic observations on these lines. I don't think these have been pursued in biology properly since. As to the tactile side, the male cannot lactate and he does not have mammary glands against which the baby can put his head. I was thinking here of the soft monkey, hard monkey work.

Hendrickse: On this question of a biological difference between male and female in relation to child-rearing, we must surely accept that there is a difference. The only question is, how long does it persist? After all a male cannot become pregnant and a woman can; and processes initiated in pregnancy do not stop immediately the baby is born. The whole process is tied up not just with the development of the baby, but also the development of the woman, along a line different from that of other women who aren't pregnant. There are psychological as well as physical changes in the pregnant woman which persist, and which in primitive rural society are essential for the survival of the group. The lion cub that is born to a mother who is incapable of breast feeding is a dead cub, and so it goes for all the mammalian species. Only man has invented an artificial method of providing physical nutrients, but this is one aspect alone of human development. The psychology of a woman at the time of birth is totally different from her psychology six months or six years later. I am sure this is all tied up with the whole process of infant rearing but how long this persists, how long this is essential for 'natural' human development, we don't know. One suspects that it is not a matter of hours or days, but a much longer period during which the ideal rearer of the infant is the female and not the male.

Miller: Theoretically it would be possible to rear a male who would be a good mother. The only problem is that males who were so reared would become uninterested in copulating with women.

Rapoport: We have no real evidence on whether children can be successfully reared from a very young age by men, but this practice does exist as a variant pattern in our society now. There are fathers bringing up infants, and there is probably room to do research on the effects of this. Women don't have to breast-feed babies now, and it is surely possible to imagine that babies don't have to be brought up by mothers. This doesn't mean there aren't differences between men and women, and it doesn't mean that the pyschological state of the woman isn't different at the birth of the baby from other times. But equally the psychological state of many fathers is different at the time the baby is born, and throughout the whole conception period—as expressed in such primitive rituals as the couvade. We need to question more and more some of these assumptions.

Rossi: From a biological point of view only one question is important. The whole construction of a woman's body is completely dedicated to this main function of being a mother and being connected with the child. The men have to fulfil other functions in the family.

Newson: We are not talking about women's bodies any more than about men's bodies; we are talking about minds and about bringing up children, which is a long long process. Secondly, the idea has been put forward that if a man were to bring up a child on his own, without a woman, his own sexuality would be in jeopardy. I don't know any evidence for this and I think it is one of these bogeys which get thrown around as a defence reaction to maintain the *status quo*.

Miller: The evidence is always indirect but a boy brought up totally by his mother, who is constantly presented with the mothering role, is confused sexually. When women are pregnant they undergo profound emotional changes; you can tinker with the culture as much you like, but you will not alter these. When women give birth they also go through emotional change; cultural engineering will not affect this.

Sjövall: The differences between men and women are a commonplace from a psychosomatic point of view. There are obviously some close relations between anatomical equipment and personality structure. In my country there are certain radical circles in which it is shockingly indecent to refer to these particular differences. They come very close to the situation described in Huxley's *Brave New World*,[5] where the concept of indecency was shifted from sexual matters proper to those of motherhood and childbirth.

Weiss: We are discussing the limitations in family form imposed by biological givens, and that issue was explored notably by Margaret Mead,[9] beginning in the middle 1920s. At that time she was arguing that there were no essential biological differences, that the only differences were the results of cultural development and elaboration. Recently I think she has qualified this judgment.

Hendrickse: It is perfectly possible for children to be reared by non-mothers, male or female. As a purely physical thing you can start a production line almost like the battery hens. But I am convinced, and the proof will show with time, that you will thereby change the very nature not only of the child but also of the rearing party. There are biological determinants in all this and our little experiment in modern development is but a millisecond of time in human evolution. We are playing around with a very fundamental biological mechanism which we do not understand, and we are not sure we shall want the end product.

Stone: The question of whether and how far men can play a mothering role is one which does not really concern us. We are not short of women to play a mothering role. The crucial situation with which we are faced is that we are now grossly overpopulated. And we are still bringing up half the population on the basic assumption that women have only two possible roles: to minister to men, and to bear and bring up children. All the propaganda against having too many children will fail unless something is done about this basic social outlook. Then add to this the increasing span of life. Increasingly people are living longer after the child-bearing and child-rearing ages. If we bring up half the population with the conviction that they have this role only, and certain ancillary things that we graft on to this role, they will then have all the years from 40 to 90 in which they cannot fulfil that role at all, following twenty-five years during which they are expected to fulfil it not more than twice.

Reynolds: With the increasing divorce rate I would have thought it is important, especially in the legal profession, to know whether there is any potential harm in leaving the child or children with the father. So I think it *is* relevant to discuss males rearing children, and some monkey data may be relevant here. There are at least three species of monkeys in which males share in the rearing of young, although never as far as I know from birth. It usually starts at about one year of age. Among Hamadryas baboons infant females are taken over at the age of about one year by sub-adult males and reared thenceforth by those males, eventually becoming their mates.[8] In some groups of Japanese macaques, some of the males take a share in rearing youngsters from the age of one year.[6] In Barbary macaques not only do males take over infants and care for them for short periods, but they also use the infants as part of their own interrelations with each other.[3]

Rossi: How will the increased period of adolescence influence the human family? Life gets longer and that might be one of the reasons to change the system, because a smaller group of people must now work for a larger group who start to work later and live longer.

Comfort: The gain in longevity may be divided into two parts. There is the gain in longevity which represents a gain in lifespan without a gain in vigour. In other words you go on being old for longer. But also in future there may be a longer period of adult vigour when the state of being old and therefore being dependent will be postponed for a number of years. I think we have to make these two extrapolations.

5: Marriage and The Family in the Near Future

ROBERT S. WEISS

I AM going to speculate about the way in which family life may develop in the near future in the more industrialized societies, especially the United States, and I shall do this by considering the likely implications of significant economic and technological developments and of what appears to be a newly dominant individual ethic in these countries. The general conclusion I shall propose is that family life will increasingly be organized around marriage, rather than around parenthood, and that the marital relationship will become both more important to the well-being of participants, and more fragile. My conclusions are, of course, speculative. Nevertheless I hope, to paraphrase Duncan,[3] that by directing attention to potentially important issues, the forecast may be useful even if not entirely accurate.

What I shall describe is what may come to be the dominant form of family life. Yet I assume there will always be great variations among individuals in the kinds of kinship ties, friendship ties and other relationships they maintain, and consequently in the form they give to relationships within their households. As a consequence of the developments I shall describe, there may in the future be even more variation, more opportunity to choose alternatives, than there is at present.

The developments in the society which I believe will have most impact on the form and functioning of the family include: (1) increased affluence; (2) increased reliability of income; (3) longer schooling for men and women; (4) widespread distribution of contraceptives; and (5) the further development of an ethic of self-realization. Let us consider each in turn.

INCREASED AFFLUENCE

In the United States there has been a steady increase in disposable personal income over the years. Although the shape of the income distribution has changed hardly at all, the distribution as a whole has moved ever upwards on the scale.[14] This will undoubtedly continue. One effect of increased affluence will be to reduce familial interdependence by relieving the married couple of the need for careful financial planning, and by furnishing the resources for individualized activity.

One of the surprising findings of statistical study of divorces has been that these are more frequent in the less affluent sector of the society[7,8] even though the cost of litigation and divorce-motivated migration makes them harder to obtain. The functioning of low-income families, both during the Depression and now, suggests that difficulties with money account for much of the trouble they experience. Increased affluence should bring many of these families above what might be called the trouble line: the level below which insufficient funds requires of a couple the closest of coordination yet sets them at odds with one another, since for one to have something extra the other must go without. In this respect increased affluence will remove one source of tension which might otherwise result in marital instability. It is one of the few ways in which the future of the family looks brighter, but it is an important way.

Increased affluence will remove one of the pressures which now lead some married women in the lower economic stratum to work, but at the same time it will increasingly free women in higher strata from responsibility for home tasks so that they may redirect their energies however they wish: to school, to a job, to public service, or to an enriched social life. It will make it possible for them to hire maids and other service personnel to perform the cleaning and cooking tasks. It will also provide the second car with which other tasks can be delivered to a servicing centre, which might be especially important if household help becomes scarce. And women will not only delegate to maids or laundry centres the routine tasks associated with maintenance of home and family, but also will delegate to nannies, baby sitters, child-care centres, and nursery schools the demanding and at times exhausting tasks of surveillance and management of young children. As motherhood becomes more nearly a part-time job, and it becomes increasingly possible for a woman to pursue occupational and avocational interests, the interdependence of the husband and wife will be lessened. While this interdependence is a source of friction when there is not enough money, it is also a bond when money is more plentiful, and its weakening reduces the justifications for the marriage.

Increasing affluence will also reduce the extent to which individuals live as members of families rather than as members of marriages. In the United States doubling up of families is already so rare that the census in 1970 will no longer collect statistics on it.[10] However there still are many families in which there are secondary adults—grown children, single aunts, widowed mothers—and we may expect the number of these to decrease drastically.[11] People use money, when they have it, to buy space. When there is enough money, a grown son or daughter will go off on his own rather than live at home and contribute to the family finances, a single aunt will have her own flat, an aged mother who is unable to live entirely on her own will be given an apartment adjoining her daughter's house rather than a room in her daughter's house. The married couple will be on their own, without other adults in their household, throughout their entire married life, and without anyone else at all in their household, including children, through many years.

INCREASED RELIABILITY OF INCOME

At present it appears that members of the managerial and professional stratum of our society think of where to live as a career decision, and that in contrast members of the blue-collar stratum give greater weight to proximity to family and friends. When the Baker Chocolate firm ended its Boston operation a few years ago and moved to a more modern plant a thousand miles away, virtually every one of its executives pulled up stakes and moved with it, but very few of its blue-collar personnel moved, although some of the latter were comparatively well paid and could not expect the same wages at the bottom of the seniority ladder in a new plant. This kin-based immobility of blue-collar workers is by no means irrational traditionalism, nor a happy-go-lucky freedom from economic concern, but rather expresses a well-founded recognition that a manual worker has no job guarantee should hard times come. For the blue-collar worker security has traditionally been found in his family rather than in his firm, to the extent that it could be found at all.

As government social welfare programmes or the implementation of the concept that a worker has a property right in his job rule out hard times and loss of income, there will be a weakening of the bonds which at present hold a young blue-collar couple to the neighbourhood of the parents of the wife or, less frequently, the husband. Blue-collar workers will then display the same kind of geographical independence of the extended family that is now shown by the more middle class. They might be even less tied to kin: young middle-class couples generally count on help from their more established parents, but there would be less differential in resources between young couples and older couples in the blue-collar world, where incomes have a much gentler upward slope.

The consequence of moving away from kin is not that kin no longer help one another; the obligation of kin to help continues. Rather it is that with geographical distance kin can no longer routinely intermesh their routine tasks, and no longer routinely rely on one another: a woman and her mother can no longer shop for one another, a man can no longer ask his father-in-law to help with a plumbing repair. Although kin obligations continue, actual exchange of services is much reduced.[1, 13]

The reduction of frequent regular exchange with kin reduces the emotional warmth of kin ties, and this tends to isolate the nuclear family emotionally. In addition, under conditions of widespread mobility it is harder to maintain old friendships. With this weakening of bonds to the past, the partners in the nuclear family must rely on each other for a sense of the continuity of their selves.

The weakening of bonds to the past facilitates change and a striving for self-realization. In the middle-class this will express itself primarily in relation to job and career, but blue-collar workers may well be more concerned with their family lives and their leisure pursuits. We might find blue-collar workers moving not to the best job, but rather to the most attractive area of the country.

GREATER LENGTH OF SCHOOLING FOR BOTH MEN AND WOMEN

It is becoming social dogma that virtually everyone in the society can be helped occupationally by additional schooling. We may expect this to continue, and we may also expect that with increased affluence an even greater proportion of our population will be enabled to go beyond college to graduate and professional schools. Extended education has serious implications for family life because it requires postponement of entrance into the occupational world to the late twenties or early thirties, and because like other socialization experiences it changes an individual's values and concerns. Fundamental choices in the aspects of the self which the individual will value, and in his mode of life, remain uncrystallized well into his adulthood. Under these circumstances it will be difficult for individuals to commit themselves in marriage, or if they do, to be sure the marriages will last. Nevertheless, individuals who could easily live together without formal ceremony are likely to feel themselves impelled towards marriage, partly as a statement of their sincerity and present committedness, partly to better present to kin and others their sense of being a couple. At some later point husband or wife or both may discover the marriage is blocking rather than facilitating their development. We may expect that one consequence of protracted schooling will be vulnerable young marriages dependent for their continuation on the continued compatibility of two changing people.

An increase in the number of women who possess specialized educations will produce further problems. A woman who is trained as a botanist or a classicist or a physician will require an opportunity to perform in her speciality if she is to maintain a sense of professional identity; and certainly she will not find a basis for a sense of competence in keeping house.[15] However a career commitment by a highly specialized woman will create difficulties for the equally specialized husband she is likely to have: he will be forced to withdraw some energy from work in order that he may participate in the joint management of the house and family, not to mention sociability with his wife's colleagues.[12] Household tasks will not be assigned once and for all on the basis of what is a man's work and what is a woman's work, but instead there will have to be weekly or even daily planning for the management of family responsibilities within the joint professional schedules; and this, too, will absorb energy which in a more traditional family might be available to the man's career. The husband may desire the family to move towards a more traditional form, but for the wife this would represent an attack on her professional self.

Some fortunate men and women may be able to organize their work so that it, like their family life, is shared, and there is no loss of energy in the dual career pattern. But in most couples one might expect this pattern to generate tension. Whereas in a traditional family form the husband can see his wife as facilitating the realization of his professional aims, and the wife may possibly see her husband as facilitating her familial aims, the dual career family is likely to be nearer the zero-sum game in which the gains of the one are losses for the other.

CONTRACEPTION

Although we now have a number of reliable methods of contraception, there appears to be a cultural lag in their adoption, particularly in the low-income sector of the population. As one piece of evidence, the rate of illegitimacy has climbed steeply over the past twenty-five years.[10] Material collected by the Laboratory of Community Psychiatry, Harvard, suggests that one reason contraceptives are not used by young people from families of the respectable poor is that even their possession would be an admission of premeditation. Often enough the result of the failure to use contraceptives is a forced marriage between young people who more or less intended to marry each other anyway, although not so soon. With further distribution of contraception, we may therefore expect an increase in the average age at marriage. Since early marriage and childbearing produce lasting economic disabilities,[6] this should give young people more chance to establish themselves before beginning parenthood.

In general, the most important consequence of the widespread distribution of methods of contraception will be to make it possible for young couples to decide deliberately whether and when they will have children. We may expect couples, especially those in graduate or professional training, to begin families later in their lives, which will tend to slow down population expansion, even without a reduction in family size. It will also mean that parents will be older, and quite possibly more distant from their children, and so more willing to contract out responsibilities for caring for them. This, along with the resources made available by affluence, and the career motivations supplied by advanced schooling, will reduce the importance of the parent–child relationship within the family, and add to the emphasis on the marriage as the central core of familial relationship.

FAMILY—3

THE ETHIC OF SELF-REALIZATION

In the families we are hypothesizing, the tasks of child care will be delegated in good part to specialists. The child may spend most of the year in a school chosen to develop his potentials, and much of the summer in a camp chosen in the same hope. Some of the time not in school will nevertheless be absorbed in classes, in theatricals, in sports, in art. In all these activities the child is likely to sense that his obligation to his parents is not to contribute to the management of the home, but rather to utilize to the fullest the opportunities they have made available to him for realizing his potential capabilities. In this way will the child learn an ethic of self-realization as a moral necessity.

Separation from the kin group in college and later will support the image young people have of themselves as unconnected individuals rather than representatives of a kin alliance. This will be reinforced by the conduct of the classroom. There the individual will be exhorted to attend to his own development, and graded on his success in doing so. The result of these social influences will be the development of individuals whose outlook expresses another form of the Protestant ethic, in which each individual is responsible for testimony to his own inner light. In the perspective of this ethic, over-adaptation to family may be thought near to immoral. A woman who sacrifices an artistic or a business career for her family would be seen as having been false to herself, unless of course it was the family she fundamentally cared for. This ethic makes fidelity to a marriage always contingent on the contribution of the marriage to the self, and whether it is a desirable or an undesirable ethic it must give rise to marital instability.

CONSEQUENCES OF THE FOREGOING

The family form which would be the consequence of the developments I have just described is an isolated nuclear family without secondary adults within the home, in contact with kin and with many friends, but without emotionally intimate ties to either. In this form collaboration in managing the family is a less important function of the marriage for the partners than is the maintenance of an emotional tie. Indeed, the need to intermesh plans and schedules is a source of some discomfort: task division must be managed by frequent discussion and negotiation rather than being set, for the most part, by the adoption of traditional responsibilities. This is a family form which gives primary place to the marital relationship: there are only a small number of children, quite possibly born rather late in the marriage, and though each child was wanted at the time of conception, responsibility for child care is to a very great extent contracted out to service personnel.

There is fairly good evidence that the family form I am describing would be only an extension of a shift which has taken place in the last fifty years from a more traditional marital form, in which primacy was given to shared responsibility for maintenance of home and family, to a form in which emotional intimacy was given primacy.[2] This trend is evident in the changes we are making in our divorce laws. In the past, our laws held that a marriage must continue so long as each partner properly met the responsibilities of his or her role. Today, more and more, the emotional compatibility of the couple is the issue, and in many jurisdictions a marriage may be dissolved if a court decides it has 'broken down'.[5] What has happened is not that our laws have become more indulgent, but rather that our ideas regarding the nature of marriage have changed.

The traditional marriage based on responsibilities to the home and family had a tendency to persist in the face of difficulty. Should the woman be a poor housekeeper, or a man a poor provider, the other partner might be resentful, but the marriage could be maintained for a time at least. In contrast, a marriage based on the maintenance of an intimate emotional tie depends on continuing trust between the partners, and a continuing belief by each partner in the other's commitment and understanding. A relationship of this sort is vulnerable to disruption by any event which leads to loss of faith, or respect, or caring for the other. This sort of marriage has less tendency to persist: participants know quickly when it has gone sour, and they cannot simply do their part and wait. A woman can much more easily continue to behave as a wife in a soured marriage which depends on role performance than in one which exists primarily to provide emotional intimacy.

These marriages come about in part because of the absence of intimate ties between the marital partners and their kin or friends. The consequence of disruption of the marriage will be the virtual emotional isolation of the marital partners. Emotional isolation is a difficult state to accept, perhaps especially so for people who subscribe to the ethic of self-realization. One response to it may be to attempt to supplement the now limited provision of the marriage by an extra-marital sexual liaison, since sexual involvement can quickly establish a sense of emotional intimacy, and can thereafter reinforce a sense of mutual commitment. Other approaches to supplementation of a near-empty marriage may also be tried: the use of drugs, including alcohol, in social situations; participation in therapy groups or other structured social forms which promise to bring individuals close to one another, such as cruises and theatre games. But of these approaches to supplementation, extra-marital liaisons are very likely the most easily initiated and, at least in their beginning, the most satisfying. Yet the reason-for-being of these extra-marital liaisons is their capacity to provide emotional intimacy, and so they will inevitably attack whatever remaining intimacy the marriage affords: it seems likely that an extra-marital liaison will, if anything, hasten a decision to divorce.

The divorce rate in the United States has been increasing steadily and we may expect that with these developments in marriage its increase will continue. At present the divorce rate is about three times what it was fifty years ago, and although we have only imperfect statistics on divorce and hardly any statistics on separation and desertion, it would appear that the chances today of a marriage ending for some reason other than the death of one of the spouses is better than one in four, and perhaps approaches one in two.[5] (It appears that there is about one divorce to every four marriages, and there may be as many separations and desertions, together, as divorces.)

We may expect that in the near future the probability of a marriage ending by desertion, separation or divorce will reach, if not exceed, one in two. Increasing frequency itself will make divorce increasingly acceptable, and so lead to greater frequency. With this likelihood of divorce we may expect a good deal of public attention to the issue, some of it directed towards strengthening the bonds of marriage, some directed in a contrary fashion towards amending the divorce laws to make divorce a less expensive and easier procedure. The outcome of these two opposed themes may be courts which require divorcing couples to attend conciliation hearings but which, if these fail, award divorce virtually on petition.[1]

The greater accessibility of divorce may actually encourage marriage. Young people who have decided to live together in any event may opt for the greater stability, security and social convenience of marriage, on the assumption that if it doesn't work out they can always get divorced. They may well use this nearly explicit escape clause; young marriages have always been poor bets, and as we noted earlier, if each of the partners is still studying, still developing and changing, their chances of lasting are likely to be poorer still. Because of this it will become generally understood that marriage among young people is not necessarily forever. A pregnancy will then have the special significance of an announcement that the marital pair believe their marriage will last, since in a time of effective contraception the pregnancy will be assumed to have been intended. The pregnancy, rather than the initial vows, will signify the commitment of the pair to the permanence of the union.

We may develop a system which resembles that once proposed by Judge Lindsay in which our laws would recognize two kinds of marriage, an easily breakable one in which it is forbidden to have children, and a nearly unbreakable one in which children are permitted.[9] We are not likely actually to adopt this in our law, but I think we will come close to adopting it in our shared understanding of the nature of marriage. We shall, of course, continue to find couples who have children in the belief that their union is permanent, and yet later get divorced, just as we now find couples taking vows of permanence in all good faith and later finding they cannot keep them. But we shall increasingly find that young couples recognize the instability of marriage and decide not to have children until they are more sure of themselves.

With marriage a source of so much difficulty, individuals will certainly consider alternative ways of organizing their lives. Some couples will live together without formal marriage. This will represent even less of a commitment to permanence than marriage without children, and will make dissolution of the relationship easier to manage. Very likely this will be the choice particularly of very young people who are not yet sure of their future. Among somewhat older people the social advantages of marriage are likely to lead a couple to take a chance on it. But even among the very young, sharing a household without marriage is an available choice only so long as there are no children. With children, a woman is apt to want either a marriage, with some commitment to permanence, or else her own household. In the latter circumstance, a man with whom she is emotionally intimate would not share living quarters with her, but rather would be a boy-friend, with a place of his own.

A boy-friend relationship might be defined as one in which a woman and man are emotionally committed to one another, but maintain different households. This seems to be the form most often assumed by intimate ties when the woman already has children. The essential difference between marriage and a boy-friend relationship turns out to be that in marriage the man has rights in the woman's household, indeed in most families is head of that household, whereas in the boy-friend relationship he has only those privileges granted him by the woman. There is no shared commitment to maintain home and family; should the woman and her boy-friend drift apart emotionally, the relationship is over. As long as the woman and her boy-friend are getting along, the boy-friend may take most of his meals with her and her children, may stay the night, may take care of the children now and then, may drive the woman when she goes shopping. Should either the woman or the boy-friend say he or she no longer cares for the other, at that moment everything ends. The man can no longer come for meals, has no further right to direct the children, will no longer be asked for favours.

Because of the woman's responsibilities for child care, the site of the boy-friend relationship will ordinarily be the woman's apartment. The consequence of this locating of the relationship in the woman's home is that the man is without rights in the setting in which the couple spend most of their time: he cannot express his moods, except as the woman will tolerate them, cannot insist on any way of managing the home or the children, cannot demand that he be given privacy, cannot take space for his activities, cannot have friends in. As a long-term arrangement, the boy-friend relationship may be less satisfactory for the man than for the woman, and in a committed boy-friend relationship, where the couple expect to be together indefinitely, the man might well press for marriage.

Still another approach to resolution of the problems of establishing a relationship which will provide the functions of marriage is the commune, which in its extreme form may be a kind of group marriage, in which property is held in common, and it is understood that individuals are emotionally and sexually available to one another. At the Laboratory of Community Psychiatry of Harvard, we have insufficient experience with this social form to evaluate it, but in the few reports I have heard it appears that in most communes, despite ideological commitment to the contrary, pairing is almost unavoidable. Individuals find it difficult, perhaps impossible, to have unquestioning trust in several people at once, and find themselves developing special reliance on just one other person. With this pairing, in a communal setting, come not only the usual problems of maintaining an intimate tie, but special problems as well, stemming from an ideological context which does not give the pair its support. One result is that older couples go on their own or move to a 'couples' commune, to protect their relationship. If these reports prove true in general, it would suggest that group marriage is no answer. Perhaps preferable would be intentional communities, in which pairings are recognized, but the emotional distances among pairs are reduced. Yet intentional communities, like kin groups, reduce an individual's freedom to find that job or that living situation in which he can realize himself most fully. They require geographical, if not social, immobility.

The conclusion would seem to be that marriage will become more and more difficult, but that alternatives to marriage, though they may be preferable for some individuals, will hardly constitute solutions to marriage's difficulties. What might we advise as social policy? How does one prescribe for a hopeless situation?

A desirable strategy would seem to me to be to continue a process of search for solutions, and to be aware that any solution can only be temporary. So long as a situation is being worked on, it is being managed: the resentments it sets going are being aired, and tentative solutions, compromises, and indulgences become possible, because there is general recognition that whatever is agreed to is temporary, and general acceptance that movement is in itself important. A permanent solution, on the other hand, leads to trouble: its disadvantages are inescapable, and resentment toward them will grow.

From this point of view we might recognize as proposals for temporary solutions attempts to make a dual career family work by having the man stay at home half the time, or reconstructionist attempts to send a woman back into the home by declaring that her self-realization can be attained only through motherhood. Living together without marriage, or boy-friend relationships, or communal arrangements, could also be seen as proposals for temporary solutions both in the lifetime of an individual, and in the development of the society. Perhaps for some individuals one of these temporary solutions would be a permanently desirable alternative; they might find in it a balance of advantages and disadvantages which will be suitable for them through their lifetimes. From this perspective, the more alternatives available, the better.

Given an ethic of self-realization, and an economic and social structure which makes its pursuit possible, marriage must inevitably suffer, although possibly individual life may be enhanced. One can only hope for a tolerant society, with many alternatives, whose members recognize that every solution is faulty, but who are nevertheless willing to continue to explore possible modifications of existent forms.

DISCUSSION

Newson: Your whole proposition hinges on the importance of self-realization—the importance of being yourself; but there is a contrary way of looking at this, in terms of giving yourself away to someone else. In the end the question comes down to basic Christian ethics. It may be that you have to lose yourself to find yourself, and have to have this commitment in order really to be yourself.

Weiss: This sort of resolution will certainly be proposed, especially for women, as has happened traditionally. Women will be told that their true careers are as wives and mothers; that they should realize themselves through giving to their husbands and their children. This may work for a time until women discover this isn't a true career at all, but is exactly what they *don't* want. They will then say, as many are saying now, that they don't want to be locked away in suburbs. They may come to distrust the idea of self-realization through the family as a male propaganda campaign against women, and decide that women have to interact with each other to find their true selves through the development of careers which express what it is to be a woman. And this will resolve the problem for a while, until this also is found to be unsatisfactory.

Ali Baig: This definition of self seems quite incorrect if it is related to self-realization. Is it 'ego' or something higher? We have been talking of marriage, which is measurable, without the factor of meaning, which is not measurable. Similarly we talk of sex, since copulation is measurable, excluding the factor of love which is not. Perhaps something unique happened historically that has given India another dimension in marriage and family life. The Dravidians, who were the earliest inhabitants of the sub-continent as far as we know, were a matriarchal society. The Aryans who invaded India some 5000 years ago were nomadic, aggressive and patriarchal. Regardless of the profound disturbance this must have caused then, today the blend gives both man and woman distinct functions and responsibilities. The *Rig Veda* says "The wife is the home and the *only* place of rest". That gives woman a rather meaningful function. Women in India know this. This function specifically is to be the ground for the spiritual growth of her mate. Women accept this as a positive value. There has also been no historical conflict between science and religion, as there was in Western society during the Middle Ages. Modern education and scientific development conformed perfectly with India's ancient understanding of supernatural phenomena. The rational mind and religious belief and practice therefore did not conflict. This has deeply affected the life of the people, who recognize themselves as a part of cosmic forces. The main object of life thus is growth; and the object of marriage is the spiritual growth of your partner. Man in this context must develop spiritually with woman as the matrix to help him achieve this. In this relationship her self-sacrifice—and there is considerable giving up of the ego—is positive. The strange institution of the *arranged* marriage becomes possible to understand only where this ability to give up is understood. 'Giving up' is the most formative discipline in human existence.

Mahatma Gandhi has written about this in detail in his autobiography, *My Experiments with Truth*.[1] He married Kasturba when she was ten and their first child was born when she was 14 years old. Her life judged by Western standards was one of total submission. His love was possessive, demanding and even dictatorial. But her surrender was part of his growth; she could have been called an insignificant woman during her life, but at her death he ceased to live in a sense, since his whole being was in her. I think many people would be grateful to be loved and needed so wholly. It is growth related to the divine, and the only human *experience* we have of this kind of divine surrender is in the surrender of one person to another. The sexual act is actually our only worldly experience of this. Life based on the ego alone has no meaning. We come into the world imperfect; the discipline of marriage helps us to change—or at least gives us this opportunity. Earthly life is thus supremely important, and marriage has a real function. The stability of the parents is also a profoundly important element for the growth of the children.

Miller: Mrs Baig is saying something that is missing from your scheme, Dr Weiss, and that scheme is riddled with inconsistencies. To bring up children both collaboration and emotional intimacy are necessary, quite apart from the extended network that children require. The needs of neither men nor women are met in your scheme, because in fact the present clinical evidence is that a woman in an intimate relationship, usually long before the man, begins to feel that she wants to make it permanent. She wants to have a child; and this does not fit in with the scheme you have drawn. Self-realization is not possible without important emotional connexions with other people. With only nuclear families, and no extended social nexus, society will probably end in a welter of self-destruction.

McLaren: What about the position of children in Dr Weiss's scheme? Both Dr Miller and Dr Weiss assume that the decision by a couple to have a child is evidence that they think their union will be permanent. I am not sure this is always so, even today, and I am certainly not sure that it will continue to be so, however much one might think it should. Longer schooling for men and women is going to mean that although emotional maturation may be accelerated, the part which Dr Weiss referred to as identity crystallization will be retarded, and I presume one is unlikely to get stable unions formed until this identity crystallization has occurred. I very much doubt whether people will put off having children until that time, and from the biological point of view one doesn't want women to put off having children too long—the late twenties are all right, but not much later.

Referring back to Dr Fox's paper, the nuclear family with the permanent male came about because the male was necessary for the economic support of the woman and child or children. If the woman herself increasingly becomes an earner, or the State provides economic support for the woman and child, we shall perhaps see the development of a system like that in Dr Fox's diagram 6, where the mother and children live together, without the father.

Fox: With respect to Dr Weiss, that is the boy-friend relationship with the semi-permanent rotating male!

McLaren: Is the effect on children necessarily bad, providing that there are these male extra-familiar adults?

Weiss: Another alternative I didn't describe is a continued relationship with the ex-husband, which may be a fairly stable arrangement but is almost always extremely ambivalent.

Stone: Surely Mrs Ali Baig was really putting forward a rather more extreme example of the Christian ethic. The idea of realizing yourself only by giving yourself away has always been sold more successfully to women than to men. In marriage a man does not give himself body and soul to his spouse, as a woman is expected to do. These ideas are all based on the assumption that the human spirit exists in men alone and not in woman at all. If a woman's function is to be the ground for the spiritual growth of her mate, this presumes that she cannot have and should never expect any spiritual growth of her own. This means either that there is no spirit in a woman to grow, or that if there is, it should be killed off. Dr Weiss makes the same assumption when he suggests that

3*

women might collaborate with each other in developing careers which would express what it is to be a woman. It has never been suggested that men's careers are directed towards expressing what it is to be a man rather than a woman. This assumes that humanity is men, and that women are simply ancillaries to men—that they are always means and never ends.

Weiss: I feel like a white liberal being attacked by the black militants with whom he had always thought himself allied!

Sjövall: What I was going to say has already been said by Dr Stone, but I think that self-realization is a tricky thing and self is not ego. Self is a wider concept, and the idea that the self-realization of woman should necessarily be some kind of a surrender or sacrifice to another being is rather unfortunate and would not work out very well in our present social arrangements.

Comfort: Is the Hindu view perhaps being misunderstood here?

Ali Baig: The patriarchal element has certainly been rather exaggerated! What we have in India is a blend of patriarchy with a society that is mother-dominated, in spite of the seeming surrender to the man, women's physical care for male well-being, and the necessity for a male child. The matriarchal system dominates because woman is looked upon as the source of strength. She is never considered a weak element. But in giving up her ego aspect, she also gains, and this is not far removed from the pure Christian ethic.

Sjövall: This sounds very similar to the refusal of Swiss women to take on voting power because they feel they dominate the field from the domestic scene anyway.

Reynolds: Dr Weiss assumed that certain developments in the socio-economic sector have necessarily certain implications for kinship relationships. I wonder if this determination is justified? If a concerted effort were made in the mass media to stress the importance of kinship links as the basis of what you should do with your life, the situation could be reversed. I think this has been happening in Russia during the last decade, with articles in the press about caring for the older generation of grandparents.

This leads on to my second point which concerns the boy-friend relationship. I wasn't quite clear how much this relationship already exists in the United States. It certainly exists and is well-documented in the West Indies, where M. G. Smith[5] calls it 'extra-residential mating', I believe. There you have exactly the same *physical* situation as Dr Weiss described with the women and children in one place and the man coming in to visit, but there is not necessarily any emotional involvement between the man and the woman with children.

Weiss: The description I gave of the form and function of the boy-friend relationship is based on a close study of interviews with a small sample of no longer married women. I have no information about the frequency of this relationship in the United States.

Himmelweit: I agree with Dr Weiss about the effects of affluence and increased dependability of income on marriage, but I think that he sees both schooling and the ethic of self-realization in old-fashioned terms. The idea that a person will only crystallize when he or she has finally chosen a job is true today, but will not necessarily be true tomorrow. I believe that as jobs recede in importance people will want a wider range of opportunities of expressing themselves. As a result they will be less concerned about excelling in any one way. At the moment everything is geared in a single direction. If you are a mother, you have to be an exceedingly good mother; if you are in a career, you have to be in an exceedingly good career. Such attitudes produce a great fall-out of misery and unhappiness with clear-cut signals of failure.

I believe the friendship relationship will become more important. For instance, if we look at the more radical students today and the solutions they find for living together, one characteristic they share is that they retain most of their old boy-friends or girl-friends as friends so that they have close emotional ties with them but perhaps no longer sexual ones. They have great concern for one another and this extends to quite a number of people—usually not their families, but it may extend to people in their own age groups for whom they take an unusual degree of responsibility. A young person knows that he or she has the homes of many friends to go to as of right. This pattern will become even stronger. Your alternative solutions are perhaps couched in too narrowly sexual, and too narrowly economic, terms, without allowing for this emotional spillover.

Newson: In the long run it is totally unsatisfactory for the average man to pin the whole justification of his life on his career prospects, on what he can achieve by *doing*. Both men and women need this other *giving* relationship and want to create an area of warmth and intimacy somewhere. And where else than in a family kind of setting would you have a group who feel very strongly that they are emotionally committed to one another?

Adams: The idea of self-giving, rather than being seen as submersion in another personality, should be understood in two other ways, first in interpersonal relationships and second in the relationship of the individual to the society around him. In the interpersonal relationship self-giving is not necessarily a surrender of the self, but is rather, when adequately understood and practised, a fulfilment of the self. Likewise the general ethical and social-psychological significance of the relationship to the larger community beyond the family is of extreme importance for the understanding and fulfilment of the person. Let me give an example from the history of religion.

In the primitive Christian community attention was given not only to interpersonal relationships (and to individual salvation) but also to broader associations. The family was understood in the context of the social order. Thus the early church developed a radical criticism of the State; it also developed all sorts of philanthropic concerns. The churches had credit unions, and local congregations assumed the obligation for the vocational education of orphans. The status of women and of the slave was raised by assigning responsibilities to them in the congregation. The manifest function of the church was the eternal salvation of souls, but a latent function turned out to be training in the skills of organization.

In modern democratic society, beginning with the left wing of the Reformation, associations analogous to the small congregation developed, namely the voluntary associations—the middle associations between the family and the community or between the family and the State. Through these organizations public opinion was given social and political reality and function. The middle organization became an indispensable instrument of democratic society for the development of new sensitivities with regard to the common good. These new sensitivities elicited philanthropic activity and organization and also political action.[4] Max Weber's study of *The Protestant Ethic and the Spirit of Capitalism*[6] has done us a disservice in so far as it identifies 'the Protestant ethic' merely with an ethos of hard work and frugality and of individual economic success. The Neo-Calvinists had a genius for forming associations, and these associations were often concerned with politics and the public welfare; indeed, many of them combatted 'the Protestant ethic' as delineated by Max Weber. The Quakers were conspicuous in devising voluntary associations concerned with overcoming social evils and with effecting legislation to that end.[2]

In the democratic society these middle associations that stand between (and connect) the family and the community or the family and the State provide a major means of self-giving which fulfils both the individual and the society. We might say that they provide both psychotherapy and sociotherapy.[3]

These middle organizations, formal and informal, occur also in the youth culture, where they provide the means of achieving independence and autonomy in face of the family, and the opportunity for self-giving that relates youth to the political order.

Miller: Dr Weiss said that economists expect society to become more affluent. In terms of the rise of gross national products in the West this may be true, but it is by no means certain that affluence will be distributed throughout society. It is perfectly possible that in fact we are reconstituting a type of feudal society in which the means of production and affluence will basically be concentrated in a few families. I don't think we can necessarily assume the spread of affluence even in America. Surely the evidence is that more and more of the means of production continues to get into the hands of fewer and fewer people.

Weiss: The nature of the income distribution has been essentially unchanged over the last fifty years.

Miller: I know, but I am talking about the ownership of the means of production.

Weiss: The Marxist might expect something different, although different Marxists might expect different things.

6: Environmental Planning and Its Influence on the Family

SU ROGERS

Is the quality of the immediate and general environment an important influence in terms of human behaviour? This is such a vast subject that, except for some opening remarks, I shall limit my discussion to the immediate environment and its influence on the family; that is to those four walls and a roof that enclose the individual family—the single dwelling unit, the domestic shelter. I shall also assume that in the future the family will be in a very fluid situation.

The physical environment is certainly one of the most important influences directing our whole pattern of behaviour, our psyche, our health. Correlations between bad housing conditions, slum areas, overcrowding, and the incidence of juvenile delinquency, nervous disorders and divorce have been illustrated innumerable times. In the same way, it is easy to prove that children living in dwellings which lead directly to a busy road are maimed or killed in much higher proportion than those who live in areas where pedestrians and traffic are segregated. Similarly, a Ministry of Health survey[3] has shown that the incidence of respiratory infections and psychoneurotic disorders is abnormally high in young mothers living in high rise flats—Point Blocks.

In the post-war period, much has been said about the ills of our present environment and we know how essential it is to change it. Sadly, we are still creating the conditions we have criticized so strongly; we are still creating the inhuman city, the never-ending suburbia. Yet we need not enforce upon ourselves an environment so foreign to our natures that we end up fighting it rather than benefiting from it. We talk at great length about the population explosion and the shortage of natural resources, but I find it comforting to know that the population of the world could still stand shoulder to shoulder on the Isle of Wight.

For the moment we have the resources, and we have the land. What we lack is the economic/sociological/architectural/political organization to make those resources into the most useable, functional and at the same time, most pleasant form. The findings of the Centre for Land Use and Built Form Studies, at the University of Cambridge,[1] show that if we demolished all our existing buildings and started again, the population of 62500000 predicted for the year 2000 in England and Wales could all be housed in individual houses, each with their own gardens, with a minimum plot size of 20 × 100 feet, in a total of two million acres (809 372 hectares) of urban land. This area is only half of that expected to be classified as urban in the year 2000 if we continue to develop our urbanization in the same manner and at the same speed as now. There are slightly more than 37 million acres in England and Wales; so two million acres represents only 74 per cent of the total. This would of course only be a real possibility if the pattern of land ownership were controlled.

I am not advocating that each family should have a house and a garden in a plot 20 × 100 feet, thus achieving the sort of Utopia envisaged by Ebenezer Howard 70 years ago,[4] but I want to illustrate that the control of the environment is still very much a real possibility. Looking at it another way, city densities are now $2\frac{1}{2}$ times lower than they were at the beginning of the century and distances between essential community services are no longer determined by walking distance but by vehicle time, thus spreading out those services and patterns of relationship which were once the key to the city core. We travel the greater distances by car or bus which, in their turn, bring pollution to the atmosphere, danger through conflict with pedestrians and other vehicles, and nervous strain in getting to places on time. As the city spreads itself, less is left of the real country, but by the year 2000 the population of England and Wales could still be housed at 77 to the acre within a 20-mile radius of Trafalgar Square if some comprehensive plan could be adopted.

I quote from the introduction to Chermayeff and Alexander's *Community and Privacy*[2]: "It is perfectly possible to rebuild deliberately the human environment in such a way that the ultimate result will be the widening and deepening of the life of the species as such, the augmenting increase of life scope, aesthetic enrichment in the most profound sense. This is the only kind of creative evolution of which we are capable." I hope we are capable of that.

SYSTEMS OF ENCLOSURE

Except for those of the privileged few, existing systems of enclosure, whether in Point Blocks, suburbia or urban slums, do not adequately answer the basic and conflicting human needs. The last really adequate national survey of the state of our buildings was in 1964. It showed that 15 per cent of all housing was structurally unsound and should be condemned; only 35 per cent was in a good state of repair; 18 per cent had no indoor water closet, 17 per cent had no hot water supply and 22 per cent had no fixed bath. The statistics are shattering.

We all know that damp basement flats breed bronchitis and rheumatism and that overcrowding breeds nervous disorders and family tensions, and is a hazard to health in terms of infection. Such immediate results of the physical inadequacies of shelters are predictable and measurable in terms of human suffering. But what of the less measurable factors? What of the damage or otherwise done to our spirits by living in a square box, perfectly serviced and maybe with adequate space (that is by the standards of the Parker Morris report[5]), but surrounded by a concrete jungle and highly dangerous because of the constant conflict between hardness, speed, noise, dirt on the one hand and the softness of the human body and of our thoughts on the other. Those four walls limit who is to come, who can go; they limit the size of the family, the freedom of expression, the way of life.

The systems of enclosure have to be fundamentally re-thought, not only in terms of bringing them all up to the right environmental standards—which is basically a question of economics—but also in terms of the less tangible factors. I want to question the basic solution of confining the physical enclosure of the family to those four walls. Assuming we have adequate resources to provide the right environmental standards, computers to compute those ideal standards, and robots to do the work, I would like to consider three criteria for planning the domestic shelter of the future. They are flexibility, freedom of choice and zoning.

(i) *Flexibility*

The four walls of the average home remain throughout their existence static and immovable, whereas the people who live inside grow, multiply and contract; not only do they vary in number, but their needs, abilities and mental attitudes also change. Let us look for a moment at a typical nuclear couple, a young married couple with at first no children: they probably both work and need a shelter which will reflect their independence from their parents, and where they show off their proud possessions, but which is cheap to maintain, easy to clean, etc., and therefore moderately small. They then have a baby; at first his demands do not fundamentally alter the parents' physical organization of space for he can, if need be, sleep under the dining-room table. Very soon the child asserts himself, he makes a noise, a mess; he has lots of possessions. More children follow—the noise, the mess, the possessions multiply with the children. The original shelter is no longer big enough, whatever the organization inside.

The children develop into teenagers; they no longer need supervising, they want to come and go as they please. Their record players, or their computerized music, make even more noise and they need privacy. The children gradually leave home: our couple are alone again, probably not yet 'old', and now wishing to enjoy their new-found freedom. The wife may go back to work, and although they will want more space than they did at the beginning of their married life, they will not necessarily want to clean and heat, say, four empty spaces. The house should be able to shrink. One of the couple dies and the other is left alone, incapable of coping either mentally or physically. He has to go into care because none of the children, who by this time all have several children of their own, have any room.

We all understand this pattern of life cycle very well, but to expand the home as the family expands has been until now all but impossible, very expensive, time-consuming and messy. Now at last we are no longer tied by the limits of technology, although no house-building concerns have as yet recognized this. Materials need not be tied to the ground, and structures can span economically from external wall to external wall, freeing the space inside for flexible use. (Figs. 1 and 2).

Walls can be unclipped, added to and refitted over a weekend. Houses can even be supported by air and the pneumatic house can grow as the family grows, and *vice versa*. This is not something of the future either: we are at the moment building two of these extendible flexible houses ourselves, and our reasons for doing so are just those I have described above.

A typical client wanting a house was a bachelor doctor with a large collection of modern paintings. He wanted a real bachelor pad, surrounded more or less by an art gallery, and that is what he got. By the time he moved into his house/pad, two and a half years after our original briefing, he had a wife, one and a half children and an *au pair* girl, all accommodated in his art gallery, which was unfortunately totally unsuitable and totally unchangeable because the house was built out of bricks and mortar. Since then we have added one room to the roof and one in the courtyard, both at great expense and inconvenience. The *au pair* girl sleeps in the garage!

How much better to be able to go to your local department store and buy an additional 200 square feet of shelter over the counter! We are very close to the point where shelters can be marketed off the peg in this way: just as men come to lay the new carpet, so there will be men who will clip or zip on one's extension. A second-hand market for the unzipped extensions might even be envisaged.

A house should be a 'general purpose' shell, not designed around the specific needs of one family, but capable of adapting to any needs and capable also of allowing for individual expression in terms of fabric, form and use.

(ii) *Choice*

This flexibility in the size and organization of our shelters immediately leads to the second criterion of freedom of choice. Young and Willmott in *Family and Kinship in East London*[6] describe what happens to family life when people move from an old tightly knit neighbourhood to a new housing estate. The housing in the old neighbourhood was inadequate in terms of sanitation, space, light, etc., but for generations the same families had lived in the same few streets. Most belonged to a very active extended family where responsibilities, festivities, debts and illnesses were to a large extent shared by that extended family of aunts, uncles, grandparents, siblings and so on. Those who wanted such small pleasures as an indoor water closet or running water had the choice of moving to a modern house on a new estate, "Greenleigh", 20 miles away, outside London, where they had to break their ties with their extended families because of the physical distances; or they could stay in their slum house in Bethnal Green, with the companionship which went with it.

Young and Willmott found that few of the families who moved to Greenleigh, and especially the wives, failed to find it very lonely. They had had such a tight kinship structure in Bethnal Green that they saw the mother or other relatives several times a day and found it strange in Greenleigh that there was no one they could call on in illness, confinement, etc. Many of these couples admitted that they stayed in Greenleigh 'only for the kiddies'. Such a kinship structure, which most sociologists agree has enormous value, was totally and successfully disintegrated by rigid planning rules and inflexible structures. In the new postwar estates and new towns the planners only provided the three-up, two-down house —maybe with different facades or an extra bedroom for a large number of children, but basically incapable of housing more than the nuclear families for whom they were intended. Not only were the houses rigid answers to a single problem, but the whole conception of the towns and estates made them incapable of expansion, so that when the first-generation children grew up, married and therefore wanted their own independent accommodation, there were no sites left in Greenleigh for more building: another migrant generation was then on the move, with no chance to establish any roots which could lead to the reconstruction of the extended family. For the family to remain a stable unit, it must be able to choose its own pattern of kinship, to determine itself where its own boundaries lie, to accommodate three or four generations if that is how it is structured.

We talk enough in this country about our treatment of old people and how we banish them to homes for the old, but if we can provide a shell in which old people can be accommodated within the family, for preference independently, perhaps more families would take on the responsibilities and even find enjoyment in looking after their own old people. We must provide a shell within which the family can do as it likes, a mobile shell which it can lift up and 'plug-in' to whichever community centre, or non-community for that matter, the whims, economies and needs of the moment lead it.

(iii) *Zoning*

In the same way as a shelter needs to extend and contract during one life cycle, so it needs to be organized differently inside, not only to accommodate different numbers of people at varying times, but to reflect and satisfy the differing needs of individuals. Parents' needs differ fundamentally from, and conflict with, children's needs. Children create noise, dirt, untidyness; parents want peace, quiet, order. In planning the domestic shelter now, no attempt is made to zone the different areas for different uses—the parent's living space is traditionally the childrens' playroom. The family still needs a *hearth*, a communal meeting space where they are drawn together, where the common functions such as eating are shared, where they can exchange ideas and experiences and where the mother can supervise the young. This hearth can act as a buffer zone between the noise and dirt of the children and the quiet and cleanliness of the parents. Both generations need and enjoy their privacy, and will appreciate their meeting point all the more. Much research has shown that overcrowding in the home tends to break up the family. I would suggest that this is due not only to physical overcrowding but to a lack of proper zoning, a lack of organization, so that no realms are defined for differing activities. Teenagers may perhaps not leave home so soon if they have privacy within the home, their own entrance so that they can come and go as they please, and can enjoy being a member of the family unit rather than have it forced upon them by their physical enclosure.

With shelters that can be inflated or clipped together come also enormous savings in both time and the cost of materials. Either the government has to accept its role as the nation's house builder, no matter what system it uses, or the free-enterprise market has to provide a housing package which does not cripple the purchasers with debt repayments lasting 25 years. Perhaps the economic saving generated by the non-custom-built shelters, by not having to piece together a hundred thousand different components for each house we build, is our main hope of introducing some sanity into our construction industry, of introducing some fluidity into our housing policies and the resultant shelters. Houses are, after all, less complicated shelters than cars—why can they not be marketed in the same way?

Figures 1 and 2 show one way of putting some of these ideas into practice. Figure 3 is another solution.

To conclude, the influence of environmental planning, of the immediate environment on the family, is self-evident. It is important to turn this from a negative and passive influence to an active manipulative one. Not only must we provide the right body temperature, the correct number of rooms, but also a place where people can enjoy growth, self-expression and freedom, where the family can be as big or as small as it chooses, and where the limitations are not those of the four walls that enclose them and the visual chaos beyond, but rather limitations of their own choosing.

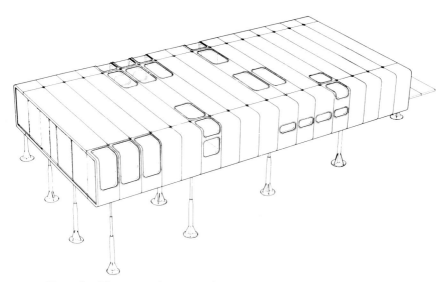

FIG. 1. Zip-up enclosure: adaptable, extendible, demountable, high environment housing system. (Designed by Richard & Su Rogers, Architects)

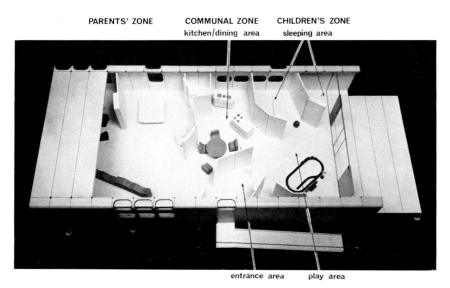

PARENTS' ZONE   COMMUNAL ZONE   CHILDREN'S ZONE
                 kitchen/dining area   sleeping area

entrance area   play area

FIG. 2. Zip-up enclosure: showing the flexible interior. (Photograph by Richard Einzig, Brecht-Einzig Ltd., London)

Fɪɢ 3. Moment Village (Archigram Group, London)

Fɪɢ. 4. Drop City, U.S.A.

DISCUSSION

McLaren: You spoke mostly about separate unit dwellings. Since smaller numbers of children per family are inevitable, and the extended family group will be increasingly important if children are not to suffer from 'sib-deprivation', can you suggest how to meet this challenge architecturally? Could there be something between community living and separate boxes?

Rogers: Of course communal services for child-minding and so on are architecturally a real possibility. Anything architectural is a real possibility, and that is the point I am trying to make in terms of family size. A lot more work of this kind has been done in Sweden than in this country.

Comfort: Family hotels, in other words.

Rogers: We are now building community schools in Britain; these will be community centres where not only children learn but mothers work at the same time, and where adults can come to learn in the evening. Such a school is really an architectural enclosure for a mass use.

Comfort: But administratively we seem to be moving away from this rather than towards it. These are the technological mass architectural possibilities but such things as our present planning regulations make it increasingly difficult to do this even experimentally. It is all right for Drop City! Fig. 4.

Rogers: Two things are involved; one is the mortgage system by which at the moment you can't get a mortgage for anything which is not completely traditional—not even a steel house. The other is, as Dr Comfort said, the planning laws, but I think there is a very real possibility to change those laws if there is enough pressure to do so.

Reynolds: The pygmies in the Congo forests live in a rather similar way to some of your designs in that they base the positions of the dwellings, which they reconstruct every year when the village is re-formed, on kinship relationships and on friendships and antagonisms. One effect Colin Turnbull[8] describes is that if people fall out with each other they simply move apart, and one implication of your suggestion might be for example that teenagers would decide not to live with their parents. This might lead to an even greater fragmentation of the family than we have at present, where people are forced to live together.

Rogers: The point I am trying to make is that if the teenagers want to live apart, they should perhaps be able to live apart. At the moment we are forcing our family patterns by the habitat we have and it could be that this is not the right answer. It may be made even worse if teenagers live apart, but I would like freedom of choice for teenagers and for everyone.

Miller: I would question the psychological validity of that!

Adams: Real freedom of choice would entail living arrangements that permit depth and scope of experience together as well as forms of privacy. It is a striking fact that in the Israeli *kibbutzim* today where parents are permitted to be with the children only at stated times for an hour or two, both the parents and the children feel that the experience together is artificial and superficial: the time together is interpreted by both children and parents as playtime when the interpersonal relationships and the roles of the respective age groups are limited in range and quality.

These observations suggest that the crucial problem is generally not merely freedom of choice but rather that of contriving significantly structured freedom of choice with respect to togetherness and also to privacy or independence.

Rogers: It is probably a question of central land control and this may be an ideal, but there is always the hope that as the next-door neighbour is contracting you are expanding.

Adams: In what way can aesthetic values be taken into account in this kind of housing, both in the interior of the shell and with respect to the outdoor environment? The question is inescapable and imperative, for the physical arrangements, interior and exterior, transmit aesthetic values or their opposite.

Rogers: I knew this question would come up! Of course we are not saying this is an aesthetic answer. The aesthetics of the house is not a technological problem. It might be more logical to have inflatable furniture because it can go in a suitcase, if you have a house which would go more or less in two suitcases; but you would still have the choice of having furniture which could fill two vans.

Fairbrother: As a landscape architect I am horrified to think what is going to happen to the outdoor environment with all these things being put up and pulled down. But leaving aesthetics aside, these would all have to be fundamentally suburban houses, yet you presuppose endless space around every house where it can simply expand like an amoeba.

Rogers: These houses can also stack.

Fairbrother: Yes, but then you say that nobody wants to live in tower blocks.

Rogers: I agree that landscape is a very important factor in the whole of our environment. In the 'moment' villages (Fig. 3) there are hard areas and certain pre-planned soft areas of shrubs or flowers on which you could never put your inflatable house base. These act as buffer zones between the house and the noisy areas, the roads. There is always that control, but there are also many other areas on which you can put your 'moment' dwelling.

Ali Baig: There is also an economic factor. Affluent societies may buy clip-on units over the counter, but what of societies with a population problem as in India, where the extended family is the normal family and there is no margin to buy extra units? The land area in India is very large, but land itself has become extremely expensive.

Rogers: I don't know what the system of land control is in India, in terms of government housing, but in a way flexible housing is a much more logical answer for very poor countries, because if the government accepts responsibility for providing shelter for the community this is a much cheaper way than providing custom-built houses for each family.

Ali Baig: The Indian Government can only undertake a limited responsibility because its economics are limited too. But in radical designs for human environments it is surely essential to plan some area of privacy within homes. In India one place that serves as a small point of refuge is the prayer room. Refuge areas should be part of modern design.

Henriques: The equation between bad environment and delinquency was mentioned, but is this really correct? If we look on drug taking as characteristic of delinquency and compare Bethnal Green with Welwyn Garden City, it comes out the wrong way. Welwyn Garden City is a good environment compared with parts of Bethnal Green but the incidence of drug taking in Bethnal Green is probably considerably lower, whereas delinquency has grown over the years in surburban areas where people are relatively affluent compared with old areas. There are a number of very good reasons for this but we must be careful not to assume too swiftly that everything that flows from what we say is a bad environment must also be bad. Bad conditions may have a very positive value, because in themselves they may promote harmony and cooperation. In the Caribbean when people are removed from very hard conditions and put into a relatively good environment they become in short time just as irresponsible and feckless as the people living in the good environment.

And don't we perhaps make rather too much fuss about privacy? This is a beautiful notion; I enjoy it, you enjoy it, perhaps all here enjoy it, but there are people in the world who don't enjoy it at all. In fact their whole life is spent in escaping from a privacy which they might even equate with loneliness, and they don't want to be alone. In the normal Caribbean household people wander in and out the whole time. The immigrant comes here and he will attempt to live in the same way in the English urban setting. He expects, if he has neighbours, that he has the right to wander in and he is disturbed when he finds the doors closed. I think the whole notion of privacy is a middle-class phenomenon.

Raveau: I would like to underline what Professor Henriques has just said. It is true that the rate of road accidents is higher near a busy road but I don't think you can use this as an analogy and say that mental pathology depends on the place where you live.

Rogers: I said there was a high correlation.

Raveau: Yes, but it is not as neat as the impression you gave. One projective test in psychology is to give a model of a small village to a child, and he has to build up the world according to his own problems and ideology. I felt that your proposition was based not on a real study of people's needs, but on a certain concealed ideology. I am not entirely happy about the idea of changing the structure in which people live. Various studies have shown that when people work in a place where you keep changing the walls and surroundings, they develop a high degree of anxiety and the standard of the work is very low. This is especially true for children at school. This desire to change, to live in a kind of fluidity of form, has to be approached with care.

Rogers: I must have made myself misunderstood. Nothing that I have shown is in opposition to what you are saying. I suggested no solution and I don't think that what I have shown is necessarily the answer to what people want. I haven't done a field study of the world population or housing. All I want to show is that there should be a choice and that housing must not dictate our behaviour patterns by the physical enclosure; I want to show that it is now technically possible to have houses which are not tied to the ground.

As to privacy, I think that if people want privacy they should be able to have it. At the moment in most of our environment, in most of our shelters, you can't have privacy. You may have family privacy, but not individual privacy. There are very few children who have a room of their own in this society, and I think that should be a choice. I like the point that people should be able to come visiting, and there is an area in the house where if you want to receive people you can do so. But perhaps you don't always want to be in when your visitors come, and therefore there should be a private area where you don't have to receive visitors.

Comfort: Options, in fact.

Rogers: The whole thing should be options. There shouldn't be an inflexible system which doesn't provide individual choice.

McLaren: There is some confusion about privacy in the discussion. Some people have equated privacy with solitude, but I believe Mrs Rogers is using it merely in the sense of separation of different family functions. Teenagers, children and parents each need their own separate accommodation, within which they may be very gregarious. Perhaps one could envisage some sort of housing which was connected in two dimensions, so that in one dimension you were connected with the rest of your family, your children, your parents, but in the other dimension teenagers, for instance, would have connexions between different family units—a sort of continuous teenager basement down a terrace of houses, for example.

Miller: Our unit of low-cost housing does not necessarily seem to be highly related to human needs. I think it is arguable whether human needs are to sleep 'en famille' as they did in the 12th century, or to sleep in separate cubicles. In low-cost housing the food preparation and service area is often much too small to allow this to be the warmth giving locus for family love which it should be. Adolescents have a need for relative withdrawal from their parents. They can do this relatively easily and safely when families live in a village. In a city they can no longer do this with safety in many neighbourhoods; adolescents may be driven into the streets because privacy in the family living unit is impossible. I think it is a pity if we do not see Mrs Rogers' paper as an extraordinarily important contribution. The problem is the production of social change in society. Many architects indicate that many changes can now be made; without social change, society seems so paralysed that it is unable to conceive of putting changes in building design into practice.

Rossi: In my experience, especially in Latin populations, people like to be together and are afraid of isolation, which will prevent communication between them.

Rogers: The problem of the people who went to Greenleigh was that they were totally isolated from their extended family because the Greenleigh house would take only the nuclear family. It would have been far better if the town could have taken the whole extended family.

Rossi: Of great importance for the creation of a desirable atmosphere for the family is an optimal ratio between the human beings and the space they are living in.

Rogers: I too think this is very important and a lot of research has been done in this country in terms not only of actual space but also height in relation to making people feel they have space in very small rooms.

Rossi: In children's hospitals where children have to stay for a long time, we do not know what is the best room size.

Rogers: If you had an inflatable or mobile or 'clip-on' hospital, you could choose.

Tavuchis: Mrs Rogers need not defend herself about the importance of choice. Something that may be peripheral to your interests but that is central to mine is the cross-cultural definition of privacy. What kinds of either physical or symbolic barriers do people in different cultures raise? What are the tolerable levels of abrasiveness of extended interaction with people? What are the real consequences of high densities? Most of the studies have been based on animal populations, lemmings or rats,[3] rather than on human populations, but the speculation about human populations and what happens under various degrees of pressure is very basic to the question of where the family is going. So what are the definitions of privacy, cross-culturally? What about people who don't fit into these definitions?

Comfort: Lack of space often provides an excuse for a family that doesn't want to look after their old people.

Tavuchis: Another really crucial point is the rootedness in society. What are the alternative bases of rootedness, of belongingness, in a society where not only is geographical mobility often demanded by a persons's occupation, but where it is also highly valued and people actually desire it?

Rogers: The next generation will be able to be really mobile, not just within a country or even within the world. In my paper I was talking about the real future, not just the next ten years, but 50 to 70 years from now when many of our assumptions will be quite different.

Reynolds: The American anthropologist E. T. Hall suggests very strongly in *The Hidden Dimension* that the existing living arrangements in a society to a great extent determine the needs of the people living in those arrangements.[6] This would seem to have rather serious implications for your own thesis, in that you are saying that certain of our needs are not being met by the current situation and we should build according to these needs. In other words, you are giving the needs some sort of primacy over the cultural setting, and Hall's work tends to argue against that.

Miller: Yes, but Hall's work takes no note of breakdown. In parts of the United States the rate of psychological disintegration among young people seems to indicate that the culture is failing to meeting their growing needs. It is true that people adapt themselves and then say they need what they have got. Nevertheless the evidence, not from the formal statistics of mental illness, because these regrettably show nothing, but from the obvious increase in drug dependency in younger and younger people, the increase in violence in the black ghetto and among alienated middle-class youth, surely indicates that developmental needs are not being met.

Reynolds: I don't think it follows necessarily that it is the spatial element which is responsible for mental or psychological breakdown. The two may be correlated but not as a cause and effect relationship.

Leach: If we ask ourselves whether the human species is adapted to any special way of living in relation to buildings, the answer must clearly be no. The human species is very ancient and it has only lived in buildings of any kind very recently. Therefore, whatever it is adapted to, it is something very different from anything we are living in now. Hall has suggested that any particular group becomes culturally adapted to the patterns of building arrangements which are customary in that group, and that this interlocking is really tight. In other words, although the possibilities are very varied, any actual situation on the ground represents an adaptation of the social system to the environment, which has been mediated by a particular pattern of building conventions. In the ordinary circumstances of the past, the historical change of society, the adaptation of the social structure, and the adaptation of the architectural arrangements have all proceeded simultaneously. There has been continuous mutual modification. But now Mrs Rogers is insisting that we are not in any way bound by the restrictions which have been accepted in the past. The modern architect is capable of meeting even our most outrageous demands. We need not be hamstrung at all by architectural conventions. We are free to modify society in any way we choose and the architect will be quite happy to come along behind to fit the material environment to any pattern of social arrangements that we care to propose. This is a fantastic possibility which is directly contrary to all our past experience. In the past the radical social reformer has always had to console himself by saying: "This is the best that we can do in the (material) circumstances." Now Mrs Rogers is saying that we can do anything we like. This is a fascinating situation.

Stone: Could you tell us more about possible densities? To what extent would you be able to reach the kind of density that would enable you to abolish commuting? Today the woman often lives in a surburban ghetto and the man spends up to an eighth of his day in purposeless and very uncomfortable commuting.

Rogers: At 77 people per acre, the figure I quoted for being housed within a 20-mile radius of Trafalgar Square, each family could have a two-storey terrace house with its own garden front and back. This does not allow for road space, but that figure is merely a statistical one. The whole population of England and Wales would not in practice be concentrated at one point. But supposing we had 250 such communities, each with a population of 250 000, with a central core of shops, offices, schools, etc., with a radius of quarter of a mile (400 metres); around this core there could be residential clusters also with a radius of quarter of a mile each. The person living furthest from the centre of the central core would be about threequarters of a mile away. All of these 250 000 people would live within easy walking distance of each other and of all social facilities.

Weiss: I like the idea of increasing the degrees of freedom available to an individual or a society, but I am very sceptical about being able to predict the implications of any new design or social form, because too many things are involved. Single elements of design rarely have one and only one consequence. Consider, for example, density. A high-density living situation could be either a housing project or Park Avenue, which has one of the highest densities in New York. The same high densities have different meanings because there are different kinds of control of space and different social definitions as to what it means to live in these places. In general we shall not be able to predict with assurance the consequences of design, because it is a complex interaction of elements which must be dealt with. What is absolutely necessary is to find an analogy to what one wants to do in one of the variety of architectural forms and social forms which exist now, and see what are the consequences of that analogue. If you are interested in what difference it makes if you have flexible extendible housing, take a look at a situation where people have something like it and see what happens there. The only analogue I can think of—and I am not sure if it is close enough—is trailers and trailer or caravan lots. I think by far the best strategy for estimating the consequences of any innovative form is to find analogies to it in the present and to take a look at what happens there.

Pirie: People are not well adapted now to the environment we are making and are trying to make. Speakers have adduced increasing drug addiction and teenage violence as evidence for this. I cannot see that that has any bearing on the issue at all. The North-West American *peyote* cultists are drug addicts and they are quiet. I think the opium addicts of Hong Kong are quiet and peaceful also, gradually rotting and causing no trouble. Much of human history has been a teenage riot, and it seems to me much more likely that the present violence is simply the reaction to improved nutrition in Britain and the U.S.A. Any region where delinquency is very low is almost certainly a region of malnutrition and in such an area any properly fed juvenile would automatically be a teenage rioter.

Miller: One really can't let Dr Pirie get away with that; there are quite clear regional differences in things like drug taking and delinquency rates which are not related to nutrition.

Pirie: Welwyn Garden City is better fed than Bethnal Green.

Miller: Yes, but some affluent communities in Upper Michigan have little delinquency or drug problems, and other regions in Michigan are equally affluent and have enormous problems of delinquency and drugs, You cannot relate this to food.

Abercrombie: The amount of light might also affect people quite a lot. In the Middle Ages people went to bed at nightfall and we now stay up through the night. Judging by the way plants and mammals are affected, this is one of the things to look at. Another factor I would guess at is communication, because the rate at which news flies round the world now must surely affect the way the people behave.

Comfort: Another is education. I think an educated public can only be consulted, it cannot be governed.

Fox: Density is important, but you can't simply take density figures *per se* as indicating anything. The difference between the equally high densities of Manhattan and Harlem, where the density is much the same and yet the behaviour is totally different, seems to me very simple. The high-density rich in Manhattan can very easily get the hell out, whereas in Harlem they can't. The Pueblo Indians live in densities that are about as high per square yard as has ever been known, but they spend a great deal of their time out hunting, and doing various things, and this, I think, is the crucial difference.

Stone: Surely cultural differences play a considerable part. In New York and San Francisco I was told that there were never any juvenile delinquents in the Chinese areas. I understand that this is now changing and I wonder what the influences are: is it the influence of the mass media?

Tavuchis: In San Francisco among the Chinese you have yet another disadvantaged poor group with a large proportion of unmarried males and the problem of the inevitable second generation conflict with a gerontocracy holding on to job opportunities. This nice image that the Chinese take care of their own is simply not true, at least not in San Francisco. It is extremely difficult to find out whether this reflects on the general trend or is something specific to the acculturation patterns of the Chinese.

Ali Baig: High density and crowding is constant throughout urban India, but we do not have a large degree of disintegration such as juvenile delinquency. There is a distinction between delinquency and the state in which the young person has gone beyond all correction. The delinquent child in India does come from high-density urban areas, but this is not the main problem; the removal of the natural function of the child within the family by the changed patterns of economic life and education is the real culprit. The child in rural areas has a 'function' from a very early age: he has no childhood perhaps, but a real function to perform as soon as he has strength enough to help in family life. Here there is never delinquency.

Borrelli: It seems to me we are romanticising the old village life. We can never really understand what social control means in a small village because our only experience is as town dwellers. We think the ideal is to be found in the country, but the ideal of country people is to come to the town to find a different dimension for their life. Hate of the town is a problem we have not yet digested. I am not sure that kinship as such is necessarily a centripetal element of communal life. In the South of Italy we have no sense of community life but we have many social problems, because of the tremendous emphasis on kinship. Kinship in such a case is a destructive element, because the family becomes the centre of life through kinship, and groups of families govern the towns; thus there is no real community spirit and we are left with a skeleton of feudal life.

Rogers: But can you separate this from your church problems in the South of Italy? Kinship or social behaviour there is surely tied up with the very strong influence of the Church?

Borrelli: Not really, because the Church may perhaps control things from the top, but it hasn't very much influence in village life.

Sjövall: Is there a power structure?

Borrelli: The power structure works very well through the kinship structure.

Weiss: Is the kinship structure active in some ethical way?

Borrelli: Banfield[1] talks about immoral familism and I think his analysis is correct but not his conclusions. It is really true that a man's family role is important in the power structure in the South.

Comfort: Is there any analogy to this in India?

Ali Baig: There was a feudal power structure in India, but this male role is more comparable to that in Iran where the tribal kinship role is very strong and exclusive. Feudal systems surviving in India depend on religion and caste superiorities, not strictly male roles, but they are not part of the modern power structure which is more political and not based on kinship.

Newson: To some extent things are as they are because people want them to be like this, and the idea that we should all have free choice is upsetting, even to us. If you want to know how people would like to live, one way to find out is to go and see how people with a lot of money actually spend it.

Fox: You are implying that people with relatively free choice would be in the same position as people with a lot of money; we need to study the anthropology of the rich.

Reynolds: The great danger in giving people freedom is what Durkheim described as 'anomie'. Durkheim said that what man thinks, what man does, is simply what culture puts in him to think and do; Durkheim's arguments lead to the conclusion that increased personal freedom to think and act leads to an increased sense of responsibility at a personal level, and to an increase of anomie and in the sum total of human misery.[4]

Borrelli: Anomie is not a typical phenomenon of the town. For instance in the 16th and 17th centuries the gypsies and the circus people were actually rejected by all towns because the towns were full up. They had left their villages and were not allowed to go back, so they adapted to their situation through their trades. I don't think pilgrims are only a religious phenomenon; some people leave their homes because they are unsettled and want to escape.

Miller: Mrs Rogers introduced an unintentional parameter, which is that freedom of choice may make people anxious. This group has demonstrated this, because the concept of complete freedom to choose in terms of architecture has made us all go round in circles. If this group cannot cope with freedom, heaven help society if everyone suddenly has total freedom to choose how they are going to live.

Rogers: I actually had that idea in my paper and I eliminated it because I thought it really would not need discussing here. Of course there will be some direction. Because we can buy house extensions over the counter, I hope architects would not be eliminated. We can direct, we can guide, we can give finite examples of finished houses. People need not use freedom unless they want to; what I am talking about is not really so very different from the existing system.

Fletcher: I am shocked at a lot of what is being said by a group of social scientists who seem to have arrived at criteria for judging the freedom to be allowed to others. I am not sure whether these are ethical or socio-psychological criteria, whereby they are prescribing the limitations of human freedom of choice in terms of something they call happiness, or harmony, or what.

We now have this infinitely greater degree of opportunity to transform our environment rather than adapt to it, but one of the crucial distinctions between man and all other animal societies has always been that man is not confined to adapting himself to an environment. He has the qualities of mind and creative activity to transform his environment to the limit of his circumstances and his technical knowledge. It is one of the common bases of all sociological theories that as man's knowledge increases, his degree of control over the natural and social environment increases. Everything points to the reconstitution of our institutionalized relationships in such a way as to provide high levels of personal status in society, with high degrees of correlated personal responsibility. High degrees of personal status and responsibility carry high levels of anxiety, but anxiety is not necessarily a bad thing. We tend to compare these higher degrees of anxiety badly with earlier situations of close kinship groups and communal relations because we think something has gone wrong with the family. This is totally wrong. It seems to me that all these improvements in status and responsibility have freed members of the family enormously. I have in mind Laslett's book, *The World we have Lost*,[7] where he shows the most harrowing degrees of human misery and constraint in families in pre-industrial conditions in Britain, when people probably died at the age of 35, or had nine children—seven of whom might die at birth.

Weiss: It is quite well established from research surveys that the more money a person has, the happier he is likely to be.[2,5] I think Durkheim[4] was referring to a sudden access of wealth as a cause of personal disorganization. Possibly there should be a qualification to the first principle; the more money the better, but if the money comes suddenly people need orientation to be able to make use of it.

Tavuchis: If you gave your paper to a non-academic audience such as Bethnal Green-ites, Mrs Rogers, I wonder what their response would be compared with ours?

Rogers: It would be very interesting; but we don't realize strongly enough that people find it very difficult to make a choice about their physical environment without experiencing that environment. People have very little imagination for the three-dimensional feeling of space, and they cannot understand what it would be like to be enclosed by a shell different in any way from their usual environment. They just cannot envisage things through pictures, but if they can actually go into these new houses, they react completely differently.

McLaren: There are marvellous opportunities at the Ideal Homes Exhibition. You could tape-record the comments.

Rogers: Our house on legs was built for the Ideal Homes Exhibition, but we didn't bother to tape-record the comments. It didn't seem to be worth while because that is a particular audience, very much concerned, for example, with comfort.

Fox: I want to pronounce a kind of valediction. I have had a lot to do with architects one way or another, and my general impression has always been of their total arrogance and irresponsibility about what they do. These are terribly important people in our society; they decide how we are going to live and what the quality of our life will be, but they mostly seem concerned with how their drawings will look to other architects and how well they will look in the architectural journals. They build these structures but never live in them. If they are motivated by anything other than their own sense of aesthetics, then it is by some notion of how people *ought* to live: they build their tower blocks according to some *ad hoc* sociology they think up themselves; or they design universities on the same basis, with lots of coloured drawings showing how people are going to bump into each other in quadrangles. They do no research into how people actually function in such structures once they have won design medals. But Richard and Su Rogers seem to be architects directly concerned with how people are really going to live and with the need to consider future alternatives to the kind of patterns for family living we have at the moment. The kind of architecture we are persisting with just keeps stamping the same old pattern on society but now we have this new approach to architecture, which really takes account of how people live and what people need. This is extremely encouraging.

7: The Family and the Law in 1970

OLIVE M. STONE

THE intending reformer of family law needs not only energy but also much patience. When one looks at recent and current reforming legislation, it is remarkable how much of it represents an extension of reforms initiated or business left unfinished during the 1930s.

In 1933, for example, the law regarding offences against and by children was consolidated in an Act which is still in operation, although much amended, expanded here or nibbled at there by later Acts. The Children and Young Persons Act, 1969, which will be brought into operation in parts from time to time, is only the latest of these many amendments of the 1933 Act.

The year 1935 marked a further stage in the legal emancipation of married women by freeing husbands from responsibility for their wives' torts or civil wrongs and including married women among the general body of adult people who might own property, instead of the 'separate' property with which propertied families had, during the eighteenth and nineteenth centuries, protected their daughters before they allowed them to marry. By a symbolism which may have been accidental, the Law Reform (Married Women and Tortfeasors) Act, 1935, severed the married woman from the old legal trinity of infants, lunatics and married women, and classed her firmly with tortfeasors, or those who are answerable for their own actions. The Matrimonial Proceedings and Property Bill, now passing through the House of Commons, will shortly enlarge the powers of the courts to deal with the property of both parties on a divorce, although under the Bill these powers will still be exercised in the court's discretion, subject only to legislative exhortations and not to rules of any kind.

The Matrimonial Causes Act of 1937, successfully promoted by Mr A. P. Herbert, as he then was, introduced grounds for divorce other than the classic one of adultery; grounds for nullity of marriage other than the classic physical incapacity to consummate it, and also for the first time made adultery a ground on which the poor might complain to the magistrates' courts and ask for a separation or maintenance order or an order for the custody of children. Some class distinctions centred on adultery still, however, remain with us. For example, adultery is still an absolute bar to maintenance in the magistrates' court as it is not in the High Court. The Divorce Reform Act, 1969, which will come into operation after the end of this year (1970) clearly marks the most recent stage in a path opened up by Sir Alan Herbert, and I will return to it.

The year 1938 saw the first modern encroachment on irresponsibility in disposing of one's estate after one's death, often called freedom of testation. This lawyers and laymen alike had previously and quite falsely persuaded themselves was one of the distinguishing marks of the English common law. On the contrary, the customary reasonable part for a widow from her deceased husband's movable property was one of the rights guaranteed by Magna Carta, which was abolished for the City of London by legislation as late as 1724. The landowner's widow was entitled to her dower until 1833. After an initial period during which the Bench showed its dislike and distrust of the Inheritance (Family Provision) Act, 1938, its provisions were extended in 1952; in 1958 they were extended to former spouses whose marriage to the deceased had been annulled or dissolved and in 1966 they were extended to enable the court to order provision by way of lump sums which might exhaust the whole of the deceased's estate. The Family Provision Acts do not, however, provide for a *legitim* or compulsory share for the deceased's dependants, as in most Civil Law Systems. They merely permit a surviving or former spouse, a son under the age of 21, an unmarried daughter of any age, or a son or daughter who by reason of incapacity is unable to maintain himself or herself, to apply to the court which may, if it thinks fit, make provision for the applicant from the estate left by the deceased.

During the 1940s, when much national energy was diverted from both the law and the family, the judges in a series of decisions extended the protection of the Rent Acts to a wife and children, even though they had been deserted by the tenant, who was also the husband and father. This kind of protective legislation was taken further by the Matrimonial Homes Act, 1967, which gave the husband or wife of the owner of a matrimonial home the right to register a possessory charge or apply to the court for an order for possession of the home. I find two main objections to this Act. In the first place it offers protection for the husband or wife of the owner, including the young, able-bodied and childless spouse, but not to the owner's children in the home in the care of anybody else. Secondly, if the possessory charge is to be effective, it should be registered before friction arises between the parties to the marriage, and the knowledge by the other party that such a charge has been registered would itself seem fairly abrasive.

At the end of 1947 the House of Lords cast the mantle of legal acceptance over the use of contraceptive devices in marriage by finally holding in *Baxter* v. *Baxter*[1] that the use of such devices did not prevent consummation of the marriage so as to enable the courts to annul it. Twenty years later the National Health Service (Family Planning) Act enabled local authorities, with the approval of the Minister of Health, to provide contraceptive advice and services, and the Abortion Act, 1967, enabled reputable medical practitioners to move into a field formerly largely reserved for the back-street bungler. Despite the various attacks that have been mounted against the Abortion Act, I find it difficult to believe in the possibility of a return to the *status quo ante*. In view of the population explosion an intensification of this area of permissiveness must be expected, coupled with restrictive measures such as immigration control. The first major post-war family legislation, prompted by the brutality shown to some foster-children during the war, was the Children Act, 1948, which placed the responsibility for all children in its area finally on the elected local authority, gave it power to supervise and when necessary receive into its care children deprived of a normal home life, and with the parents' consent to vest parental powers in itself to the exclusion of the parents. The organization of local authority services is now, of course, under review, following the report of the Seebohm Committee on Local Authorities and Allied Personal Services[11] and the functioning of the Children Acts is now almost inextricably entwined with that of the Children and Young Persons Acts.

In 1951 the House of Commons granted a second reading to a Bill that, if enacted, would have allowed either party to a marriage to have it dissolved without the consent or matrimonial fault of the other if the parties had been living apart from each other continuously for seven years immediately before the divorce petition was presented. This provision for divorce by unilateral repudiation, coupled with a prolonged period of separation, is the most controversial of the 'facts' on which an English court may find that a marriage has broken down irretrievably and therefore grant a divorce under the Divorce Reform Act, 1969, which will come into operation after the end of this year, 1970, just twenty years after the House of Commons first accepted the principle. The period of separation under the 1969 Act has now been reduced to five years where there is unilateral repudiation of the marriage, and to two years where both parties consent to the divorce. Three newly-formulated kinds of 'fault' may also, under the new Act, constitute facts on which the court may find that the marriage has broken down irretrievably and therefore dissolve it. These are: (a) that the other party to the marriage has committed adultery and the petitioner finds it intolerable to live with him or her; (b) that the other party has behaved in such a way that the petitioner cannot reasonably be expected to live with him or her, and (c) that the other party has deserted the petitioner for a continuous period of at least two years immediately preceding the presentation of the petition, instead of three years as at present.

A similar principle of divorce without fault and without the consent of one party, sometimes as the sole ground, and sometimes with alternative 'fault' grounds, is now in operation in many highly developed countries including Australia (since 1959); New Zealand (since 1954); Canada (since 1968); West Germany (since 1933); the Soviet Union, Poland, East Germany, Czechoslovakia and Hungary, and the American State of California (since the beginning of 1970). The Californian provisions are the most recent and the most radical to date. California now provides only two grounds for divorce: (1) Irreconcilable differences, which have caused the irremediable breakdown of the marriage, and (2) incurable insanity. In an effort to avoid the spite and malice, frequently buttressed by perjury, which constitute one of the strongest objections to the 'fault' system of divorce, the Californian statute now provides that the alleged irreconcilable differences must be pleaded generally. Specific acts of misconduct are, I quote: "improper and inadmissible, except where child custody is in issue and the evidence is relevant to establish that parental custody would be detrimental to the child", or where the court decides that such evidence is necessary to establish the existence of irreconcilable differences. The Act also lays down that the community property of the parties, which in general includes all property acquired by either during the existence of the marriage, shall in all cases be equally divided between the parties on divorce, irrespective of their behaviour during the marriage. The lack of any such general principle in the English Act will, in my view, largely frustrate the avowed object, that of eliminating as much personal bitterness as possible from the divorce proceedings. The object of most of the bitter and frequently false accusations commonly hurled across the divorce court is not primarily to question whether one of the parties did indeed commit adultery, or whether he deserted her or she him or whether they agreed to part to their mutual relief. It is primarily to question whether, after the divorce, the former husband must continue to maintain the former wife, and if so, to what extent. In this country, unlike California and seven other south-western States of the Union, we have no system of matrimonial community of acquisitions during the marriage. The general principle is that what the husband earns and acquires during the marriage is his alone, and what the wife earns and acquires during the marriage is hers alone. But there is an additional principle that a husband must maintain his wife. Thus the woman who owns property or earns income during the marriage is absolutely entitled to retain that and demand that her husband maintain her in addition. The woman with no property who devotes her energies to the household during the marriage will, if the marriage is dissolved, be entitled to none of the property which the husband has acquired during the marriage. He will probably be ordered to maintain her, but no effective method of enforcing the payment of maintenance orders has yet been devised, and if the former husband sets up a household with another woman, whether he marries her or not, because of her nearness to his bank balance or pay cheque, her needs and those of any children she may have will take precedence over the claims of the former wife and her children, however strong these may appear in law. Moreover, the law still regards a husband's primary liability as that of maintaining his wife, so long as she does not commit a matrimonial offence, and comparatively small amounts are customarily added to any maintenance order for the maintenance of the children, although the low maxima for maintenance orders in magistrates' courts were abolished by the Maintenance Orders Act, 1968. I suggest that the primary liability should be seen as that of both parents to maintain the dependent children they brought into the world, and that the kind of order commonly issued by the magistrates' courts, that the husband should pay the wife £3 per week for her maintenance, and a further £1 per week for the maintenance of each of two children aged six and eight years, is an absurdity. Any man paying a total of £5 per week is not maintaining two children of school age, and I find it absurd that the law should buttress the illusion that he is maintaining not only them but the wife or former wife as well.

The extent of the additional burden which the new Divorce Reform Act will, after the end of 1970, place on public funds is by no means clear. At present the major burden on public funds is cast by the large numbers of women who do not resort to the divorce court, but are satisfied with applying for a maintenance order, with or without a separation order, in the magistrates' court. Even if a maintenance order is made, no effective means of enforcing payment has yet been devised and, if no order is made, the children must clearly be maintained at public expense. The new rules for divorce, which include a licence to remarry, will simply enable such marriages to be dissolved after the parties have been living apart for two years if both agree, or for five years if one party objects. The charge on public funds will increase only if, having remarried, the man fails to support the second or any subsequent wife and her children if any, and she is unable to support them. Social scientists seem far from agreement on the extent to which men who do not support their families may be encouraged by legal aid and the new divorce rules to enter into a succession of marriages leaving a succession of wives and their children to be supported at public expense. In the meantime, however, a committee has been set up under the chairmanship of Mr Morris Finer, Q.C., to examine the needs and problems of one-parent families, and some further information and recommendations may be anticipated.

The acceptance by the House of Commons in 1951 of the principle of unilateral repudiation of marriage coupled with separation of the parties led to the establishment of the Royal Commission on Marriage and Divorce, which sat until 1955. Although the Royal Commission was unable to agree on any of the major questions of divorce without fault or matrimonial property, its report[3] directed attention to the interests of the children whose parents were involved in divorce proceedings and led to amending legislation on this and other matters during 1957 and 1958.

Considerable activity followed on the law relating to children. In 1958 new adoption legislation was enacted following the report of the Hurst Committee.[2] The 1958 Act for the first time enabled Local Authorities to act as adoption agencies. It also slightly extended the grounds on which the court might dispense with the parents' consent to the adoption, where they had "consistently failed, without reasonable excuse, to fulfil the obligations of a parent". Difficulties are still being experienced on the question of parental consent to adoption, and following a report made in 1968 by the Standing Conference of Societies Registered for Adoption, a committee was appointed in July 1969 to enquire into the difficulties arising under the 1958 Act, and also the question of long-term fostering of children.

In 1957 the Affiliation Proceedings Act consolidated with minor amendments the nineteenth-century Bastardy Laws Amendment Acts, and this Act, which is still in operation, retained the old quasi-criminal terminology for affiliation proceedings. Section 6 still provides that an affiliation order shall be effective only until the child reaches the age of thirteen unless the court expressly provides that it shall continue until the child reaches the age of sixteen. Thereafter the court may, on a new application, continue the order, but for not more than two years at a time, and in no circumstances beyond the time at which the child reaches the age of twenty-one. The age of thirteen seems quite irreconcilable with a school-leaving age of either fifteen or sixteen. The Legitimacy Act, 1959, provides a sharp contrast both in content and expression. The Act of 1959 provided for the first time that affiliation proceedings should be classed with domestic proceedings instead of criminal proceedings, as previously. It also extended the operation of the Guardianship of Infants Acts to illegitimate children, and empowered a putative father to apply to the court for the custody of his illegitimate child. The 1959 Act also reduced the number of illegitimate children by providing that every child is legitimated by the subsequent marriage of his parents, even though one of them may have been married to another person at the time of the child's birth, and that the child of a void marriage is to be treated as legitimate provided at least one of the parents reasonably believed that the marriage was valid either at the time of the ceremony or the time of the act of intercourse resulting in the child's conception, whichever last happens.

Ten years later the law regarding children, including illegitimate children, was carried considerably further by the Family Law Reform Act, 1969, most of which came into operation at the beginning of this year. The first part of the Act implemented the recommendations of the Latey Committee on the age of majority[7] by reducing the age of majority from twenty-one to eighteen years, whilst enabling the courts to order maintenance for those under the age of twenty-one. The second part of the Act implements and indeed goes beyond the recommendations of the Russell Committee on the Law of Succession in relation to Illegitimate Persons.[5] It gives the illegitimate child the same right of succession to the property of either of his parents who dies intestate as a legitimate child. The Scandinavian countries have already made comparable provision, and so did New York in 1965 and Western Germany in August 1969. In my view incomprehensibly, the English Act gives the parents an unqualified reciprocal right to succeed to the property of an illegitimate child who dies intestate. Of greater practical importance is the power to apply to the court for provision under the Family Provision Acts for the maintenance of an illegitimate child from the estate of a deceased parent. Any affiliation order ceases to operate on the death of the payer, and formerly the courts had no power to order that the child be maintained from the deceased parent's estate.

Probably the potentially most important provision relating to illegitimate children, however, is that abolishing the rule of judicial interpretation of documents by which all references to a child, son, daughter or other words of relationship mean a legitimate child, son, daughter etc., unless a contrary intention clearly appears. To hold that an illegitimate child is not a child of either parent comes close to saying—as the English common law never has said—that an illegitimate person is not quite a person. The Act also abolishes the strong presumption that the child of a married woman is the child of her husband, and now provides that in any civil proceedings the paternity of a child shall be decided on the balance of probabilities. Part III of the Act, providing for the use of blood tests to determine paternity, is not yet in operation, and a committee of the Home Office is now studying its implementation. It will be essential to ensure that people competent to administer the new and highly sophisticated blood tests will be available within a reasonable distance of every magistrates' court, so that a woman with a young child does not have to travel far to take the test. These provisions for the reception of scientific evidence on matters on which the law formerly relied on presumptions is a welcome sign that the lawyers are making some efforts to understand and utilize a more scientific approach.

The establishment in 1965 of the Law Commission, under the chairmanship of a High Court judge of the divorce division, has ensured at least the beginning of a thorough review of the whole of our family law. The Law Commission has, during the last few years, produced a fairly constant flow of reports and working papers on various aspects of family law. The Matrimonial Proceedings and Property Bill and the Law Reform (Miscellaneous Provisions) Bill, both drafted by the Law Commission, have both passed through the House of Lords and are now on their way through the House of Commons. The Administration of Justice Bill will, amongst other things, reorganize the High Court by transferring the jurisdiction over divorce and other matrimonial causes and custody of children of the present Probate Divorce and Admiralty Division to a new Family Division, which will also take over the jurisdiction of the Chancery Division and the Queen's Bench Division in respect of children. No change is, however, being made in the organization of the lower courts. One result will be that, although appeals from magistrates' courts over the custody of legitimate children will in future go to the Family Division of the High Court, appeals in affiliation proceedings will continue to go to quarter sessions, as will appeals from the juvenile court in respect of neglected and delinquent children.

The Law Commission has also assisted in the drafting of such private members' Bills in the field of family law as the Matrimonial Homes Act, the Abortion Act and the Sexual Offences Act, all of 1967. The last-mentioned was, of course, the Act which provided that homosexual acts in private between consenting adults should no longer constitute a criminal offence.

There has also been a new approach to statistics about the family. In 1956 the Royal Commission on Marriage and Divorce referred to the unsatisfactory condition of the statistics about matrimonial proceedings in magistrates courts, which until 1967 were published in the Criminal Statistics issued by the Home Office. The Royal Commission agreed that: "the grounds on which the orders were made are not shown; the total number of separation orders made is not given; the total number of orders in force throughout England and Wales at the time of making the annual return is not made available", but it concluded that the value of the additional information did not justify the trouble and expense of collecting it.[3] Three later committees[7, 8, 10] have condemned the inclusion of the old uninformative table of matrimonial proceedings in magistrates courts in the annual volume of criminal statistics, and they were included in the Civil Judicial Statistics for the first time for the year 1967, published in 1968.[12] The statistics are still very defective and still show the total of orders made under particular statutes rather than for particular objects, such as the maintenance of young children, but at least the defects are now acknowledged to be important. The Lord Chancellor declared in the House of Lords on February 22nd 1967: "I have been struck . . . at the low level of our statistics. I certainly do not know more than about one-tenth of the facts relating to judicial administration which I ought to know if I am to do my job properly."[13]

To sum up: In 1970 English law preoccupies itself far less than it used to do with the private sexual activities of citizens. On the other hand, it is far more mindful of the welfare of children than it was. Those who reach their eighteenth birthday are treated as adults. The position of illegitimate children has been improved but needs further improvement. It is still, on the whole, cheaper for a man to have an illegitimate than a legitimate child. Next year marriage *de jure* will be brought more closely into line with marriage *de facto*, with consequences which few are prepared to predict with confidence. In one area only is the married woman still regarded entirely as a satellite of her husband, and that is the area of taxation, which includes domicile. We have declared a movement towards equal pay, but only for the same or broadly similar work and not work of equal value.

An indication that the law does not contemplate any drastic change in the role of the family in the near future may be found in the many compromises and reformulations that took place before the publication of the Children and Young Persons Act, 1969,[4, 6, 9, 11] which seems unlikely to be the final word on this subject. The fact is that there seems to be no general agreement on the best way of dealing with neglected or delinquent children. No substitute for the family in the upbringing of children seems in sight.

DISCUSSION

Tavuchis: In the United States, responsibility for maintaining indigent relations has tended to become much narrower. What is the situation in England? Is the general lack of interest in adult sibling ties reflected in common law and in enacted law? To what legal extent are we our brothers' or sisters' keepers?

Stone: The British National Insurance Act of 1946 makes a woman responsible for maintaining her children and a man for maintaining his. Responsibility is limited to two generations, and under the public act the man is not responsible for maintaining his wife's children although he may be responsible under civil or private law. Both here and in the U.S.A. the basic idea is that a man should maintain the woman with whom he cohabits (and any children she has) and in indigency there is therefore an inquisition into the man in the house.

Children are not publicly responsible for maintaining their parents, and certainly no responsibility for each other rests on adult siblings in Britain.

Weiss: If 'the man in the house' rule is enforced anywhere, it is only in southern states as a means of keeping black families off welfare. At one time this was a very serious problem because the woman could not in fact depend on a man who was just a boy-friend; the boy-friend relationship generally does not obligate the man to contribute to the woman's household. If she went off welfare she was destitute.

Stone: When I was in the U.S.A. in 1966 they talked in the north about raids at 2 a.m. to prove that the man was actually living there. Certainly in the south the welfare people would try to say that such a man should keep all other dependents in that house.

4*

Weiss: They assumed something like a common law marriage. But there is a distinction between a marriage, even one without a ceremony, and a boy-friend relationship. In the latter the man is not obliged to contribute to the woman's home. Things in the States have changed in the last few years; in the welfare organization I know best, the Boston department, a man in the house would at one time have been considered responsible for the house, but this is no longer necessarily the case.

Miller: Does a common law wife exist legally in England and if she does, does she have any rights?

Stone: There was never a 'common law wife' in English law. In this area the English and American views of the history of common law are quite different. In England if a man and a woman were living together openly as husband and wife this raised a presumption only that they had been validly married. I think any canon lawyer would swiftly crush the idea that a man with a lawful wedded wife according to the canon law (which was also the common law of marriage) could also have a so-called common law wife.

Miller: Does this then mean that if a man dies intestate, his common law 'wife' and/or illegitimate offspring have no claim on his estate?

Stone: His illegitimate offspring have a claim from the beginning of 1970, under the Family Law Reform Act, 1969, but if the mother is not his wife then she is his mistress and has no claim. He can of course always provide for her in a will.

McLaren: The situation is different in Scotland. Scottish law allows you only one wife, but she can be a common law wife, and in intestacy the common law wife can inherit property if the judge decides that the couple have been living together as man and wife. The Kilbrandon committee which recently scrutinized the marriage laws of Scotland specifically recommended that this irregular form of marriage should be kept, giving the court power "to declare as marriages, with all the social and financial consequences, associations which have been marriages in all but name, the parties to them having accepted and discharged all the duties arising from the married status, save only the ceremony of matrimony".

Henriques: What decision has been made about immigrants with more than one wife?

Stone: We have recently had an interesting paper from the Law Commission on polygamous marriages.[4] The shocking situation at the moment is that the English courts will not entertain any matrimonial proceedings, including maintenance applications, in respect of people whose marriages are potentially polygamous. For example, *Sowa* v. *Sowa* [1961][5] concerned a couple domiciled and married in Ghana by a potentially polygamous marriage. After they came to this country the husband deserted and failed to maintain the wife and child. The wife applied to the magistrates for a maintenance order, which was refused. On the second appeal Lord Justice Harman in the Court of Appeal said he concurred in the dismissal of "the lady's appeal". This was not 'the lady's appeal' on her claim, but a claim for maintenance of an undoubted child by his undoubted parent.

Leach: The trend of these legal enactments seems to express a general feeling that somehow in our society the mistress, the 'common law wife', and the illegitimate child have all been getting a raw deal. Consequently we have been modifying our traditional rules in such a way that the social status of the child comes to be defined more and more by biological rather than by legal criteria. I am struck by the fact that the exact contrary is universally the case in primitive societies. Among primitive peoples there are always very precise rules for deciding who is the legal child of Mr X or the legal heir of Mr Y but biological facts play only a very small part in such criteria. Our modern society is so heavily dependent upon artificial contrivances that it might well have been expected that we would be moving into an era of intensified legal fiction whereby we could recognize all sorts of new categories of foster fathers, foster mothers, deputy parents and so on. Instead we actually seem to be moving more and more in the direction of literal biological definition. This may get us into a dilemma. The flexibility implicit in legal fictions can be very valuable, but we may deprive ourselves of this flexibility if we insist on identifying legal parenthood with biological parenthood.

Fletcher: What impresses me enormously about these legal reforms is the continual movement towards a legally precise recognition of personal responsibility for actual parenthood, and this seems to me to be the vital nub of the family bonds we nowadays have to consider. These are not only bio-psychological, factual and sociological but crucial *moral* responsibilities. The reforms of the law are reconstituting more and more our social relationships—both within and beyond the family—to give precise effect (in terms of rights and duties) to known personal statuses and known personal responsibilities. It seems to me that this is not just a legal reconstituting of the family, but of the whole fabric of society in relation to modern industrial conditions, and on the same grounds of personal responsibility in human relationships. I would like to know why Dr Leach doesn't like this?

Leach: I find this a most extraordinary attitude. Fortes[2] has reported a Tallensi maxim which translates as: "Copulation and marriage are not the same thing", and similar valuations have been reported by anthropologists from all over the world. It is only in Christian ideology that we encounter the dogma that sexual intercourse should be wholly encompassed by the institution of marriage. The much more normal attitude is to regard marriage as an enduring legal arrangement but to treat copulation in itself as a temporary and trivial social incident. Certainly moral responsibility must lie within the legal institution of marriage but to argue that moral responsibility must automatically flow from any casual act of cohabitation seems to me most extraordinary.

Miller: Another important aspect is that copulation is not now necessarily related to impregnation; impregnation can now be almost a volitional act on the part of the woman. Illegitimacy is often seen where the woman has chosen to be fertilized without the man being aware that she was making this choice. A woman need not tell her cohabitee that she has stopped taking the pill. She may therefore become pregnant as it were under false pretences. The issue of moral responsibility for illegitimacy and birth then becomes extremely complex; the law at present grossly oversimplifies it.

Fletcher: But procreation must now be regarded as a responsible act, and you are saying that a woman is sometimes dishonest about it. The moral and legal supposition must still be that parents, whether of illegitimate or legitimate children, are responsible. Dr Stone's point is that the law is coming with greater precision to insist upon personal responsibility for fact, rather than upon legal fictions which Dr Leach appears to want extended.

Stone: I can't sufficiently stress that there are conflicting elements in the law here. The concept of 'child of the family' has introduced a new form of fictional parenthood through acceptance into the family. I don't think the law worries too much about moral responsibility; it may be largely a question of from whom is the money most easily extracted. Unmarried women managed to acquire certain rights over their illegitimate children because they were stuck with the children and could be made responsible for their maintenance. In days before blood tests you couldn't tell who the father might be.

Fox: You still can't. All the blood test establishes is whether the man is *not* the father, not whether he necessarily is.

Stone: The Law Commission has pointed out[3] that where uncommon blood factors are present, the incidence of possible fathers could be as low as one in fifty million. In *Aspinall* v. *Aspinall,*[1] a case on nullity, the man admitted that there had been some kind of sexual play before marriage but he said pregnancy couldn't possibly have resulted. It was shown that he could be the father, and also that something like 2·27 per cent of Western European males could be the father. This is negative but pretty cogent.

Fox: Circumstantial evidence!

Comfort: Does the man need something like the equivalent of third party insurance here?

Weiss: In the American system a paternity suit may be pressed even if the man has no funds. There are many men in American prisons who are guilty only of simultaneous impoverishment and fatherhood, two conditions which taken separately are not crimes but in combination can get one jailed.

Reynolds: There are recent modifications in other areas in the law which indicate that in our legal dealings we are trying to pin responsibility for their acts on particular individuals. I am thinking of the breathalyser test, and of the use of scientific evidence to establish the actual or most probable identity of the person responsible for an act of rape or incest.

Stone: But can one say that we are trying only to pin down responsibility? Until 1968 in England the worst possible advice to give a young man as far as his pocket was concerned was that he should marry the girl. It was much cheaper and carried much less responsibility to have an illegitimate child than a legitimate one. In so far as we want to try and protect the family (however we see the family), this is not the sort of thing to be encouraged in the law.

Borrelli: In Italy a young man is obliged by law to marry a *minor* if she is carrying his child, or else to go to prison. Therefore we have many meaningless marriages and yet the whole society is quite prepared to accept this as a normal solution. Our legislation also says, officially, that if a man has a child from another woman then the wife has to accept his child as her own, because the other woman doesn't exist as a wife.

Comfort: Adultery is in fact a criminal offence in Italy.

Stone: What percentage of cases of adultery are ever prosecuted in Italy?

Borrelli: It is very low. I would say Italian law is still male centred.

Stone: Pressure on the man to marry the girl, or pressure on his wife to accept another woman's child, is the kind of distortion that arises from exonerating people completely from responsibility for an illegitimate child. Isn't it better to say to a man: "You need not be stuck with this woman but you are stuck with this child and you must at least maintain him until he is independent"?

Fox: Even the 'biological father' of the child is itself a legal fiction. Nobody knows who the biological father of a child is. Three people can be involved: the partner, the father of the child—that is, the actual genitor, and the man on whom it gets pinned. The law reduces it not to a biological relationship but to what society will accept as evidence for being the biological father of a child.

Borrelli: I wonder why we always emphasize the father's responsibility for the upbringing of the child? Why doesn't the woman have to take half the responsibility?

Weiss: There is a punitive element as well. At a court hearing some men get a lecture as well as a continuing fine.

Stone: I am interested that so many men are in prison for the 'crime' of fatherhood in the States. In 1965–1966 I was told that the New York man would pay up rather than go inside. Whereas in England if the alternatives are to maintain the wife or to be maintained in idleness by the State, men apparently prefer to go to jail. In 1958 the jails were so full of such men that there was nowhere to put the real criminals, and we had to find some other way to enforce maintenance.

8: Biological Regulation of Reproduction

ANNE MCLAREN

MAN is remarkable in many ways. One feature that distinguishes him from other mammals is the relative lack of synchronization between mating and ovulation. In most mammals, female receptivity is confined to the period of oestrus, when the eggs are shed. In a few, such as the rabbit, the non-pregnant female is sexually receptive at all times, but ovulation only occurs in response to a sexual stimulus. Earlier observations on monkeys and anthropoid apes suggested that mating could take place throughout the female cycle, but it now appears that even in captivity rhesus monkeys show a marked increase in sexual activity near mid-cycle,[11] while in the wild the overwhelming majority of copulations, at least in chimpanzees, take place at or close to the time of maximal sexual swelling.[9] In man, although some indications of a behavioural rhythm still persist,[17] the great majority of matings take place outside the fertile period.

The biological importance of synchronizing mating and ovulation is clearly great, since evolution has produced elaborate signals of female receptivity (e.g. the sexual skin in primates, such as our fellow-anthropoid the chimpanzee) and effective barriers to coitus in the non-fertile period, both behavioural (e.g. the aggression towards males of the dioestrous hamster) and anatomical (non-patency of the vagina in many rodents except during oestrus). When synchronization is relaxed, the spermatozoa may be stale by the time the eggs are shed, or the eggs may be stale by the time the spermatozoa reach them. Laboratory experiments have shown that either eventuality decreases the chances of normal development, fertilization of stale eggs in particular leading to polyspermy and high embryonic mortality.[1] This factor must contribute to the high rate of pregnancy wastage in our own species, though the attempt by German[6] to explain in this way the increased incidence of Down's syndrome (mongolism) with maternal age has been widely criticized.[1]

If mating outside the fertile period is reproductively hazardous, why has natural selection permitted it to occur in our own species? The answer may lie in the importance of sexual activity in the maintenance of stable pair matings and family cohesion, and the importance of such a system in the evolution of human society. The case for the relational and recreational aspect of sexual activity has been well argued by Comfort.[3]

We may carry the argument a stage further. The biological evolution of mankind has already produced a partial separation of sexual activity from reproduction; social evolution is now completing this process. If the world population explosion is to be checked, sexual activity must no longer be thought of as primarily concerned with procreation. In the next part of this paper, I shall be discussing the means of achieving sex without reproduction. Later, we shall see that the other side of the coin, reproduction without sex, will also need to be taken account of in the future.

REDUCING FERTILITY

If the population of the world is to be kept within reasonable bounds, the most urgent form of regulation of reproduction is of course its prevention. In industrialized countries, the issue of contraception is viewed mainly in the context of family planning, that is the spacing and limitation of births in the best interests of children and parents. Contraceptive methods therefore require to be fully effective. The problem is also a social one, since much further increase in the population of, for instance, this country would overload hospitals, schools, roads, housing, recreational facilities and so on. In underdeveloped countries the problem is at present primarily a social one, and is aggravated by the threat of mass starvation if the rate of population increase is not checked. Contraceptive methods need not be fully effective, but must be cheap, and easy to apply.

The various contraceptive measures available at present, including abortion and sterilization, as well as those which may be developed for future use, have recently been authoritatively reviewed.[15] All these measures have disadvantages. The contraceptive pill is relatively expensive, requires continuing positive action and has undesirable side-effects (though its dangers are considerably less than those of pregnancy). Intrauterine devices, though they are cheap to produce and have the great advantage that, once in place, no further action is required, need to be inserted by medically trained people and are not tolerated by some women. Nonetheless, it is difficult to escape the conclusion that the main problems now are economic, political, cultural and psychological, rather than scientific. Given the money and the will, effective campaigns to reduce fertility could be put into action in every country, based on existing methods of contraception.

Again, the problem varies from country to country. We do not know how many children women in industrialized countries will want to have if economic factors cease to be a deterrent, but it will almost certainly be more than the 2 to $2\frac{1}{2}$ per family that is required to maintain a constant level of population. A radical change in social outlook will therefore be needed: excess breeding will be viewed with the same social disapproval as excess drinking or eating, and the ethical and aesthetic advantages of small families will be stressed. Such a change would not be hard to bring about if the power of the advertising industry were harnessed to this end. In underdeveloped countries education is a factor of prime importance, plus of course the availability for women of jobs other than child-rearing. What of 'social', mass-acting contraceptives? Dr Homi Bhaba, Director of the Indian Atomic Energy Commission, stated in 1959: "What is necessary to solve (India's) population problem is some substance, an additive which can be put in drinking water or food, which will reduce fertility 30 to 35 per cent, just a general reduction. This would effectively reduce (our) birth rate to optimal limits." No such additive is known at present, and clearly exhaustive safety tests would be needed before anything of the sort could be contemplated. A foretaste of the opposition that such a measure would arouse can be seen in the passionate campaign against compulsory fluoridation of drinking water to prevent dental caries. But liberty of the individual and freedom of choice are already luxuries that not all societies can afford, and 'freedom to breed' may become an increasingly unappealing slogan.

The even more radical solution of making an entire population infertile so that procreation was only possible by taking some positive countermeasure, would ensure that every conception was a deliberate act and every child a wanted child. Governments might be tempted only to allow selected individuals to reproduce, which, as with any form of positive eugenics, would raise moral and social problems of great complexity.

Looking ahead, one can foresee a time when the most common sibship size will be two, with many couples, more than at present, having a single child only. The increasing importance of the extended family group in such a situation was discussed earlier here by Professor Miller.[12]

INCREASING FERTILITY

Infertility causes an enormous amount of unhappiness to individuals, since about 10 per cent of all couples in Britain and America, for instance, are affected. If social attitudes change so that fewer women regard childbearing as their primary function in life, the distress associated with sterility will diminish, but the problem will remain great. A further reason for seeking ways to increase fertility is of course the importance to the world's food supply of animal breeding, both of existing farm animals and of new species which it may be possible to domesticate.

Much can already be done to alleviate infertility. Treatment with pituitary gonadotropins ('fertility drugs') will induce ovulation, at present to a not always predictable extent. Foetal and neonatal deaths due to Rhesus incompatibility are already much reduced in number and may soon be eliminated. Some cases of infertility, in both male and female, may be caused by immunization against spermatozoa: these cases are only now beginning to be identified and treated appropriately.

Artificial insemination with the husband's sperm, A.I.H., is used where the woman has some anatomical defect which prevents entry of sperm into the cervix after normal coitus, or where the man is impotent, or produces too few sperm for normal fertility. In the last case, the sperm can be concentrated, either by centrifugation or by the split-ejaculate method, and inseminated directly into the cervix, or they can be accumulated by deep-freeze storing over a period of several months. The more common situation is where the husband produces no normal sperm, so that insemination has to be carried out using sperm from a donor, A.I.D.

It is almost impossible to get reliable data on artificial insemination, because the entire subject is shrouded in secrecy. It was estimated[13] in 1957 that 100000 babies had already been born in the U.S. as a result of artificial insemination, and that 6000 inseminations a year were being performed in Britain. Most of these would involve A.I.D. rather than A.I.H. Even if these figures were a gross overestimate, it is clear that the technique is widely used to alleviate infertility.

The companion technique of egg transfer[8] is a routine procedure in laboratory animals and some farm animals. Several groups in Britain and the U.S. are interested in the possibility of applying it to women, but so far no transfers have been reported. The ideal patient would be one whose Fallopian tubes were blocked, rendering her sterile, but who has normal ovaries and uterus and a fertile husband. By analogy with A.I.H., such a procedure could be termed E.T.W. Unfortunately, however, few cases of infertility fall into this category. Most women with blocked Fallopian tubes also have multiple adhesions involving the ovaries, making it difficult or impossible to obtain eggs from them. In such cases, as well as in women who are infertile because they produce no normal eggs, it would be necessary to transfer an egg from a donor, a procedure which we may term E.T.D. In the not very likely event of transferred egg and sperm both being derived from donors, we could refer to E.T.D.D. Table I summarizes the contributions that the two parents make to babies conceived as a result of these procedures.

TABLE I

BIOLOGICAL CONTRIBUTION OF PARENTS TO OFFSPRING ACQUIRED IN VARIOUS WAYS
(For explanation, see text)

	Coitus	Paternal genome	Maternal genome	Maternal environment
Normal conception	+	+	+	+
A.I.H.	−	+	+	+
A.I.D.	−	−	+	+
E.T.W.	−	+	+	+
E.T.D.	−	+	−	+
E.T.D.D.	−	−	−	+
Adoption	−	−	−	−

In animals, the egg is fertilized in the reproductive tract of the donor female, and the subsequent transfer operation presents no great difficulties. In women, it would be exceedingly difficult to recover the egg after fertilization, and in any case blockage of the Fallopian tubes would preclude fertilization. It will therefore be necessary to fertilize the human egg *in vitro*, outside the body, and it is at this stage that most of the technical problems arise. There is no lack of potential material, since each ovary contains many thousands of eggs. Most of these are still too immature to be fertilized: they can be matured either by treating the patient with hormones before the fragment of ovary is removed, or by maintaining them in culture for a few days after removal. *In vitro* fertilization has been achieved in rabbits, hamsters and mice, but development of the fertilized eggs is by no means always normal, and tends to be associated with heavy embryonic mortality.[2] There have been a number of claims of *in vitro* fertilization of human eggs, but the published evidence suggests that so far only the early stages of fertilization have been achieved,[5] and no normal development has ensued. It may well be several years before the first living E.T. baby is born, and several decades before the technique becomes part of routine gynaecological practice.

At this point we may ask, what is the point of bothering with artificial insemination and egg transfer, and indeed with the alleviation of infertility in general, when the world is suffering from too many babies and there exists the obvious alternative of adoption? One answer is that medical ethics demands that the doctor do whatever he considers is in the best interests of the individual patient, whether or not it is in the best interests of society; a second answer is that adoption is not always possible. In 1957, it was reported[13] that about 900000 childless couples applied for the adoption of a child each year in the U.S., but only 80000–90000 children were available, i.e. only one baby to every ten or eleven couples. As contraceptive measures get more effective and more widely used, the number of unwanted children will decline and even fewer babies will be available for adoption. Also, adoption societies have very stringent regulations as to which couples are suitable to adopt children, and often these rule out couples (e.g. those who have an older handicapped child) that the doctor judges would make excellent parents.

Artificial insemination differs from adoption (Table I) in that at least the mother's genes are transmitted to the child, and the mother also has the satisfaction of carrying and giving birth to the child. One risk with A.I.D. might be that the husband would resent and reject a child who inherited another man's genes and not his own; but the experience of gynaecologists who have used this technique seems to be that, provided the couples are carefully selected beforehand, the husband accepts the child as his own. One of the few published followup studies is that of Weisman,[18] who selected 87 couples for A.I.D. Seventy-four women became pregnant, 69 produced normal healthy babies and 41 were followed up. In only one case was there any psychological difficulty, and Weisman concludes: "The most valuable finding of the follow-up survey was the healthy psychological relationship of the family unit having a child derived through artificial donor insemination." In particular, he found that the A.I.D. children did not have the personal and social problems of some adopted children. Many of his couples came back for a second and even a third A.I.D. child; this is also the experience of other workers in the field.

Problems of psychological adjustment should be rather easier with E.T.D. than with A.I.D., since the parental contribution is more evenly shared (Table I), the father contributing to the baby's genetic constitution and the mother providing the prenatal environment.

The legal situation of adopted children is clear. In England, although hereditary titles are not passed on to adopted children, the laws of inheritance of property in no way distinguish adopted from ordinary children. The same has been true in Scotland only since 1964; before that time an adopted child had rights of inheritance from its natural parents but none from its adoptive parents.

For A.I.D. children, the legal situation is very confused, since there exists no relevant statute law and very little case law. Two main questions arise: (1) Is A.I.D. classed as adultery, and can it therefore be used as grounds for divorce? (2) Are A.I.D. children illegitimate, and hence possibly discriminated against in inheritance and death duties? In 1928 Lord Dunedin ruled that fecundation ab extra could constitute adultery; in 1945, Willink, as Minister of Health, stated that A.I.D. was tantamount to adultery, both on the part of the wife and of the donor, even if the husband had given his consent; an opposite decision was taken by Lord Wheatley in 1958. The Royal Commission on Marriage and Divorce, in 1956, recommended that A.I.D. should not be considered as adultery, but as "new and separate ground for divorce" if the husband had not given his consent. The variously worded forms of consent that most doctors get both husband and wife to sign before insemination is performed have little legal bearing on the adultery issue, nor on the question of whether the child is illegitimate. They may indeed have an adverse effect on both issues, since they make explicit the fact that the husband is not the biological father of the child. On the other hand the consent form makes it clear that the husband has accepted the child as one of the family, and he would therefore be liable for maintenance for the child in the event of a subsequent divorce.

The Report of the Feversham Committee on Human Artificial Insemination, published in 1960, sets forth majority and minority opinions.

The majority ruled that a child born as a result of A.I.D. was illegitimate, while the minority considered that such a child should be regarded in law as legitimate, and for the purposes of registration be deemed the child of a husband who had consented to the insemination of his wife by a donor.[14] In fact every child born from a marriage is presumed legitimate unless proved to the contrary. It is open to the husband to dispute paternity at any time, but once he has acknowledged the child as his own, the court is less likely to find in his favour.

The legal situation for egg transfer, E.T.D., babies will presumably be simpler than that for A.I.D. babies, since the husband's sperm is used and therefore no question of adultery is likely to arise. But if the husband can dispute paternity in A.I.D., what would be the legal position of an E.T.D. mother who disputed maternity? In the case of the husband, "acknowledging the child as his own" is a rather imprecise phrase; would a woman who gestated an E.T.D. baby thereby automatically "acknowledge it as her own", or would some postnatal acknowledgement be required?

The confused legal situation underlies much of the secrecy which at present surrounds artificial insemination. From the point of view of the welfare of the family, it would seem eminently desirable that legislation should be introduced to the effect that a child, conceived by an insemination to which both parents have given their written consent, should have complete legal equality with an adopted child or a child conceived normally.

MODIFICATIONS OF THE REPRODUCTIVE PROCESS

In spite of frequent newspaper reports to the contrary, there is as yet no way of predetermining the sex of a baby. We know that whether a fertilized egg develops as a male or a female depends on whether the fertilizing sperm carried an X or a Y chromosome, but we have no means of separating or differentially inactivating the two populations of sperm. Many different research groups are working on this problem, and the solution, when it comes, will be of considerable economic importance in animal breeding.

If the solution were one which could be applied to our own species, if necessary with the aid of artificial insemination, the chief social effect would be a reduction in family size. Many couples would like one son and one daughter; if they could choose the appropriate sex for their second child, they might leave it at that and have no more children. In societies where male (or female) children were of economic value, the social implications of sex determination might be much greater. One sex would be preferentially selected, with consequent distortion of the sex ratio. An excess of males would reduce the rate of population growth, but might increase the level of aggression of the society. The sex ratio might oscillate for a few generations.

The technique of amniocentesis, in which a needle is inserted into the amniotic cavity during pregnancy so that foetal cells can be withdrawn and examined under the microscope, offers a means of identifying the sex of a baby before birth. In theory the pregnancy could then be terminated if the sex was not the desired one, but in practice the test can only be done fairly late in pregnancy, by which time abortion is no longer a simple operation. If the technique were improved, so that it no longer carried the risks which it does at present, and could be performed earlier, it might prove useful for identifying embryos carrying major chromosome abnormalities known to be present in one or other parent. As a method of regulating the sex of children, it would remain a messy and unsatisfactory procedure.

Euphenics and eugenics need not occupy our attention for very long. Euphenics, the attempt to correct genetic defects during development, would include, for instance, curing a defective embryo by injecting some chemical substance such as ribonucleic acid (RNA). This is still a very long way from being practicable, even in animals, and in any event it seems unlikely that it would be worth going to such lengths to save an individual abnormal embryo. As for positive treatments to improve the quality of our species, one suspects that for the next few generations, very much more rapid progress will be made by studying the neglected fields of child upbringing and education than by tampering with the bio-chemistry of the unborn.

Eugenics, the attempt to alter genetic constitution by breeding, means encouraging some people to breed and discouraging others. Genetic counselling, in the case of hereditary diseases, will become more wide-spread and effective as our knowledge of human heredity increases. Selective breeding for desirable traits has of course been carried out for purposes of animal improvement for thousands of years, but has not been deliberately applied in our own species although the techniques were available. Unless the structure of society changes drastically, there seems no reason to think that it will be applied to any greater extent in the future. Even if a cooperative population could be found, and the ethical and social problems of deciding what traits are desirable could be over-come, the rate of genetic progress would be very slow.

A faster rate of genetic advance would be achieved if genes could be altered biochemically, in a controlled way, as can be done to some degree in bacteria at present. This process of 'genetic engineering', termed by Lederberg 'algeny' by analogy with alchemy (the attempt to alter ele-ments in a controlled way), is at present still in the realms of science fiction as far as higher organisms are concerned. Advances in this field might well revolutionize animal and plant breeding in the twenty-first century, but are unlikely to find any application in our own species for at least a hundred years.

Another possibility, which is also still in the science fiction category but which may turn out to be less technically formidable than controlled alteration of genes, is nuclear transfer, sometimes called nuclear cloning. In principle this consists of taking the nucleus, which contains the hereditary material, from an ordinary body cell such as a skin cell, and substituting it for the nucleus of a fertilized egg. This has been done in Amphibia and the embryo has been shown to develop normally, once technical hazards are overcome. Since an adult can donate a virtually unlimited number of body cells, as many individuals with an identical genetic constitution can be manufactured as there are eggs available. Nuclear transfer may well be accomplished in mammalian material within the next few years, opening up a fascinating field of research on the extent to which the resulting individuals resemble the donor of the nucleus rather than the donor of the egg or the recipient uterus. The first practical applications may be to multiply the numbers of champion show dogs or race horses,[4] but once egg transfer becomes a routine procedure in our own species, the opportunity of combining it with nuclear transfer is unlikely to be missed. A woman having an E.T.D. baby could be given an egg containing one of her husband's nuclei, or one of her own nuclei, or a nucleus from some great statesman or artist who was phyloprogenitively inclined. Unlike normal parenthood, in which a selection of the hereditary characteristics of two parents are transmitted to the progeny, with nuclear transfer the child receives the entire hereditary constitution of a single donor.

Using the newly developed technique of fusing mammalian embryos (for references, see McLaren and Bowman[10]), it might even be possible to combine the nuclear contributions of two eminent donors within a single transferred egg. What would be the artistic achievements of a Picasso and Epstein chimaera? Or shall we find that environment and upbringing turn out, after all, to be of over-riding importance?

To complete our survey of twenty-first century reproduction, we must briefly mention two possible substitutes for the normal processes of reproduction, namely parthenogenesis and vitriparity. Parthenogenesis, or virgin birth, involves the artificial activation of the unfertilized egg, giving rise to an individual with a mother but no father. Common among lower animals, it has recently been achieved in mammals,[7, 16] but the parthenogenetic embryos died early in gestation. Even if this hazard were overcome, it seems unlikely to become of any great significance unless women become markedly more misandric than at present. Vitriparity, gestation of the embryo entirely outside the body as in Huxley's *Brave New World*, is still a long way off. The problems are largely if not entirely technological, but none the less formidable, and no social pressure exists to overcome them. For the limited amount of reproduction that the society of the future is going to think proper, viviparity will continue to give satisfaction.

I shall end with an example to suggest that modifications of the reproductive pattern do not always exert a negative effect on the stability of family life. In Britain and the U.S., the human breast, while acquiring a new role as a mainstay of the entertainment and advertising industries, has largely ceased to play a part in the nutrition of the young. This radical change has been accompanied by surprisingly little protest or outcry. One consequence of bottle as opposed to breast-feeding is that both parents can and often do participate. Is it not possible that the advent of the bottle, with the consequent strengthening of the father–child bond, is making a positive contribution to family stability?

SUMMARY

The process of reproduction can be checked, stimulated or modified. By the end of this century our abilities in all three directions will be greatly increased. Barriers to fertility control will increasingly become political, social and psychological, rather than biological. There is as yet no prospect of 'social' fertility control, e.g. contraceptives in the drinking water. Stimulation of fertility, as far as our own species goes, will presumably be restricted to the treatment of individual fertility. Egg transfer, already a routine procedure in laboratory and farm animals, will almost certainly join artificial insemination as part of the gynaecologist's repertoire by the end of the century. The psychological problems that these procedures raise are aggravated by the uncertain legal position of the children that result from them.

Most forms of genetic engineering are likely to remain theoretical possibilities unless a radical change in social organization occurs. A method for predetermining sex would diminish the number of single-sex families and probably help to reduce the birth rate, but would have little effect on the overall sex ratio, except in societies where one sex or other is preferentially valued.

Of all the suggested modifications to the natural process of reproduction, the two most liable to interfere with the present-day concept of the family are nuclear transfer and vitriparity. The first is unlikely to become accepted clinical practice for at least thirty years, and the second is an even more remote prospect.

DISCUSSION

Stone: The legal position of children conceived by artificial insemination involves two separate kinds of question, one concerned with the behaviour of the spouses and the other with the effect on the child.

Adultery is clearly defined as "voluntary sexual intercourse between persons of opposite sex, one at least of whom is married to another". It is therefore quite clear, and has been judicially held, that artificial insemination does not amount to adultery. But in my view A.I.D. without the consent of the husband would constitute behaving "in such a way that the petitioner cannot reasonably be expected to live with" the wife; and in England after the end of 1970 this will constitute a ground on which the court may find irretrievable breakdown of a marriage and grant a divorce.

In matrimonial causes we now have the useful fiction of a 'child of the family' in respect of whom the court may order maintenance and award custody. This includes not only any child of both spouses, but any child of either who has been accepted by the other as a member of the family.

As regards succession, illegitimate children now have, under the Family Law Reform Act 1969 s. 14, the same rights as legitimate children to succeed to the property of their parents who die without making a will, but such children must prove the fact of parenthood. In cases of A.I.D. the mother's husband would clearly not be the child's father, and the child would therefore have no right to succeed if the husband died intestate, if anyone contested this right, but he could always be provided for by will. I would prefer to leave to the judges the question of whether a woman who had consented to bear a child could subsequently repudiate her parenthood of that child. We do not need both a strong and intelligent judiciary and legislation to deal with every individual who seeks to avoid moral obligations. I hope we shall not exclude non-written evidence of consent. Writing is merely a useful kind of evidence, but in my view it should be open to the court to find on other evidence that consent had been given.

Tavuchis: On the question of sex ratios raised by Dr McLaren, data from large national samples in the United States show clearly that parents with two children of the same sex tend to want and usually have more children.[2]

Comfort: Have you any comments on jet pilots and stress in relation to sex ratio? Snyder in America found that pilots flying high-performance jets had an excess of female offspring.[1] He analysed this statistically, comparing them with their previous reproductive performances when they were flying conventional aircraft, and found that there was 250 per cent excess. A recent article in the popular press related the sex ratio to psychological and physical stress in the father. Choosing the sex of one's children may happen sooner than you imply.

McLaren: I predict that somebody will come up with a method in the next five years, but it may take a long time before the method can be translated into clinical practice. Sex ratio is a very difficult subject;

over the last 20–30 years there have been a large number of claims that look good statistically, but when the experiment is repeated the effect disappears.

Borrelli: A very important issue today is to know the scientific viewpoint about when a human embryo should be considered a human being. We are losing our sense of mystery about an embryo; we are starting to manipulate it and from the legal point of view this is a fundamental issue. We need to know legally when that embryo is considered a human being, because we could not then manipulate it so easily as we do now. I am not talking about the ethical point of view, although I would like to; but every legislation talks about murder of human beings. If an embryo is a human being and it dies, or more likely is killed, do we have any responsibility? We should decide honestly as to when an embryo is a *persona humana*, from the legal point of view. From then on it should be untouchable or it must at least be protected in the same way as every other human being.

McLaren: Some possible points one could take are birth, which seems to most people far too late; 'quickening', when the embryo starts moving, which is when the mother tends to feel she is carrying a human person; the time of implantation; and, of course, fertilization. From the point of view of contraception, most people would be happy with a method that prevented implantation but not so happy with a method that produced abortion after implantation.

Borrelli: Perhaps my question is naive, but I wanted a scientific view of when the human embryo should be considered a human being.

McLaren: The process of development is a continuous one and I was giving not an answer but various alternatives to choose between.

Newson: A straightforward point about development is that in something like four weeks the embryo has all the recognized organs, which is an extremely short period compared with the length of the whole pregnancy. Another point concerns the *social* implications of being a human being. I don't see how you can talk about this except in terms of social interaction.

Borrelli: Dr McLaren mentioned that when the mother feels that the embryo is a person, then he becomes a person. This seems too late to me because the legal status of that human being cannot depend on the consciousness of his mother.

Comfort: This is bound to be arbitrary. Many doctors would say that the embryo becomes a human being when it is capable of independent existence. This puts it later than implantation but earlier than quickening.

Hendrickse: This raises a very interesting point. The ability to keep the embryo in existence outside the uterus seems to be increasing all the time. As our knowledge of basic biochemistry improves I am sure it will be possible to move the date of viability, which is for humans technically still at 28 weeks of gestation, back earlier and earlier in pregnancy. This is where the problem arises: at which point is an act which favours the death of an embryo, whether by commission or omission, equivalent to infanticide?

Stone: Do we really want to draw lines and say on this side it is X and on the other side it is Y, when in fact no dividing line can be drawn? This is something we should try not to do.

Reynolds: If it ever came to the point where it became illegal or just morally unacceptable to have more than, say, two children, one might be forced to decide. Then, once conception had occurred, it would be necessary to know at what point it could be terminated without offending against the moral code. This point would have to be defined.

Rossi: In Switzerland we consider the moment of implantation into the uterus as the beginning of a new human life.

Sjövall: This is an arbitrary question but it is of great importance and there are different views around the world. For instance, two years ago the Grand Mufti of Jerusalem made a famous statement which is taken as authoritative from the Islamic point of view. What he called the formed state of a human being, that is the beginning of human life, in his opinion appears around the 120th day of pregnancy.

McLaren: That seems very late.

Borrelli: I must insist that I am not talking about the ethical issue. I am saying that scientists have a duty to concentrate their studies on this question. This problem has to be dealt with scientifically and it is important that an agreement be found scientifically.

Hendrickse: Let me give you an extreme example. We talked about an infant being capable of an independent existence as a human being. At present, if we entrust the care of some infants directly to their mothers those infants will not survive because they require special care which can only be provided in highly scientific units. One can project this back and back as our scientific knowledge increases. We do not know what the limit of our capabilities is for maintaining life outside the natural environment of the womb. For this reason, I think it is impossible to answer the question you have asked.

Weiss: A number of us have said this is arbitrary. I think that what that means in practice is that it is a matter of social definition. And social definitions change with time and change by cases. This question is not necessarily limited to pre-birth. Some societies in some circumstances have defined those already born as non-human for the early part of their lives.

Hendrickse: Even in present-day West African society a child born with certain malformations, even those which do not directly threaten life, may be at great risk because of total social rejection, and may be 'allowed' to die. We know too of other cultures where children at birth have traditionally been subjected to a ritual of exposure.

Abercrombie: The necessity to accept arbitrary definitions at one time and reject them at another perhaps helps in this problem of when a human being is a human being. It arises when the evolution of the human species is considered—when is a monkey a man? Culturally it is thought reasonable to discuss when to kill and when not to kill, but it is only recently that we have been able to talk about when to create and when not to create. The recent correspondence in *The Times* about the so-called 'test-tube' babies included a statement of anger that scientists should dare to create; yet thousands of people do just that every night. A cultural lag which came out during our earlier discussions is the slowness with which people will accept ideas, compared with the immense emancipation we get as soon as we can consider alternative ways, alternative basic assumptions. In Dr McLaren's marvellous exposition she spoke of vitriparity as not happening for a hundred years or so. She was thinking in terms, I imagine, of a technological difficulty which may well disappear at any moment. Since we can get to the moon, we can also make vitriparity possible if there is sufficient social pressure. And this social pressure could very well arise, because vitriparity would be one of the most emancipating things to happen to us. Think of the biological tightness of the human womb, for instance, or the possible effects of female hormones on a male child. The expansion of human possibilities is something we ought to be teaching people about. We ought to be preparing for the revolution in culture values.

Comfort: The traditional method of human population control in most societies is infanticide, and it is rather striking that we have come a long way from that in a relatively short time.

Rogers: Adoption is a pretty important kind of social behaviour for the future. When you said only one in ten babies available were adopted, Dr McLaren, isn't this a rather artificial statistic, since it happens because only pure white English babies are socially acceptable?

McLaren: White Anglo-Saxon Protestant!

Rogers: If advertising can influence people to reduce the number of children, then an advertising campaign ought to be able to get people to adopt all these thousands of black or half black babies, and the babies with a small malformation who normally would be acceptable to the parents who had given birth to them. If people would adopt these babies instead of worrying too much about having their own, this would go a long way towards solving the orphanage problem.

Fox: It also makes a great case for an increase in illegitimate births; there is clearly a hiatus between supply and demand!

McLaren: Actually, more and more illegitimate babies are being kept by their mothers and not offered for adoption.

Miller: We are beginning to talk as if people can really be engineered merely by an advertising campaign. This is simply not true. It is clear from clinical studies that the wish to father children is important to adult men; and the wish to conceive and carry the baby is important for women. To be pregnant is to be feminine. This has a great deal to do with the aetiology of many illegitimate births. It is very nice to think about the advantages of vitriparity but I am not sure what this does to reinforce a sense of feminine identity! I am particularly interested in the follow-up of A.I.D. that Dr McLaren mentioned. The problem of adoption is that its results in terms of successful child-rearing may be grossly over-estimated by over-enthusiastic social workers in both Britain and the U.S.A. For example it is apparent that a sterile father has many problems in relating to his pubertal and presumably now fertile son. Sterile mothers may have difficulty, when their daughters reach puberty, about their daughter's fertility. The envy they may feel about their daughter's fertility may lead to some adoptive mothers living vicariously through the behaviour of their child. A mother may unconsciously provoke her adopted daughter to have an illegitimate child. Equally, adoptive fathers, when they are the sterile marital partners, may appear to be doing everything possible to influence their son's sexual behaviour, either positively or negatively. In the A.I.D. study I wonder whether the contact with the father went on past the son's puberty. Trouble so obviously may start in adoption when the offspring becomes sexually mature. We are talking as though people are highly rational; they aren't.

Fairbrother: You don't have to be sterile to have problems with adolescents, however!

Ali Baig: Adoption outside India is still opposed because of our karmic heritage. (*Karma* is said to be the sum of the self that goes on for life after life. In other words, death of the physical self is not an end.) A bill on adoption is before the Indian Parliament now. Indian children are in constant demand for adoption in other countries, but this faces considerable public opposition. Even people with Western scientific backgrounds feel that a child will suffer more by losing his karmic continuity in a foreign environment, even if he is well cared for, than by remaining in misery in his own. No one seems concerned about the humanitarian side. They feel a child must not have its *Karma* altered by going into a totally different psychic environment.

Weiss: Is this a predestination issue?

Ali Baig: Not predestination but the sum of past existences, which have a bearing upon future existence, something to do with spiritual continuity and growth. This is one of the reasons why there is such a resistance to conversion to Christianity for instance.

Comfort: Weren't the Buddha and the founder of Jainism both in a sense adopted?

Ali Baig: There is no objection to adoptions *within* India. If an orthodox Hindu family adopts a child of Hindu parents the *Karma* remains undamaged!

9: The Development of Contraception: Psychodynamic Considerations

THORSTEN SJÖVALL

IN trying to discuss the family and its future intelligently, not only do we face the natural hazards of making projections into the future, but our very starting point, the human family, is ill-defined and complex, both in its historical and its contemporary manifestations. It is also completely bound up with the human predicament at large. I shall therefore abandon any rigid attempt at exactness in favour of some speculative boldness. The area assigned to me may seem comparatively simple and clear-cut, but I believe that the subject of contraception, where human knowledge and inventiveness converge on basic human drives and emotions has a crucial and complicated position in contemporary problems.

To take one example, it might be argued that there is no better evidence of the Freudian dictum that civilization has to be bought by the repression of basic drives than the present increase in world population. For the first time in history human procreation, previously regarded as an unquestionable asset, has turned into a deadly threat. This is a direct consequence of death rates being curbed by medical technology, which again is only one of many cases where even the 'beneficial' products of human knowledge and inventiveness are showing their reverse side in a staggeringly unprecedented way. The fact that the very creativity of man, from his biological reproductive capacities up to the most sophisticated accomplishments of applied knowledge, appears to be potentially so self-destructive, is one of the most frightening predicaments of our time.

Those who try to evaluate the situation are divided into two camps. The pessimists have it that man, like other species, is subject to evolutionary laws which are now, perhaps in some Darwinian fashion, exercising their inevitable selective powers, to the detriment of our surplus numbers. According to this view, mankind is a self-limiting, germ-like growth on the surface of the globe, dependent on random mutations for an essentially unpredictable future existence.

The optimists, on the other hand, hold that man is the first species capable of steering his own evolution, even against previously immutable natural laws. The remedy they usually advocate against the destructiveness inherent in human knowledge is more knowledge, holding to the age-old maxim *simila similibus curantur*. This homeopathic recommendation is at first sight surprising, but this optimistic view refers not so much to 'pure' knowledge as to the still more human quality of wisdom, which may be defined as knowledge plus an ethical superstructure. It is another notable paradox of our time that, along with continuing secularization, there is a sincere and increasing interest, particularly among the younger generation, in the moral condition of man.

I shall therefore present here some reflections on the broad psychodynamics of knowledge and wisdom, as they relate to human procreation and its control. Two definable items in this area have had a particularly formative influence on the human condition. The first was the cognitive connection between sexual activity and procreation—that is, the discovery of fatherhood. The second was the technical dissociation of sex and procreation, made possible by modern contraception. The first step belongs essentially to the past, the second to the present and the future.

SOME SOCIAL-ANTHROPOLOGICAL FACTORS

Motherhood has always been self-evident: a true and important historical difference between the sexes. Admittedly, we find some *social* conceptualization of human fatherhood as far back in history as we can go. A woman and a child, and a man to look after her: that is Margaret Mead's definition of the basic human family. But at this stage, whatever might have been dimly realized as *biological* fatherhood seems to have remained at a prelogical, psychodynamically unconscious level of mental functioning, from where it exercised a rather insignificant influence on emotional and social life. This is assumed to be the situation in certain human groups, even today.

An explicit knowledge of biological fatherhood is a late accomplishment in the history of mankind, appearing only in comparatively sophisticated civilizations. However and whenever such knowledge emerged in any civilization, it is likely to have had a profound impact on social, personal and emotional relationships between its members. The prestige and economic values ubiquitously ascribed to fertility and children may be assumed to have prompted males to compensate for the inevitable uncertainty of biological fatherhood, as compared to motherhood, by putting various restrictions on female freedom. The average male superiority of sheer muscle power may have been the simplest tool for achieving this goal. But this is only one of a number of innate secondary sexual characteristics that have been emphasized, elaborated and institutionalized in human societies. To this should be added a host of purely socially determined and clearly man-made distinctions between maleness and femaleness, all of them having some potential strategic value in the age-old battle between the sexes. Thus, the discovery of biological fatherhood may well have initiated and/or reinforced a complex structure characteristic of higher levels of civilization, with the effect of consolidating the differential status of man and woman. In Western civilization this has too frequently, and quite subtly, tended to emphasize male superiority and female inferiority.

We have to remember this general background when we try to evaluate the implications of the second decisive discovery in this field, that of efficient instrumental contraception allowing for a secondary dissociation of sexual activity and procreation, based on knowledge and technology.

Historically speaking, the increasingly sophisticated methods for controlling human numbers are infanticide, abortion, coitus interruptus and barrier contraception. All these methods are reasonably 'effective', and they are all practised in various parts of the world today. Only the last two are based on knowledge of biological fatherhood and mechanisms of conception; only these are contraceptive. The extent to which people still resort to abortion all over the world is a good indication of how rarely contraceptive knowledge has been applied. One of the main conclusions in Norman Himes' admirable classic, *Medical History of Contraception*,[2] is that the desire and intention to control human procreation is clearly demonstrable as far back as historical knowledge goes, and as deeply into the recesses of human behaviour as anthropological research has shed light. Practice, however, has remained imperfect and primitive until recently.

The great innovation of our time, according to Himes, is the availability of sufficient technical knowledge, and what he calls the democratization of such knowledge. He goes on to say "Opposition to contraception and the democratization of such knowledge never has been successful whether repression came through religion or law. Will it be any more successful in the future?"[2]

Obviously, Himes did not believe that it would. Now, more than thirty years later, we are at a critical point for putting this question to the test. In the last two decades the problem of controlling human procreation has been solved, from the medico-technical point of view. What remains to be tackled lies in the realm of individual and social psychology. Attempts to implement contraception on a large scale during the last two decades in various parts of the world have not been very encouraging, and we have come to recognize that, where birth rates seem to be well under control, this state of affairs was initiated and established long before contraceptives were generally available. Such control therefore remains with individuals, who need to have a basic knowledge of the mechanisms of reproduction, and the willingness ('motivation') to put this knowledge into practice. For we have come to believe that individual knowledge and individual motivation are vastly superior to even the best-organized contraceptive services in bringing about a better balance between human numbers and available resources. This is where psychology comes into the picture. It gives new relevance to Himes' statement[2] of the importance of the 'democratization' of knowledge: not only knowledge about contraception, however, because our present experience shows that this is insufficient, but knowledge about sex and human sexual behaviour in a broader context. We can reasonably hope that this will help to provide the necessary individual motivation, which probably has more to do with wisdom, in the sense mentioned earlier, than with plain knowledge.

An interest in and a demand for public sex education has certainly emerged suddenly and simultaneously in widely separate parts of the world. However, this 'democratization' of sexual knowledge is meeting with a peculiar and stubborn resistance, probably much greater than resistance to the disseminating of knowledge in general. To establish why, we need to formulate our ideas about the role of sex in man.

THE ROLE OF SEX IN MAN

Most research and knowledge on this subject has been provided by psychoanalysis. Psychoanalytic theory was explicitly founded on biological considerations, so it tended at first to emphasize the similarities rather than the differences between man and animal. Libido and its most important manifestation, sexual behaviour, were assigned a crucial role among the basic drives of human motivation. Later were added the so-called ego drives, essentially serving self-preservative purposes, as distinct from the species-preservative ones—the sex drives. Still later, the ego drives were exchanged for aggressive drives. The dichotomy between libido and aggression as the sole and basic motivating forces of the human psyche has been retained in modern psychoanalysis.

However, the general development of psychoanalysis after Freud has been towards a loosening of its alleged biological anchorage. The manifestations of drives in man, originally assumed to be more or less analogous to animal instinctual behaviour, have proved to be so malleable by social and cultural conditions that worthwhile comparison is hardly possible. This is particularly true of human sexual behaviour, as Freud clearly recognized.

Furthermore, the recent development of psychoanalytic theory, and the whole field of psychodynamics inspired by it, is characterized by the introduction and elaboration of so-called ego-psychology. This means essentially a shift of emphasis from the internal, psychobiological reality of drive manifestations to the external, 'socialized' reality of the relationships of the individual with his environment and his fellow beings. Incidentally, a parallel is still to be found here with biology, since this discipline now pays great attention to ecology. Yet the most decisive and fateful ecological changes of our times are more or less deliberately triggered by man himself, through the whole gamut of his technical machinery. Contraception is only one case in point.

Finally, it is tempting to speculate whether the development of human psychology as a science will tend to reflect the development of the individual human psyche into id, ego and superego. Psychology seems to have passed through the id-psychology stage and is now in the midst of ego-psychology, having largely severed its ties with biology; the future may bring another shift of emphasis, this time towards a still more exclusively human 'superego-psychology'.

SEXUAL BEHAVIOUR PATTERNS

Calculations based on the Kinsey survey of 1948,[1] and a recent investigation of a representative sample of the Swedish population,[5] reveal that it takes about one thousand acts of intercourse to produce one baby. So at least quantitatively and in certain parts of the world, the link between potentially reproductive sexual behaviour and actual reproduction is scant indeed. Moreover, if the two were as deep-rootedly related as is tacitly assumed, we would expect that sexual pleasure would be impaired, at least in women, when effective contraception is practised. However, enquiries so far indicate that the opposite is true in women taking oral contraceptives.

The rather obvious conclusion to be drawn is that human sexuality has a much wider scope and potential than mere reproduction. This happens to be one of the corner-stones of psychoanalytic theory. Yet when Freud was constructing this theory in the puritan climate of his time, he seems to have been convinced of the axiomatic closeness between *mature* sexuality and reproduction. He referred almost all non-reproductive adult sexual behaviour, particularly the so-called 'perversions', to psychopathology. In doing so he joined forces, although from a different angle, with deeply engraved trends of thought in Western civilization, according to which all sexual behaviour that is not at least potentially reproductive is morally to be condemned.

There is a peculiar contradiction here because, although from an anthropological point of view all the original bans and restrictions on sexual behaviour were aimed at its practical reproductive consequences, a secondary and still more rigid set of taboos has been erected against the richly varied but essentially harmless non-reproductive practices. Whether this is mainly a result of the Christian influence I cannot tell. Nevertheless, the adamant Catholic ban on any deliberate separation of sex and reproduction seems preposterous in this light; the more so since there are good reasons for regarding this separation as a uniquely human step, away from animal conditions.

It has been said that people having to struggle continuously to obtain the bare necessities of life cannot afford to be neurotic. In other words, neurosis resulting essentially from libidinal conflicts is supposed to be a typical concomitant of affluent society. Yet in highly industrialized societies today, patterns of mental disturbances frequently cannot be described and explained so convincingly in terms of libidinal conflicts as they appeared to be a few decades ago. I can only speculate about some of the reasons for this.

The well-known explorative and curative emphasis of psychodynamics on libidinal aspects of human conflict, once prompted by a sexually over-restrictive society but still lingering, may have led to a greater tolerance of all kinds of sexual manifestations. Energies previously spent on mandatory sexual repressions may then have been released, changing the balance of individual drive and defence economics. My own clinical experience of modern youngsters, those sensitive registers of contemporary currents in our cultural climate, is that they are not very troubled by sex, whereas they are intensely preoccupied with problems of security and survival. It is as if the pendulum had swung back, giving the once discarded self-preservative drives a new and urgent importance, and this in a society where, as in Sweden, the immediate needs for external security are ambitiously taken care of. Apparently the internal sense of security supposed to ensue from this protection is easily broken down by the overwhelming inflow of information from a turbulent world, which has been drastically shrunk by modern communication. Both long-term physical survival, externally, and the experience of a stable personal identity, internally, are felt to be seriously jeopardized. In this situation, we may expect and even observe the release of aggressive drive manifestations, which so far have been insufficiently explored and understood by psychodynamic research.

My tentative formulation, from a modern psychodynamic viewpoint, of the role of sex in man would therefore be something like this. Human sexuality is a means of expressing and satisfying individual needs for safety and/or intimacy; on rare chosen occasions such behaviour will also fulfil reproductive intentions and thereby add considerably to a shared emotional experience.

This formulation does not dismiss the biological aspect of the matter, which is included, in a 'humanized' and most personal version, in the individual experience of both safety and intimacy. But it does bring self-preservative aspects to the fore, while the species-preservative ones are toned down. This view is based on the facts just related, and I put it forward in the conviction that people are more readily approached through their own concrete experiences and emotions than through the rather abstract repercussions of such phenomena on the species at large. Incidentally, the overall aims of these two biological forces, the self-preservative and the species-preservative, so far theoretically kept apart, must be made to merge even more as human technology progresses. The willingness to realize and to take the consequences of the present development towards a rapidly increasing mutual dependence in a shrinking world is, however, not a biological but an ethical matter.

Let us now return to the idea that the population explosion shows the necessity of repressing basic drives. The pessimists, perhaps including Freud, would say that a civilized saving of lives by curtailing deaths must be paid for by a further repression of sex. However, if we interpret human sexuality in its wider sense the statement is an over-simplification, because it is after all not sex but reproduction that has to be repressed. So the optimistic formulation would be something like this: our knowledge has made it possible to save lives and this has created an allegedly alarming situation. The threat should be averted by more knowledge, and indeed we have already covered some ground. Technical stumbling-blocks have been removed, and growing insights seem to call for a revision of traditional views on human sexuality. This brings us back to the democratization of sexual knowledge, so absurdly neglected in view of its universal importance.

ETHICS AND CONTRACEPTION

The Swedish family planning pioneer, Elise Ottesen-Jensen, tells us (personal communication) that one of the things that started her on her life-work some fifty years ago was the poor women asking her how the rich managed to have so few children. The answer was that the rich knew how to avoid pregnancies, and some of them even had the wisdom to make sexuality an instrument for promoting human well-being. The poor had neither the knowledge nor the wisdom, and they still have not. To most of them, the menace of unmanageable pregnancies vastly and horribly overshadows the sexual pleasures of safety and intimacy.

Informed people agree that something should be done about this. Most of them seem to think that a well-organized system for distributing contraceptives, perhaps with some matter-of-fact explanations to the 'target population', would solve the problems. But this group does not sufficiently consider the importance of individual motivation. Quite a few believe that overt coercion or even violence in terms of armed revolution are essential and they act accordingly, thereby sacrificing elementary principles of human rights and freedom. A slightly more ethical standpoint has it that the idea must be 'sold', and that any method of contraception is better than none, from a demographic point of view. This attitude disregards the reasonable right of everyone to the most reliable methods, on which alone individual safety can rest. The implication is that something beneficial is still being kept from 'the poor', be they individuals or nations.

Less informed people have more or less ingrained moral objections against systematic sex education in general, and contraception in particular. They feel, for instance, that talking to children about sex would seduce them to embark upon activities for which they are supposed to be physically and mentally immature. They seem ignorant of the fact, convincingly demonstrated by psychoanalytic research, that sexual experiences in a broader sense are a decisive reality in the lives and development of every child from birth onwards; and they seem unaware of the lack of evidence that youngsters reared in an open-minded atmosphere show more sexual misbehaviour than others.

Efficient contraception is commonly claimed to be 'against nature', and to encourage promiscuity. Again, no investigations have so far supported the latter view, at the back of which we easily recognize the old idea that non-reproductive sexual behaviour as such is harmful, immoral, or both.

Public opinion on these matters is still based largely on a mixture of ignorance and contradictory ethical arguments, the ethical confusion being probably the more serious of the two. Sexual taboos, presumably originating in primeval attempts to control reproduction, have been adopted and expanded in Western civilization to a degree that may explain our present preoccupation with sex. Consequently, many people tend to equate sexual morality with general morality, to the detriment of a badly needed widespread recognition of the broader, and possibly vital, implications of ethics.

We can observe this, for instance, in the indignation often expressed at the sight of so many sexually or otherwise mischievous youngsters coming from 'good and decent families'. In psychodynamic terms, we may say that we have a highly elaborate ethics of libido at the expense of a comparably elaborate ethics of aggression which, if we are going to benefit from our present knowledge, may be much more urgent.

When some of us in the International Planned Parenthood Federation a couple of years ago considered the responsibilities of the Federation regarding sex education, we discussed the possibility of producing a basic document on sex for world-wide distribution. This should be a careful compilation of such biological, psychological and ethical ingredients of human sexuality as could reasonably be regarded as universally valid, to serve as the foundation on which any country could build its own local superstructure.

The idea has so far not been expressed in public. Even the term 'sex education' was eventually considered too bold for world-wide distribution. However, a few months ago a group of interested people from all over the world again discussed the subject under the euphemistic title

'Family Life Education'. At the end of the meeting, they decided to continue their work under the title 'Responsible Parenthood and Sex Education'. The deletion of the word 'family', as implying too narrow a framework for a true representation of human sexuality, and the acceptance after all of the term 'sex education' as an honest description, constituted, in my opinion, a considerable ethical achievement for this group, representing as it did such vastly different cultural traditions.

A founder and leader of the IPPF, the British gynaecologist Helena Wright, ascribes so much importance to effective contraception that in her view it not only requires unprecedented efforts in sex education, but also an entirely new and ethically revolutionary code of sexual behaviour. I quote this code from her recent book, *Sex and Society*[5]:

"1. No new sex relationship should cause damage or distress to any existing one
2. No financial advantage to either side should accrue in any sex relationship which is outside marriage
3. Financially dependent individuals must not enter into a sex relationship of which their source of support would disapprove, with the possible exception of marriage
4. Fidelity to one partner to the exclusion of all other sex relationships must not be demanded
5. Neither possessiveness nor jealousy must enter into a sex relationship
6. Marriage and parenthood should be the only sex relationships which are public property. All other kinds should be of concern only to the individuals involved."

The pessimists will immediately ask whether this code has the slightest chance of being a realistic basis for general sexual conduct; and, of course, they would be hard to contradict. Yet my guess is that, if any evolutionary mechanisms of natural selection are operating on mankind, they should be looked for in the latest and most decisive development of the species, that of the mind. Here they might be described in terms of human wisdom or superego development not keeping pace with the technical accomplishments of the ego, so giving the already obviously self-destructive potentialities of the latter the upper hand. It is this apocalyptic vision that inspires my feebly optimistic recommendation for systematic efforts to create a workable 'superego-psychology' of man. Any contributions in this direction should be welcomed. The idea has in fact been emerging in different versions in various quarters. Margaret Mead, attending a Nobel Symposium in Stockholm in autumn, 1969, said that in her view the most urgent contemporary need is for a global code of ethics, and that she would devote the remainder of her active life to this problem.[3]

COMMENTS ON POSSIBLE FUTURE METHODS OF CONTRACEPTION

The fact that the problem of controlling human reproduction has been essentially solved technically does not mean that we yet have an ideal contraceptive. Such a thing is anyway almost impossible considering the varied requirements arising from different conditions in different parts of the world.

If effectiveness and medical safety together are given the highest priority, the so-called systemic or hormonal methods are the best contraceptives available today, in spite of the continuous turmoil over their possible long-term side effects, which seems to have reached a crisis now. The heat of this debate is no doubt fuelled mainly by the intense emotional charge of the subject as a whole. Ecologists tell us that our present environment is contaminated by hundreds of chemical compounds, and we have not the faintest idea of the long-term effects on the human organism. Debatable attitudes towards sex again seem largely responsible for our selection, on the scantiest scientific evidence and with little consideration of the advantages, of these particular substances for condemnation, although an estimated 20 million women are already dependent on them.

Apart from the problem of side-effects, however, it is generally agreed that the present 'pill' is far from ideal in practice. The continuous and rather complicated administration is one of the more cumbersome disadvantages. The comparatively high price is another.

In my view, a solution close to the ideal would be an efficient and harmless 'post-coital pill' for a woman to take whenever, in her opinion, a conception is possible but undesirable. Such a pill is theoretically possible and its application may not be far ahead. One disadvantage is that, according to current definitions of 'the beginning of life', it might be considered as an abortifacient. Here is another case where modern technology and other prevailing circumstances seem to call for a change of traditions, attitudes and definitions. Previously, it was convenient to equate the beginning of life with some easily describable physiological event, such as conception—the penetration of an egg by a sperm—or implantation. This has been essentially an academic question, but today it has attained enormous practical importance, since anything that could be regarded as an abortifacient would be unacceptable to very large groups of people.

Yet in our present situation the subjective experience of the woman herself should be given much greater importance, and to the best of our knowledge this is unaffected by both conception and implantation. That is, subjectively it is irrelevant to the woman whether she is using a contraceptive or an early abortifacient, and it is in our own power to re-define the beginning of life accordingly. For all practical purposes, such a re-definition is certainly badly needed.

It should be noted in this context that not only has modern technology confused the issue of the beginning of life, but also that of the end of life, as the present debate about heart-death versus brain-death testifies.

Clearly, however far technology takes us in the future, we shall probably never find the ideal contraceptive—that is one fully acceptable to all individuals everywhere. We shall always have to count on a substantial number of failures, as we still have to in Sweden. The causes of these failures are not sufficiently known yet, although it seems reasonable from a psychodynamic point of view to think of them as a regressive phenomenon. For instance, some Swedish women, in spite of all facilities available, repeatedly find themselves needing abortion, and my hypothesis is that the psychodynamic background is one of a 'biological' or regressive reaction against the ordeal of having to choose voluntary sterilization, which is essentially what effective contraception implies.

In this whole area, we always face an intrinsic dichotomy between two viewpoints which are not easily reconcilable, and which are frequently confused in discussions. One of them may be called the psychological or individual, and the other the statistical or mass, point of view. Although, from the psychodynamic or individual perspective, conception is a comparatively rare consequence of human sexual behaviour, from the statistical or mass perspective it is a catastrophically frequent occurrence in mankind as a whole. This is the magic of large numbers increasing their momentum every day. The main dilemma of the educators seems to be to explain this dichotomy in a comprehensive way to increasing numbers of people at various stages of sophistication—obviously not an easy task.

Yet if we take up a position at the statistical end, emphasizing the frequency and danger of conception, we are in a sense continuing old and traditional attitudes towards human sexuality. We are in fact extending the old sanctions of fear and guilt, thereby sacrificing the positive and pleasurable potentialities of human sexuality. We also run the risk of giving the politically harmful impression of trying to make the position seen in terms of the individual a privilege of the so-called developed countries, so denying a measure of human well-being and dignity to the less developed parts of the world.

DISCUSSION

Raveau: I am not sure that Freud implied that procreation was the only normal way to act, sexually speaking. I think that the dialectic of pleasure is the opening of a new way out of sexual perversion. Do you think that Oedipus complex in itself is transformed by the control of procreation?

Sjövall: I agree that Freud's work made it possible to humanize the whole idea of contraception, but on the other hand he definitely

5*

indicated that potentially reproductive behaviour is essential to mature genital sexuality; non-reproductive activities as an end in themselves at the mature stage are definitely referred to as psychopathological.

Abercrombie: Although very sympathetic with the argument running through our discussions that we are after all biological organisms and have sex and reproductive drives, I am very reluctant to think these cannot be modified. If our progenitors, sub-human or human, had not had these pleasures in sex and in reproduction we would not be here at all. But we would not be sitting in this Ciba Foundation conference room if we were not the 'brain children' of these progenitors as well as their biological children. The notions of maleness or femaleness, of human-ness and of what fertility is, can vary, and the modification of the biological reproductive urge into the urge to produce 'brain children' may be one of the things that we most need to think about.

Ali Baig: In India codes of behaviour have had to be altered by sheer necessity: by poverty, hunger, over-population and unemployment. Sex is not the danger, but too many people. Many problems seem to have arisen in the West through over-valuation of virginity, and so the "possession" of woman. Marriage is important in our society but for other reasons. The system of the Ghotul among Muria tribes in Central India could be a sophisticated solution for youth in troubled Western societies. They have a commune or special house where adolescents of both sexes live in a community of their own, related to their family but without all the pressures of the adult upon them. This serves two purposes: one, youth's own function in a community which has the sanctions of society and the right to joy, such things as dancing, singing and sex with no taboos; the second, and more important, is training in non-possessiveness. It is an excellent preparation for marriage which has been proved by the system.

In the last 25 years there has been an enormous social change in India. Once it was not even possible to talk about contraception; today India is full of family planning advertisements, and we have an elaborate State system of awards for family planning, but the slogans do not reach far enough yet into the rural areas where the problem is greatest. Some 90 million couples are of reproductive age, of which 35 million couples are likely to want children. In 1969–1970 nearly seven million tubectomies and vasectomies were carried out, bringing the number of couples protected against further birth by sterilization up to more than 11 per cent of the total; over three million intrauterine coils were provided, and nearly a million low-priced condoms were distributed through the match and tea selling circuits which reach the remotest areas. In 25 years contraception has been accepted by 530 million people.

Newson: Has this change affected the value placed on male children in Indian families?

Ali Baig: No; female children are cherished, but the male child is essential in Hindu social mores for the continuation of the father's spirit. We have had to modify the limitation figure in family planning because people feel a family will be endangered if they fail to have a son.

Henriques: Barbados is a very small island with a population of 270 000 and it has had the most phenomenal success in population control within the last 25 years. This is an example of methods whose success depends upon the context. In the city of Bogotá, Colombia, there is now a local law which makes the employer responsible for the pregnancies of his employees or servants. When country girls come into Bogotá to work, the employer sends them immediately to the clinic to be fitted with a coil. This is an interesting and surprising development in a Roman Catholic country, especially in a country like Colombia which is not exactly regarded as being in the vanguard of progress.

Dr Sjövall referred to Helena Wright's suggested code.[9] My own feeling about jealousy, which she mentions in her code, is that this is something which is very largely socially conditioned. In our society, if their wives are unfaithful to them many men feel obliged to exhibit jealousy in a very magnified form because this meets with social approval, although they may have no actual feeling of this nature. In Western society, notions of virginity are very much tied to property and this came about historically through the association of property with child-bearing women; hence the importance of legitimacy. It is paradoxical that in Western Europe virginity is most prized now in the dispossessed poverty-stricken countries. In Southern Italy or in Greece, in Spain and Portugal, the males of the family feel a tremendous social obligation to defend almost fanatically this very valuable possession—female honour.

Reynolds: According to Kingsley Davis,[2] contraceptive techniques and sterilization in the developing countries are used to limit family size only when people have already had the requisite number of children according to their culture's demands, usually between four and five. This makes it very unclear how advances in contraceptive techniques can make any major impact on the population growth of the world.

Hendrickse: In underdeveloped countries where infant and child mortality rates are still very high, encouragement of birth control can inspire more antagonism than support. As a paediatrician I have often been questioned about the long-term consequences of ensuring the survival of more and more children, thus adding to the population pressure. My experience in West Africa has convinced me that a first essential step if you wish a family to exercise birth control is to give them a reasonable assurance that the children they have or might have will survive. This question of guaranteed survival of offspring in fact is essential. In the emerging affluent stratum of Nigerian society with which I am familiar, there is a demand for family planning assistance which cannot at present be supplied by the agencies available. Young couples who have two or three children and the means to provide them with proper medical care see these children surviving and then a second factor comes into play, namely economic and educational pressures. These parents want to do the best possible for their children's future and they have no desire to dilute their resources with a large number of children.

There are countries where there is tremendous suspicion about the whole purpose of international interest in family planning. It is seen as a 'mean capitalist trick' to keep them in permanent subjection. A very real factor is the whole psychology of inescapable poverty, and the concept of survival by sheer mass production—that is, the hope that out of say ten children born maybe three or four will survive. To impose a limit of two or three is seen virtually as an attempt to extinguish the group.

Borrelli: In general poor people are not poor because they are numerous; for them having many children is the only possible form of investment economically. For a poor family living in a shanty in Naples, having five children means an extra income roughly similar to that of a breadwinner, since the family allowances for an Italian are an incentive to have children. A parallel enquiry I made among families of workers and shanty families in the same area showed that people in the shanties have fewer children than the workers because once the investment is no longer profitable, they start to have abortions. When the first male child reaches the age of 16 or 17 and is capable of helping the family financially the women of the shanties generally begin to have abortions.

Tavuchis: The most successful family planning programme in the world would not necessarily make a dent in the problem. In certain countries in South America with very high fertility, if all reproduction stopped today the effect would not be felt for a very long time. We would still have the cohorts previously produced to deal with, and these are for the most part consumer cohorts. This has enormous implications for economic growth and is something that countries with easy abortion and other factors that reduce fertility have had to face. We should not become obsessed with absolute numbers; these other variables are equally important.

Rossi: In India I was very impressed by the family planning campaign but I heard that this propaganda was reaching only the middle and the upper classes. The lower class was said not to be affected, so this might lead to a change in population structure. Is this so?

Ali Baig: Written propaganda is not reaching the agricultural communities, but cartoonists are much more successful and in any case news travels round India by word of mouth at an incredible speed, faster even than by radio, and this is helping to spread the propaganda. But we have some curious anomalies in the legislation. Maternity benefit acts are virtually controlled by the labour movement, so we pay limitless maternity benefit on the one hand, and on the other we pay for non-maternity in the sterilization campaign.

Fairbrother: I wonder if there is any underlying danger; after all, the human species developed by mass production and by survival of the fittest. If we do not mass produce we are eliminating survival of the fittest, and perhaps we should be frightened about what we are doing to the species in the long term.

McLaren: Certainly that has to be taken into account but I suspect the danger is exaggerated. In our society all sorts of selective factors operate which haven't been operating in the past and one must remember that survival of the fittest doesn't mean just survival but also reproduction. Babies of Rhesus-negative mothers are being kept alive now who previously would have died of haemolytic disease, but population geneticists have estimated that the rate of spread of the Rhesus-negative factors will be extremely slow.[1] Biological evolution is always a very slow process, and increasingly we are moving into an era in which it is not nearly so important as social evolution.

Fairbrother: But the non-survival of the unfittest is rare now, compared with what it was before modern medicine.

Stone: We are talking only about fitness to survive. The survival of the fittest doesn't necessarily mean preserving the most admirable.

Comfort: 'Fittest' means able to contribute the maximum number to the next generation.

Stone: Professor Sjövall mentioned that motherhood has always been self-evident, but this is not always accepted by the law. In some Latin countries recognition is required not only by the father but also by the mother and I have seen at least one case in Italy of a child being registered as the child of the father who had recognized it, mother unknown. Even English laws can produce some anomalies here.

On the question of adoption, I would like to make it quite clear that I am in favour of it. Professor Fox perhaps jokingly suggested that because of the demand, the production of more illegitimate children for adoption might be encouraged. It is difficult to reconcile this with his thesis that the basic bond is the bond between mother and child. He is now suggesting this is something that should be forged merely to be broken: that the young, the poor and the ignorant should produce children for the well-heeled middle classes to adopt.

Fox: For the child the bond need not necessarily be with the biological mother.

Stone: Although I am strongly in favour of adoption some psychiatrists today point out that where a child is born naturally, the period of pregnancy is a training period for the mother. She feels the child growing within her and adjusts to the fact that this is the child she must rear. Where the child is born in a marriage the husband is also closely involved in the training period. Where the child is adopted, this training is missing. It is true that our law of adoption has brought a great deal of happiness to fairly large numbers of people, but where adoption fails, the failure is cataclysmic for the child. A large proportion of children who attend child psychiatric clinics are adopted children.

Fairbrother: In a broadcast programme on the unmarried mother and her child we found that if any sort of pressure was put on the unmarried mother to have the child adopted, she might let the child go, but she very often went straight out and had another. You may not have to be the biological child of the mother, but the mother is still a biological mother. It works two ways.

Henriques: I have come across just such cases, but the point is that the factors precipitating the first situation continue to exist, and merely taking the child away from the mother doesn't destroy their operation. I agree with Professor Fox that maybe there should be more illegitimate children. There is a tremendous need and anxiety for adoption, but there is also the vested interest of the adoption societies. No one in the slightest degree undesirable as an adoptive parent from the point of view of the society in question will get a child.

Rogers: Surely there are enough illegitimate children anyway; we haven't got to make any more, they are just not being adopted.

Weiss: The only work on the consequences of adoption for the adoptive parents that I know was done by Russell Kirk.[4] He reports that adoptive parents seem as committed to their adopted children as they are to their natural children, although there is some difference between the mother and the father in the nature of the commitment, the mother being usually the leader in the adoptive procedure. However, grandparents treat their adopted grandchildren differently from the way they treat their natural grandchildren; therefore bonds more indirect than the parent–child bond do seem to be different, and in ways which are to the detriment of the adopted member of the kinship group.

From the adopted child's perspective, according to Jean Paton, who was herself adopted and has since become an advocate for other adopted children, there is a yearning for the natural family present among all adopted children. She may be exaggerating a bit, but according to her it makes no difference whether the relationships with the adopted parents are good or bad; there is a need for a sense of biological lineage.

Miller: The adoption procedure is completely distorted by our social processes. Adoptive parents are made to feel different by society before they adopt; they are for example instructed to tell their children that they have been adopted. There is a whole mythology around this which is very interesting in itself.

Fox: I was struck by Professor Sjövall's reference to the discovery of fatherhood, and it is still more complicated if the beliefs about what each parent contributes to the child are looked at in different societies. I think there is no society that denies or doesn't understand fatherhood, but societies may give different emphasis to the contributions that father or mother can make, and one needs to know the evolutionary reasons for this difference in the father's notion of how he relates to the children. The great need of adolescent males to father children may come from all sorts of reasons to do with their sense of their own maleness. Something which worries me about the contraceptive pill is that whenever people talk about it they talk exclusively about its effect on the woman who takes it, never about the effect on the man. The pill does not render the woman infertile so much as it renders her man sterile. I have seen this amongst teenagers and college students in America where the young males have bad enough troubles anyway about their own masculinity; they are always wondering whether they are really masculine and how to prove this. European males seem to take it for granted that if they are male they are masculine, but in America, if you render them sterile and their women infertile, they take out their frustrations on university deans and the Bank of America because they have to prove their manhood somehow. I am not being facetious; I think this is a growing problem for the male, and nobody thinks about him.

Hendrickse: What is the effect of such things as national service on the maturation of the adolescent? Is this something which aids or arrests it? It used to be an important aspect of life in most European countries, and to an extent in the United States, but it has now disappeared from life in Great Britain. Have any comparative studies been done on the total effect of this experience on young males?

Miller: Military service did provide a ready-made network in which significant relationships could be made. The dependence which is implicit in being in an army and the apparent value to society of this activity are also relevant. Adults who are seen by the social system as valuable are very important to adolescents.

Hendrickse: I would like to know more about the present younger generation in Scandinavian countries, where sex problems and anxieties have gone into the background and there are now problems of security and survival. What type of security are we talking about? Is it financial security as a group? And are we talking in terms of personal survival, or group survival in an atomic world? What are the effects of the constant feeding-in of information about serious problems in remote countries in terms of this sense of security and survival? The kind of security the young see in their countries is being challenged by what has been going on and is continuing to occur in the world outside. We go on speaking euphemistically about 'developing' countries, but the truth is that the gap is broadening and by comparison these 'developing' countries are static and even sliding. Thinking globally, this is a very urgent and nasty situation which calls for far more positive direct action than has so far been achieved by any country. I am sure the thinking younger generation, especially perhaps in the Scandinavian countries, feel their security is tied up with this splitting of humanity into those who are going ahead and those who are staying behind, for it is among the latter that the problem of human multiplication is most evident.

Borrelli: Professor Sjövall gave a new idea of an ethic which was rather revolutionary compared with the ethics most of us have today. If he was basing it on psychoanalytic grounds, it deserves more proof if it is to be offered as a basis for human behaviour.

Sjövall: The code I was quoting was not proposed by an analyst. I think it is to an extent unrealistic, and certainly representative of a very optimistic view; yet there is something to be said in favour of it, although it would mean setting our targets high. For our own mental hygiene, I am very much concerned with the need for creating a new kind of ethics, because in Sweden, a highly developed welfare society, what is definitely lacking today is solidarity and loyalty between its members. This is rather surprising in an environment where people are so extremely well off materially. The discrepancy between material affluence and what could be described as a general lack of harmony between the citizens is puzzling. My hypothesis would be that this has much to do with ethical development not keeping pace with other kinds of development. If we are not careful this discrepancy may finally kill us.

Tavuchis: What one interprets perhaps as a lack of solidarity could also be viewed as a higher degree of rationalization and efficiency of services. As we get more differentiated structures for handling different kinds of problems—runaway children, divorces, and so on—we may get a decrease in solidarity or interpersonal relationships. People feel less and less competent to do more and more things.

Sjövall: I am not so sure it is a matter of competence. A year ago a reform was made in Sweden to the effect that no patient should pay more than 15 crowns ($3) for a medical prescription, everything exceeding that being paid by the State. Many doctors were then coerced by their patients into giving very large prescriptions, sometimes worth hundreds of crowns. This is a simple and alarming case in point, because if a social reform is adopted in a country like Sweden, you would expect that at least the medical profession would show some kind of responsibility; if you do not find this measure of loyalty among a highly educated profession, what could you expect from other groups of society?

Tavuchis: The same thing can be said of society in general: the larger the organization the less one is committed. I don't see that this is specific to a socialist economy or a highly planned or rationalized economy.

Adams: We have considered the family and its future mainly in terms of interpersonal relations, to the neglect of the relations between the family and the economic and political institutions. We are living in a time when the family is being subjected to radical criticism at the hands of a youth culture and of the students in revolt against contemporary domestic, economic and political institutions. Much of the criticism directed against the family is fundamentally ethical in character. Middle-class youths see the family as an enclave concerned mainly to achieve its own narrow economic success and security; to them the family is merely an instrument of conformity and adjustment to the economic and political institutions, producing political eunuchs. One is reminded of Plato's view that the family is the enemy of justice in society at large—the enemy of the city state. One remembers also what Aldous Huxley, in the Foreword to *Brave New World*.[3] calls "excessive familism."

It is ironic that in China, where we typically think that the intent of the government is to pulverise the family, the new nuclear family in fact seems to be surviving precisely because of its relation to broad social purposes—to be sure, this is in an authoritarian society.[8]

In the modern period the self-regarding character of the family has been enhanced by notions of romantic love. The novel and the cinema have centred attention upon merely interpersonal configurations—boy meets girl, and the conflict of the triangle. This kind of novel and cinema eschews criticism of economic and political institutions.

There is a type of religion which also emphasizes individual piety and an ethos of the family which ignores the responsibility in a democratic society to participate in those social disciplines that make effective the criticism and transformation of political and economic institutions. This kind of religion generally prefers domestic theological metaphors (God as father, and man as child of God), and it neglects symbols which give a larger scope to religion so as to embrace institutional criticism and responsibilities (covenant, the kingdom of God).

In contemporary psychiatric literature one finds a similar differentiation, and even a conflict, between individualistic, bourgeois psychotherapy and a 'sociotherapy' of broad societal orientation. The latter defines 'mature personality' and mental health in a different way from the former, and looks towards the mature person's assuming socio-political responsibility for constructive participation in the democratic society. How is the family of the future to function in educating youth to meet the responsibility of attempting to shape community and other public policies? Surely we are not to assume that the family is to play no role here? Does not this area of values belong to the process of socialization that takes place in the family? The younger generation holds that the family should concern itself with bureaucratization, over-centralization of economic and political power, poverty, meaningless work, pollution of soil and atmosphere, and war. The youth are not only demanding a new sexual freedom; they are also demanding new concepts of parenthood. They do not confine their attention to sex and drugs and interpersonal intimacy. The new interest in politics among youth in the United States testifies to this, as do also civil disobedience and the vehemence of protest against war.

The family of the future, as well as of past and present, must be assessed in terms of its function within the context of the whole social order; that is, in terms of the ultimate goals of family and society. So the basic questions are: "The family for what?" and "Mental health for what?"

The same sort of question must be asked about all institutions and all scientific disciplines (including religion and psychiatry). The alternative can be only a runaway fragmentation. Religion, psychiatry and the family will be "digested by the *status quo* as part of its healthy diet",[7] and the family will become what R. D. Laing has called a neurotic "protection racket".[6]

Sjövall: One of the things you are hinting at is the grossly misleading romanticism about love and sex that the family is carrying. These youngsters are perhaps extremely disappointed and feel very misled, and rightly so, I think.

Newson: The family is the only social institution which teaches certain fundamental human values: that you must hold back and not take, that you must share. Parents have to see that violence is not done, that justice obtains in some sense in a good family. Admittedly there are all sorts of breakdowns but I do not know any other human institution which has that kind of value ethic built into it. "God help us" is all I can say if this is now disappearing. The reactions of adolescents to the family are to some extent superficial. Every child learns a basic lesson through his family, and I think this becomes apparent pathologically if it isn't properly learnt; this lesson is the terribly important relationship of the unconditional love of parents and their children, and of siblings for each other. It is your duty to care for members of your own family. The brother–sister tie is not biological, so where did that lesson come from?

Comfort: Perhaps the rejection in American society is not so much of the family as of the institutions the family is supposed to be upholding. The rejection of political parties and the like seems to me to be a general anti-establishment feeling.

Hendrickse: Perhaps because the family is the most accessible target, it is the first brick of society which the adolescents are rebelling against. What is the basis of this major discontent? The one thing that comes through time and again in my very frequent discussions with adolescents is their complete disenchantment with all the professed values of the society to which they belong, values which are enforced or ignored in terms of profit and loss. The man who has 'made it' financially is the man who is accepted in society even though the means whereby he has achieved this wealth and power may be more than questionable. I think this underlies a lot of the neuroticism of the younger generation. They look at the Church and they find that its practices conflict with their concepts of a reasonable morality; they look at the State and at the political institutions and they find similar conflicts. They look at their own families and they feel almost a sense of shame because they see their parents as part of a national institution with which they are in basic disagreement.

Comfort: We must guard against undervaluing the genuineness of the moral concern.

Miller: I think the younger generation has intensely identified with the family. We are naive if we believe that the attack is any more than an attempt to free themselves from being highly dependent. They identify with the family both positively and negatively; the moral code they produce is very often the parental moral code—only more so. This is being confirmed by studies on the radical rebels in the States. They also may identify with the very worst aspect of family life which they attack. I once spoke to a group of adults and adolescents in one of these remarkable British new towns that have been so much admired. The adolescents all sat at the back and the adults all sat at the front, with four rows between them, which said something significant about their community. The adolescents were complaining bitterly about how uncaring the adult world was, and then we got onto the subject of marijuana. I said that the problem of the widespread use of marijuana was that 12-year-old children would then begin to use it; we ought to wonder whether we want our 12-year-olds to get intoxicated on 'pot'. These youngsters who had been berating the adult world for being uncaring, said it was no concern of theirs what happened to 12-year-olds.

Weiss: We got into this issue of the general social ethic by considering what would follow from the separation of sexuality and reproduction. The other side of this is the question of reproductive behaviour. Dr McLaren's paper makes it clear that, irrespective of sexuality, having children is important, and if we are to get some sense of what the potential is for using contraception we ought to consider what the motivations are for having children. This is an almost unexplored area.

10: Changes in Concepts of Parenthood

JOHN AND ELIZABETH NEWSON

ON-GOING research at the Child Development Research Unit at Nottingham University is concerned with patterns of child rearing in an urban community; and the data upon which this paper is based derive from a long-term survey study, during which mothers are being interviewed at length in their own homes as their children reach successive age-stages. So far, we have talked to some 700 mothers about their children as they have reached their first, fourth and seventh birthdays; we are currently doing the fieldwork for the eleven-year-old level, and we intend to visit these children at least once more before they leave school. The results we have obtained so far [3,5] indicate that real and important social class differences in behaviour exist and are described by mothers in relation to many aspects of child rearing, and that these differences reflect varying preoccupations, attitudes and values according to the socio-economic level of the family. For a number of reasons, the existence of distinct class-linked attitudes to child-rearing must be relevant to the present discussion.

In the first place, any consideration of changing patterns of parenthood demands an adequate and comprehensive picture of how the statistical majority of parents are thinking and feeling on a whole variety of issues connected with child upbringing. The concerns of upper-middle-class mothers which receive considerable publicity by being discussed in the women's pages of the better-quality newspapers—the problems of securing a satisfactory *au pair* girl, for example, or how to reconcile oneself to a son's departure for boarding school at the tender age of seven—are not without interest. But we must always remind ourselves that such worries affect only a tiny majority of the whole population of parents.

In our own sample of 700 families, even though it was class-stratified to include a rather larger number of Class I and II children than would appear in a totally random population, we discovered no real nannies, only a couple of *au pair* girls, and one single candidate for boarding school at seven. Seventy-three per cent of the parents of young children in Nottingham are working-class, and half of the middle class occupy non-professional and non-supervisory jobs.

The implication of this is that, for the majority of parents in this country, child rearing today is taking place in the context of a greatly improved standard of living. When we asked mothers of pre-school children to tell us in what way their children's upbringing was different from their own as they remembered it, it was in this transformation of the lives of ordinary people, in terms of availability of something more than the basic necessities of life, that the major change was seen. Although all social classes felt that there was now a greater freedom of communication between parent and child, working-class mothers were inclined to look for the roots of this more nebulous change, too, in the fact that parents had been freed from the worst anxieties of penury and could literally afford to relax with their children.

Tobacco-worker's wife:

Our mam was stricter, we got a lot of shouting at. Well, she was worried all the time about money, where the next meal was coming from and that. And we'd be asking like kids do, "Mam, can I have a penny for this and a penny for that"— well, you're bound to get nasty if you haven't got it to give them. It gets on your nerves. Ours was a good mam, but it was the money you see.

Railwayman's wife:

I'm bringing mine up differently. For one start, we never knew where the next meal was coming from. My dad was out of work from the General Strike. Where my mother went wrong, I try to . . . you know . . . She always left us at night-time—she was working. Don't think I'm trying to blacken my mother, sort of thing, but . . . you know, we used to have two penn'orth of meat between us and a penn'orth of chips between six of us. Well, I thought to myself, my children will never be like that; and they never have been. Of course, conditions are different, but they've always got their meals on the table. My mother nearly killed me once for pinching a ha'penny off the shelf. She did, honestly—but then, you see, things were very bad then . . . They were bad old days, I wouldn't like those to come back.

Tobacco-packer's wife:

There's so much more money these days, you can afford to be silly over your children, take them for holidays, and that. I never saw the seaside till I was sixteen, my dad was on the dole all the time we was kids, but Janey went to the sea when she was four months, and she's going again next month.

We have pointed out elsewhere[4] that "child psychology is a luxury which only a small section of the world's parents can afford to consider"; that "mothers need a respite from the most urgent problems of hunger, sickness and exposure, before they can give much attention to questions of personal adjustment and maladjustment" in their children. In those countries in which the majority of parents feel they have attained such a respite, the fact that these improvements in the standard of living have occurred within their own memories means that parents are consciously concerned to give their children what they themselves missed, both materially and psychologically: "She'll have a bit better chance than what I had," said a lorry-driver's wife; and a miner's wife spoke for the majority, when she said, "Well, you try to do a bit more for them, don't you? I always think you try to do just a bit more than you think was done for yourself." Clearly, if we are to discuss changing concepts of parenthood it is important to know how rising standards among working-class families affect these parents' general attitude to their children, quite apart from the specific effects of environmental factors such as gardens, high-rise flats, launderettes and so forth.

There is, however, another way in which social class differences can throw light upon the changing pattern of child rearing. Most social commentators seem to agree that over the last few generations there has been a very profound and universal shift in the whole philosophy of parents *vis-à-vis* their children. This change from a largely authoritarian towards a largely democratic mode in parent–child relationships may be observed internationally, and within any given country it seems to be in evidence at every social level. It seems reasonable to believe, however, that changes in fashion, innovations in styles of behaviour, and new social movements generally, tend first to take root in the more informed sections of society. They then take some time to percolate down the whole length of the social scale.

This will be particularly true in the case of child upbringing, where characteristically there is a great deal of inertia in the system. The time scale is an extended one, since, for most people, ideas about how children should be treated stem in part from their own experiences as children some twenty years earlier. Other factors also oppose change, some of them clearly linked to social class; for instance, young mothers still come under remarkably strong social pressures from their own parents as well as from the older generation within the community at large, but the more geographically mobile and the better educated will be in a more favourable position to resist such pressures. Thus we can argue that changes in ideas of child rearing, when they occur, cannot be expected to influence different sections of society at the same rate, and this in turn means that, at any given time, social class differences can probably be at least partly explained in terms of a differential time-lag hypothesis. As we descend the social scale, we find a greater proportion of parents clinging to traditional attitudes and values which hark back to a more static order of society, if only because, with limited educational and financial resources, people are in no position to make radical experiments in their style of life even if they think they would like to do so.

One further initial point needs to be made at this stage: that we adopt as a working hypothesis the assumption that social class differences are patterned in a meaningful way. In other words, we believe that social class groups develop traditions, belief systems, values and techniques of child socialization which are functionally related to the sorts of lives which their members lead, and to their expectations about the adult roles in society which their children will ultimately play. This is perhaps not a very fashionable hypothesis: it is often said that a major contemporary problem for the individual centres upon his uncertainty as to who he is and where he stands in relation to people belonging to other social groups. This 'crisis of identity', however, seems to exist mainly among young people who are both socially mobile and unattached. Once people have married, settled down and assumed parental responsibilities, they still seem to acquire fairly realistic notions about their occupational status and about the style of life which they and their children can expect. This is not to argue that patterns of child rearing remain static from one generation to the next: we live in a time of rapid technological acceleration and social change. Rather, it seems necessary to assume that the way parents bring up their children is based upon a mixture of tradition—how they were themselves brought up—and an attempt to keep pace with the changing situation, insofar as this will probably affect 'people like us' in the not-too-distant future. In other words, it seems important to examine the total life-style of a given social group in order to understand, not only the ways in which child-rearing practices function, but also the adaptive ends which they serve in perpetuating that way of life.

*   *   *

Whatever interpretive framework we choose to adopt, however, it is fairly clear that, moving down the socio-economic scale, we are more likely to encounter a tradition-oriented, or 'old-fashioned', style of child upbringing. In the first place, sex roles between husband and wife are ever more rigidly differentiated as one moves away from the professional class, through the white-collar and skilled manual to the unskilled manual group. Work-roles in particular show this pattern; while most professional and white-collar occupations are open to women as well as men, and carry equal pay, there are a great many manual jobs which are exclusively reserved, by tradition, for men alone, and women at the manual level tend to be grossly undervalued. The degree of sex differentiation in the work-role tends to spill over into the division which is drawn at home between 'mother's role' and 'father's role'. Further down the scale, the father is less likely to take a share in feeding and tending the baby or in putting the toddler to bed. Perceived differences in maternal and paternal roles are also reflected in the ways boys and girls are differentially treated: parents' expectations of behaviour are more closely dependent upon the child's sex as one descends the class scale.

Other kinds of parental behaviour can similarly be seen as approximating more nearly to older traditions at the lower end of the scale. The father is more likely to be described by his wife as 'stricter' than herself, and accorded greater prestige as an authority figure. He is less likely to participate in story-telling, or to share an interest with the seven-year-old. Parents in the unskilled manual class more often resort to smacking as a disciplinary technique, and rely heavily upon their inherent status as adults, exerting as such an inalienable right to respect and obedience, and thus deliberately creating a social distance between adults and children. In line with this, they also appear to suffer less anxiety over what methods to adopt in dealing with their children, and are less inclined than other parents to be self-critical with regard to their own attitudes and behaviour.

Although, in common with other investigators, we have found in this group a preference for non-verbal methods of controlling children, we have also shown that there is a simultaneous readiness to use a verbal technique of teasing or threatening the child, in ways which depend for their effectiveness upon his immaturity of understanding. In direct contrast to mothers at the other end of the social scale, who show an almost superstitious respect for words as the agents of truth, lower-working-class mothers on the whole accept as normal the use of deliberate distortions of fact, often exploiting the child's natural fears and anxieties, in order to instil in him a salutary sense of their own power. It is perhaps significant how often such idle threats consist of a backing-up of the mother's own authority by some outside authority figure, which, being a more unknown quantity, to the child than the mother herself, is perhaps presumed to retain its effectiveness rather longer. Examples of idle threats and teases follow; they are representative.

> "I say 'A policeman will come and take you away, and you'll have no Mummy and no Daddy'."
> "I often say 'If I have to keep shouting at you, I'm going to the doctor's, and if I don't get any better I'll have to go away'."
> "I tell her God will do something to her hand if she smacks me."
> "I've told him I'll have to put him in a home if he's naughty."
> "She picks her nose—I tell her it's dirty and her nose will fall off."

The following account is an example of how a chance occurrence may be deliberately used both to tease the child and to tighten control; similar examples have been reported from other cultures.

> "After I got your letter, mester asked what it was for; so my girl, naturally enough (*sic*), she said to Freddie (aged 4), 'Oh, it's to take you away, a lady's coming to take you away'. He said 'I don't want to go away'; so I said 'Well, you'd better be a good lad, then—or else she will'. (Do you often say that sort of thing?) Yes."

On the whole, the parental attitudes and group trends that we have so far discussed are those which differentiate most sharply between different working-class groups at the lower end of the social scale: which, in fact, characterize the unskilled worker's family from those of other manual workers. They suggest a traditional pattern of child rearing which would these days be condemned by most middle-class commentators and experts, and by a majority of parents generally, as at best uneducated and lacking in psychological insight, and at worst unkind and extremely undesirable. We must, however, remind ourselves that this style of parent–child relationships has a long history and deep cultural roots. The pattern would appear to share many features with patterns adopted by economically underprivileged parents in urban communities all round the world, and in societies which are, in many other respects, very different from our own. It has probably evolved in such a way that it allows parents and their children at least to survive and cope at a certain level; and whether or not this method will be successful in producing children who are reasonably well adapted to the kinds of conditions they are liable to face as young adults, at the least privileged end of the social spectrum in our decaying city centres, is still rather an open question. It could be argued, for instance, with some cynicism but also with some force, that a socialization pattern which compels children to independence; which turns them, at an early age, away from their parents and towards the peer group; which teaches them to distrust as unreliable all adults in positions of authority; and which, to some extent, hardens and desensitizes them emotionally, will continue to serve a function in making a hard life at least tolerable for the exceptionally underprivileged. It may also, of course, make them irreclaimable to such opportunities as exist.

However, it is necessary to emphasize that the pattern of child-rearing which we have been describing is nowadays only to be found, in its essential form, in a small minority of families in our sample. Nottingham is a prosperous city with a low unemployment rate and a vigorous policy of slum clearance and rehousing on new estates. The old densely-packed terraced housing in the central districts is steadily being eroded and replaced. For the majority of children, even within the working-class group, the socialization pattern has already changed. Father has come down from his erstwhile pedestal to be a friend to his children and a help to his wife. Relationships between parents and children have already become a good deal more egalitarian and democratic. And parents pinpoint the change by their pleasure at their children's willingness to talk to and share confidences with them with a freedom that they found so much more difficult, or even impossible, to attain with their own parents. In the context of a culture in which the major attitude changes over time have already affected all socio-economic groups except the lowest, much of our work has been to attempt a description of the skilled and semi-skilled working-class style of upbringing, and to show how it still differs in more subtle ways from middle-class modes of behaviour.

                              *   *   *

At this point, then, let us consider a whole variety of interlocking ways in which the experience of middle-class children differs from that of working-class children; in other words, we will switch our attention away from differences between groups at the bottom end of the social scale, and towards a consideration of differences between middle-class children and working-class children as a whole. It is convenient to do this in terms of a number of propositions which can be backed up by both qualitative and quantitative evidence drawn from the results of our study of seven-year-olds and their mothers. Briefly to define our terms, we take the middle class to comprise white-collar workers and upwards, and the working class to include all manual workers with the exception of foremen.

(1) Middle-class children are *future-oriented*. Their parents tend to marry somewhat later, on average, than those of working-class children, and this is often quite deliberately planned in order to allow the middle-class father to establish himself vocationally on some career which will have a rising income-curve through time. The middle-class child is thus born into a family which can look forward to considerably improved standards in the future—not because everyone in the country will gradually get richer, but because middle-class workers expect to benefit from a promotion system which brings them to their peak in middle age, whereas manual workers know that their earning power is likely to fade proportionally to their failing health and strength. This is what lies behind what Brian Jackson has succinctly described as "the middle-class ethic of postponed pleasure"[2]; and it is nowhere more strongly evident than in the way children in different social groups are taught to handle their pocket money. We have calculated, taking all different sources of income into account, precisely how much pocket money is at the disposal of the seven-year-old child in the course of a week; oddly or significantly, depending on one's viewpoint, there is a perfect inverse correlation between this average figure and the social class affiliation of the child: that is to say, the lower down the class scale, the more money the child is given to spend each week. It must be remembered, of course, that the middle-class child is probably enjoying rather more luxurious living-standards, and may be receiving considerable benefits in kind such as plenty of fruit, drawing materials, outings etc.; however, the fact remains that the working-class child has more immediate spending power. His mother is also more likely to give him extra if she happens to have it, without making conditions as to its sensible use. What is more, once the money has been put into his hands (often in small daily amounts), there is considerable tolerance of his spending it at once, although there is a tradition of saving up as a holiday approaches; whereas middle-class children are generally expected *on principle* to save a proportion of their smaller sum.

(2) Middle-class children—particularly the boys, compared with working-class boys—appear to lead *more sheltered and protected lives* than their working-class counterparts. Sometimes this is the result of parents actively discouraging their children from 'playing out' in the neighbourhood or forbidding their wandering off beyond their own road

into an area where the children might be less 'nice'; but in practice it is seldom necessary for the middle-class mother to make such blatant restrictions, since middle-class areas tend anyhow to be geographically distinct and insular. It is also broadly true that the catchment areas of the state primary schools tend to reflect such social divisions. When house-hunting, middle-class parents are often strongly influenced to choose a particular area because of the reputation of the local primary school; and, even when they live outside the normal catchment area of a favoured school, they will tend to exercise the right of parental choice (allowed for by the education act, but rather seldom invoked by working-class parents) so as to allow their child to attend a 'better' school some distance from their home. Alternatively, they may opt out of the state system altogether and send their children to private schools.

When we first began to look into the question of protection, our original intention was simply to obtain some measure of children's independence at the age of seven years. To this end, we endeavoured to form a scale based on answers given to a number of different specific questions, which could be rated and then summed to yield a composite index or independence score for each child. When, however, the separate questions were analysed as a function of social class, the results were not at all consistent from one question to the next. For instance, when we asked whether the child was permitted to go to the park or recreation ground alone, we found a clear class trend indicating that, as we move down the social class scale, more and more children are permitted to do this; when we asked about children going shopping alone, there was no consistent social class trend; and when we asked about travelling alone by bus, there was a significant trend showing that a greater proportion of middle-class children are expected to cope with this. Again, whereas more middle-class children are taken and collected to and from school, it is also true that fewer working-class children ever have the experience of staying away from home overnight, for pleasure, without their parents. Thinking in terms of some global concept such as 'independence train-ing', these divergent results are not easy to reconcile. The evidence instead suggests that middle-class and working-class children are taught to be independent in somewhat different ways. Taking into account a good deal of additional evidence, one arrives at the conclusion that the work-ing-class child is taught to be independent in the sense that he must learn to fend for himself *among other children* in a variety of situations where adult supervision is likely to be minimal. He is allowed to wander further, through very much more crowded streets, in order to reach a recreation ground where, again, he is likely to have to cope with large unsupervised groups of children; and he is expected to make his own way on foot to his local school. By contrast, the middle-class child is encouraged to be inde-pendent of his own parents by learning to rely on other *adults* for help and support. Parents expect some control over his choice of companions, by selecting both his school and the location of his play. Selection of school gives rise to problems of distance; these they solve either by ferrying or by teaching him to use public transport, an adult-supervised activity. He may stay a night away from home with a friend, but it is fully understood that the friend's mother is in charge. Thus the middle-class child is introduced to independence by degrees and in a highly protected context.

At first sight, this tendency on the part of middle-class parents to protect and supervise their children so closely might appear to restrict the range of experiences to which the middle-class child has access. It is true that the middle-class child grows up without much acquaintance with a busy street life, the hurly-burly of traffic, hostile and friendly adults and a mob of neighbourhood children. Adult memories of back-street childhoods evoke a richness of mingled delights and fears: the parents of back-street children often express considerable anxiety as to the unfortunate influences from which they are powerless to shield the child effectively. The middle-class child's experience is very different, but probably no less rich. Intellectually, his parents expect to provide opportunities for his own self-expression as well as for learning; socially, they provide the formal opportunity to play both guest and host. Outside the home, there is a deliberate widening of the child's experience, again under supervision. As one might expect, middle-class seven-year-olds are more likely than their working-class counterparts to be taken on visits to theatres, concerts, exhibitions, art galleries and historic buildings; but it is interesting that it is the middle-class children who also more often attend sporting events such as football matches with their parents, and also the cinema. A higher proportion of middle-class children also go to church with their parents, belong to Sunday School and are members of organized clubs or church groups.

(3) This leads to a further broad generalization: that middle-class children are expected to *learn communication skills* of many different kinds as early as possible. We ourselves have shown how, as early as four years old, the middle-class child is effectively rewarded for his skill in verbally stating his case for arbitration; and Bernstein[1] has made an especially important contribution by his emphasis of the difference between an explicit and a context-bound use of language. The point at issue is whether the child is able to use language to communicate meaningfully, without recourse to gesture and pronominal indications of the context; such gestures in fact restrict him to communicating his thoughts only in contexts which his listener already shares. For example, the child who normally sees no need to be more explicit than "You know him, out there, well he pushed her just here all like that" is entirely dependent for communication upon his listener's ability to watch his gestures and

look out of the window to see to whom these gestures refer. He is more likely to have difficulty in putting his thoughts across in situations where the context is not available than the child who has the habit of being explicit: "That boy in next door's yard, he twisted his sister's arm right up behind her back."

It is, of course, precisely this comparative lack of familiarity with the context-free use of language which makes it difficult for many working-class adults to use the telephone effectively. Conversely, the telephone for most middle-class people, in work and at play, is an indispensable tool of communication. In perhaps the majority of middle-class households, its possibilities are taken for granted; middle-class children need little encouragement to learn its use from an early age, in order to take messages for their parents, and quickly discover its advantages to further their own social enjoyment, and indeed to break through the geographical restrictions still imposed on them at the primary-school age. Every middle-class parent of reasonably sociable children becomes irritably aware of the telephone as a successful medium for children's conversations with their peers. The working-class child, however, even if his father's job atypically demands a telephone, finds that very few of his friends have access to one, and that therefore his own use of the facility is negligible. The situation is a good example of a technological innovation which offers a specific if unlooked-for training in a communication skill, and it is interesting that the use of telephones is now encouraged as a deliberate pedagogic technique in schools for underprivileged children.

This is, of course, not the only way in which middle-class children acquire more opportunity to learn and practise the skills of explicit language. They are also read to more often from story books, frequently full length books taken on a serial basis. They more often 'say their prayers' at bedtime. They are encouraged to communicate their private fantasy life to their mothers, who have more welcoming attitudes to fantasy and imagination than working-class mothers, and therefore reward the child by their interest and approval for describing to his mother what only he *can* describe. Middle-class children are also more likely to prefer imaginative, role-playing games to the play of the rough-and-tumble variety which is the first choice of more working-class children; while it is not altogether clear why this preference should exist (factors may be parental encouragment and greater privacy and space in the home), certainly imaginative play provides a much more powerful stimulus for the explicit use of language, whereas rough-and-tumble play is well enough served by purely implicit forms.

When we turn to other communication skills such as the child's developing ability in reading and writing, we of course find enormous social class differences in the extent to which parents expect such activities to spill over from the school setting into the child's home life. That parents look upon reading and writing as a normal part of *anyone's* life, not just something one learns at school, must inevitably determine in part the child's ability to use such skills as flexible tools rather than as some kind of trick unrelated to real life. The writing of letters by children, story writing for their own pleasure, membership of public libraries and ownership of books all correlate dramatically with social class. To state the obvious, the skills of literacy are virtually indispensable to adults in middle-class occupations; and it is largely through writing letters and memoranda to one another that the professional and managerial classes exert power and influence over events and hence earn their livelihoods. Inevitably, then, middle-class parents are hypersensitive to any difficulties their children may have in learning to read and write; what is more, a knowledge of this fact brings a subtle but strong and effective pressure to bear on all teachers in primary schools within middle-class catchment areas.

(4) Turning finally to the ways in which parents attempt to control their children, the differences between the two major class groups are not simple. When the children in our sample were only a year old, there was a substantial group in all social classes, albeit a minority group (38 per cent overall), who felt that it was totally inappropriate to smack a baby of that age for any reason; and there was also a clear difference between the professional/managerial class, for whom this was a majority opinion, and the rest. By the time the child had reached four, the situation had changed somewhat: four is an age when, in all sorts of ways, the child comes into conflict with his mother, while at the same time he is still highly egocentric and not particularly amenable to his mother's reasoning. At this age, smacking is rather widely seen as appropriate, even if an unfortunate necessity, and there is no class difference in approval or disapproval of its use, although the top and bottom classes smack significantly less and more often respectively. By the age of seven, rather more parents see smacking as inappropriate, and smacking has in fact decreased over all classes; but class differences in frequency of smacking retain the same pattern.

There are also interesting divergences in the kinds of things for which smacking is thought to be a suitable punishment: for instance, at seven, middle-class parents are less likely to smack their children for untruthfulness and for rudeness; and in fact it is rather typical of these mothers that they do not like smacking for matters which they regard as serious. In our view, however, it is a mistake to place too much emphasis upon smacking as such. The discipline of the human child is accomplished primarily by means of language. Acts of physical punishment are not generally important in and of themselves; they act merely as punctuation marks in a continuing dialogue between the parent and the child. On their own admission, nearly all parents in our culture are at times driven to smacking their children; but smacks are almost invariably accompanied by a barrage of verbal pressure, and it is not without interest that in Nottingham it is this verbal 'telling-off', rather than the hitting, which goes by the name of 'chastisement'.

Is there, then, any essential difference between the social classes in their handling of discipline generally? We have shown elsewhere how the middle-class mother tries to use verbal reasoning methods in attempting to influence her child, and we have linked this preference for verbal control to her democratic intentions in her style of discipline. The ordering of family behaviour on a democratic system immediately involves a high degree of verbal interaction as disagreements are talked out and every voice is heard; whereas the authoritarian system preferred further down the scale has no need of more talk than a firm 'Do this!' Basically, the democratic ethic boils down to a *principle of reciprocity*, and this is the most important idea that middle-class parents try to teach their children: that they should have respect for the rights and wishes of other persons *as individuals*. In the end, this principle can only be taught by example, backed up by endless verbal persuasion and reiteration: "Don't do that to me, I wouldn't do it to you"; "I know you don't want to share your bike with Jane, but she's your visitor, and you'll be *her* visitor when you go to her house"; "Answer Mrs Brown when she speaks to you, you wouldn't like it if someone didn't answer you". Middle-class parents consciously want their children to realize how other people feel when they are at the receiving end of thoughtless behaviour; they expect their children to make an imaginative effort to put themselves in the place of others, and thereby to become sensitive to the impressions which they create. The whole process is a painfully slow one, dependent as it is upon the gradual growth of self-awareness and social empathy. It is a necessary part of this orientation towards an integrated rather than piecemeal socialization, that the child himself is valued as a person whose wishes and desires must be respected, and is accorded status in his own right.

With this in mind, it is worth looking at class differences in what we may call 'child-centredness'. From a number of different areas of interaction between the mother and the seven-year-old, it has been possible to draw certain indicators of a child-centred attitude, and to construct an index of child-centredness on this basis. Briefly, then responses were scored as positively child-centred, as follows: the child has a place to keep his own possessions, if only a cardboard box; his friends are allowed to play inside the house most weeks; his mother shows sympathy if he does not want to go to school (not necessarily to the extent of allowing his absence); she shows sympathy if, to escape school, he pretends he is not well; she takes complaints of school seriously, i.e. does not ignore them; she keeps or displays some of his drawings; she shares a special interest with the child; she does not punish but only rebukes or ignores rudeness to her; she is prepared to say 'sorry' sometimes when she has been cross with him; she lets him have some say in plans for holidays or outings. On this index, mothers who score 7+ out of a possible 10 are considered highly child-centred, while those who score 4 or less are rated as low on child-centredness. Class differences are in fact very marked: 51 per cent of middle-class, compared with 25 per cent of working-class mothers rate as highly child-centred on this criterion, while 15 per cent of middle-class mothers and 40 per cent of working-class mothers score low. It is possibly of interest that working-class mothers are significantly more inclined to child-centredness where girls are concerned, while middle-class mothers reverse this trend, though not to significance level. Clearly, the overall results show that the middle-class mother, in contrast to her working-class counterpart, accepts her stated principle of reciprocity as a practical way of life.

We have attempted here to outline and illustrate just a few of the characteristic differences in attitudes towards child rearing which sharply distinguish middle-class from working-class parents. We have argued in general terms that such divergences are to be expected because different social class groups have their own expectations and their own outlook on life, and these in turn lead them to attach importance to different qualities in the upbringing of their children. It is sometimes assumed that, as material living standards rise, people will instantaneously adopt specifically middle-class attitudes and ideas. Obviously working-class families want to share the good things which a modern technological society has to offer, and quickly acquire a taste for better clothes, more varied foodstuffs and consumer durables which were hitherto only available to a middle-class minority. It does not follow from this that we should expect a very rapid shift towards middle-class ideals and values generally.

DISCUSSION

Himmelweit: We have to be careful not to overestimate differences due to social background. I have made a study of the outlook, behaviour and aspirations of middle-and working-class adolescent boys in four grammar and five secondary modern schools in the Greater London area.[1] It showed there were hardly any social class differences among those attending the grammar school, and that those within the secondary modern school were small; but there were sharp differences in outlook, behaviour, and, of course, aspirations between those who went to grammar school and those who did not. It is easy to suggest that the grammar school would have exceptional children coming from atypical working-class homes, and there is some truth in this. They are, firstly, more intelligent and tend to come from smaller families; their relation to the family and the family's relation to them also seems to be warmer. But there is much more to this. After all, many of the working-class grammar school boys have brothers and sisters in secondary modern modern schools. We have re-interviewed 450 of these 614 boys at the age of 25 to learn about their subsequent educational and occupational history, present aspirations and social attitudes. The luck of having entered a grammar school, far more than their social background, determined their life chances. It must be remembered that not all who can profit from grammar school education do so; it depends on the proportion of such children in a given age group in the community relative to the number of grammar school places available.

I am urging, therefore, that social class differences be kept in perspective and other socializing experiences, produced by our educational institutions, be looked at with equal care.

I would add two further observations. When we look at our ex-grammar and ex-secondary modern boys at age 25, they differ remarkably little in outlook. Instead, differences arise due to a further socializing process within the work situation.

Secondly, a working-class parent of today knows the value of education and is very open to ideas about how to fit his child into the society of which he is a part. The difference in upbringing and outlook of present-day parents compared with those of twenty years ago in the working class, is far greater than that between middle-class and working-class parents today.

Over-emphasis on social class factors can obscure more significant relationships (e.g. the quality of parent-child interaction) and the need for reinforcing or compensatory factors provided by school and later by work. School is the responsibility of the community. It has such a powerful effect that we need to examine whether this is one of opening up opportunities, facilitating transitions and affording means for resocializing, or is instead a means of restricting opportunities.

Much social class research is done with a middle-class orientation; we may not be sufficiently alert in the McLuhan age to the new means that individuals use to become informed. Library footage may no longer be as important a criterion as the type of television programmes watched or the kinds of clubs to which the children go.

We have tended in these social class studies to forget that the child operates his own measuring instrument; he is in contact with the wider world. First he measures himself against his siblings, then in school. Today this country is the most school-conscious in the world and a child derives his rating of his own work from the school he attends and to a lesser extent his place inside the school. Where both are rewarding, he is likely to do well, provided the situation at home is not too counter-productive—it rarely is. Our experience has been that working-class children do as well as middle-class children in the same school and that this has to do with the rewards offered at school or through school and with the emotional climate of the home.

Tavuchis: Are working-class mothers less centred on boys than on girls, Dr Newson? That is not what your paper showed.

Newson: No, I would say we showed there are fewer working-class mothers who are child centred.

Tavuchis: Do these different attitudes in the working class with regard to boys and girls develop during childhood or is there a relatively constant difference?

Newson: In Nottingham it isn't true at age four, which is of course quite young, but it is there at seven years. My impression, now we are interviewing children aged eleven, is that there are very strong differences, but this is mixed up with a whole lot of things. One is the tendency to protect girls, particularly by keeping them at home and not letting them wander about.

Miller: Do you know anything about fathers?

Newson: Yes, through the interest the father takes in the child, but our information was obtained from what the mother says of the father, and we have to bear in mind that this may be coloured by their relationship. To some extent the father's participation seems to drop for working-class children, but this is complicated by the much bigger sex difference; fathers in general take more interest in boys than girls.

McLaren: Does the higher proportion of working-class girls than boys (30 versus 19 per cent) to receive 'child-centred behaviour', apply equally to child-centred behaviour from mothers and from fathers, or would the fathers give more attention to the boys than to the girls?

Newson: I have not looked at child-centred behaviour by fathers, because we hadn't enough questions, but I have looked at father participation. I deliberately excluded here the items where the father is involved.

McLaren: What was the distribution of family size and to what extent would the various points that you made also apply to different family sizes within each social class?

Newson: There is a difference between the middle-class and the working-class groups, but the big difference in size of families is in the tail end of the working class; this forms only a small percentage of the whole group.

Rogers: Do you know the part the extended family, other than the nuclear family, plays in the bringing up of these children? Do grandparents have any large role in their upbringing?

Newson: We haven't been very systematic about this. Relatives of the middle class may pay an occasional visit, whereas working-class families who live near each other often visit daily. We don't have the problem you referred to in the Bethnal Green studies, where the families have been moved so far apart they cannot commute.

Adams: In the light of what you say about differentiation with regard to personality, perhaps there would be greater respect in the middle-class group and less toleration in the working-class and lower groups for a variety of models for children to identify with. Do you see a variation there?

Newson We shall know more about this when we have analysed our data on eleven-year-olds.

Adams: I would expect a differentiation also with respect to extra-familial activities. These play an important role in the transmission of values. If, for example, the parents invest time in civic or community activities, the children may gain from the parents some sense of the responsibilities of citizenship. Here they see a model of freedom and responsibility—and also of differentiation of skills. I have heard here little reference to these aspects of differentiation; yet this kind of activity on the part of parents provides not only models of behaviour but also access to adults outside the family with whom the youth may identify. Here we see a social-psychological function somewhat analogous to that available in the extended family.

Newson: Middle-class children visit other families and more often stay away from home for pleasure. When the children go on trains they are put in charge of an adult, and I think the parents are deliberately letting the children have the experience of being controlled by other adults; on the other hand I think the middle-class child is more tightly restricted geographically than the lower-class groups.

Reynolds: In studies of the behavioural development of monkeys in the wild a process of peripheralization—of moving away from the parent —has been observed among young males to a greater extent than among females.[2] If middle-class parents are more protective than working-class parents, could it just be that middle-class parents interfere more with their sons' efforts to peripheralize, while working-class boys get away from their parents more because their parents are less protective?

Newson: I would agree that they are getting away more but I wouldn't say it is necessarily on a biological basis. I think the middle-class parents provide an environment in which they hope their child is safe. If a child is out somewhere in a city centre on his own he really has to fend for himself, but in a middle-class residential suburb people take responsibility for other children. It is more a geographical than a biological difference.

Henriques: Don't we have to define classes more closely? What is called middle class in the north of England would be regarded in London as working class and in fact working-class behaviour is altogether more characteristic of the north of England. We must be very careful about our context. The same applies to schools. I know a secondary modern school in the north of England where all the teacher does is stop them burning the place down, whereas in a secondary modern school elsewhere all is sweetness and light.

Newson: I think we need to simplify this instead of spelling out social classes. What we are looking for is the place where you get a major change in the proportion of parents who behave in a particular way; and on the whole this either comes between the professional-managerial group and the rest, or it comes between the professional-managerial group including the white-collar workers, and the rest.

Henriques: Yes, but the kind of people who have migrated from elsewhere into this category of the professional-managerial are not quite the same in terms of their behaviour as the people who originally belonged to the same group in the same area. Although they may occupy the same suburb, their behaviour and their attitude towards their children would be very different.

Newson: I think it is valid to talk of a middle-class way of bringing up children in this country, excluding immigrants.

Raveau: Earlier you said that the lower classes seem to have only the vestigial values of the higher classes. Did I understand you properly? It seemed that you were not allowing the working classes to have their own subculture and creativity, the so called 'culture of poverty'.

Newson: No; I said that vestigial traces of a much older, more primitive way of bringing up children are to be found at the bottom end of the social scale. I would agree with Dr Himmelweit that the influence of the educational system is paramount. I never know whether the permissive or child-centred attitude reached the school system via the middle class, or whether it originated in the school system and has spread from there. The general idea that you have to take the child as an individual in his own right and to approach learning from this standpoint is a very potent and a very new one, particularly if you look at the way education is conducted in many underdeveloped countries.

Sjövall: I agree about the great influence of the school. This is something that we are grappling with in Sweden in terms of building up sex education in schools. The teaching of mere facts is no problem, but when a child starts school at age seven, as in Sweden, his personality is already laid down to such an extent that it is highly questionable how far it could be changed by the influence of school.

Himmelweit: We need to be careful about our generalizations. We have no evidence that by the age of seven years the personality is formed. Why should there be such a limit to personality development? Often, of course, after the age of seven the school and neighbourhood hinder rather than help an already disturbed child. I would feel more positive about the decisive role of early childhood if it had been found that it makes little difference after that age to provide the child with a different and a better environment.

In school the child first of all has to deal with what is for him a quite new relationship: that with the teacher—a relationship continually censuring or praising. Secondly, he has to relate to the other children, and only thirdly to the actual learning situation. Once he is of school age, he spends on average far more time in school that he does in his family. But we as psychologists have paid little attention to school, although we know from child-guidance experience that a good school can tip the scales and a bad school can disturb, and that recovery is as hard from a bad school as it is from a defective home environment. I feel equally strongly that we should not generalize about middle class and working class but rather look at other dimensions and consider the family in the context of time and place. After all, English families differ from German or Swedish families in some of the values they consider important and the way in which they communicate with one another. Yet the adults, as far as adjustment or achievement are concerned, do not differ correspondingly.

11: Changing Trends in Child Development

ETTORE ROSSI AND NORBERT HERSCHKOWITZ

DURING the twentieth century both the infant mortality rate and the physical, sexual and mental development of infants and children have undergone significant changes.

INFANT MORTALITY

The statistics show that in New York City deaths of newborn babies fell from 140 per thousand births to less than 60 per thousand between 1900 and 1930 (Fig. 1). This decrease was due mainly to the decrease in infectious diseases affecting the digestive and respiratory systems.[4] However, mortality due to causes operating at the time of birth, including prematurity and congenital malformations, remained fairly constant during this period.

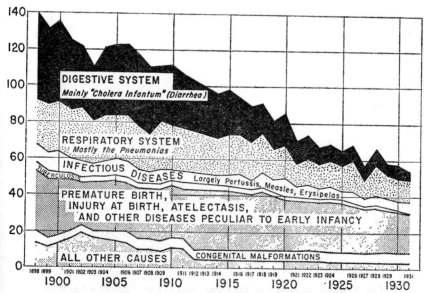

FIG. 1. Infant mortality in New York City between 1900 and 1930, in terms of the most significant causes.[4] Rates per thousand births. (By courtesy of *Pediatrics*.)

TABLE I

PROPORTIONAL INFANT MORTALITY

	1900 New York	1930 New York	1960 Singapore	1960 Sweden
Infections	64	40	41	7
Malformations	7	20	11	21
Prematurity, neonatal	29	40	48	72
	100	100	100	100

The three main causes of infant deaths (death under one year of age) are infections, congenital malformations and diseases peculiar to the neonatal phase (the first seven days of life) such as pulmonary disorders, and prematurity. By 1960 (Fig. 2) infectious diseases had ceased to be the most important of these and most deaths in children under one year of age occurred in the first seven days, as a result of diseases typical of this stage. Table I shows the changing percentages of deaths due to these three causes.

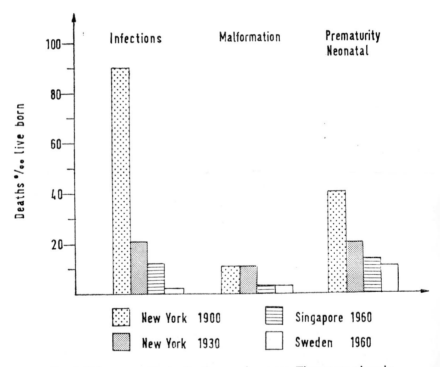

FIG. 2. Infant mortality by the three main causes. Figures are given in number of deaths per thousand live-born. (Adapted from *Epidemiological and Vital Statistics Report*, World Health Organization, 1964.)

In the future we can expect a further drop in infant mortality as a result of advances in medical knowledge about life before birth, birth itself and the neonatal period.

In the *prenatal* phase, more consideration will be given to the environment the mother is living in. The metabolic and immunological interplay between mother and embryo will be better understood, and inborn, or genetically determined, errors of metabolism will be detected early and corrected. The placenta and its many metabolic and immunological functions will be monitored during pregnancy and failures will be detected and corrected. The rate of birth injury will fall as a result of special care for 'high risk' mothers and the constant surveillance of the metabolism of the child during birth. In the *neonatal phase*, the difficult period of adaptation to extrauterine life will be eased by the possibilities of controlling and regulating circulation, respiration and metabolism in the newborn child. These efforts of perinatal medicine will have to be extended by large-scale studies continuing far into *postnatal* life in order to investigate their impact on the development of the child.

ACCELERATION OF CHILD DEVELOPMENT

Systematic recording of the body measurements and the age of onset of menstruation (the menarche) during the last hundred years has shown that both these parameters of child development have undergone a so-called acceleration (Table II).

TABLE II

ACCELERATION: SUMMARY OF THE BIOLOGICAL FEATURES

1. Weight of newborn ↑
2. Height of newborn ↑
3. Maximum weight ↑
4. Maximum height ↑
5. Growth rate ↑
6. Maximum height reached: younger age
7. Sexual maturity reached: younger age

The weight of the newborn has increased steadily in recent decades in both girls and boys. Between 1933 and 1963 the gain in weight in babies born in the province of Sassari (Italy), for example, was about 300 grammes, or 10 per cent of body-weight.[1]

The average height reached by 19-year-old boys entering military service in Sassari was 162 centimeters in 1911, and 165 cm in 1945.[8] The heights reached at different ages by Swedish boys in 1883 and in 1938 (Fig. 3) indicate that the same height was being reached 2½ years earlier in 1938.[7] The growth rate (height gain in cm per year) was faster by 1–2 cm in 1938 than in 1883, and whereas the peak of the growth rate occurred at the age of 15 in 1883, in 1938 it occurred at 13 years, nine months (Fig. 4).[7] The onset of puberty in boys at these peak years was responsible for the decline in growth rate in the following years.

The general increase in the growth rate in height between 1910 and 1950 did not continue during World War I and World War II in boys from Stuttgart, Germany, and in fact tended to decrease (Fig. 5).[7] Since the

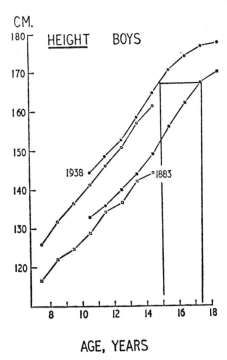

AGE, YEARS

FIG. 3. Acceleration of growth in height in Swedish boys between 1883 and 1938.[7] (By courtesy of Blackwell Scientific Publications, Oxford.)
●, ■: boys from secondary schools, aged 10–18.
○, □: boys from elementary schools, aged 7–14.

mechanisms which cause the acceleration of the rate of growth are not really clear, we are unable to explain the absence of acceleration during the two world wars; however, it is safe to assume that undernutrition may have played a role.

Parallel to the observed acceleration in growth rate, an earlier occurrence of the menarche in girls has been observed, indicating an earlier onset of puberty.[2] Between 1841 and 1949 the average age of menarche dropped from 14 to 13 years of age (Fig. 6). According to other authors[7] and to studies in the USA, Norway, Sweden and Finland, menarche occurs four to six months earlier in each decade. The acceleration in the

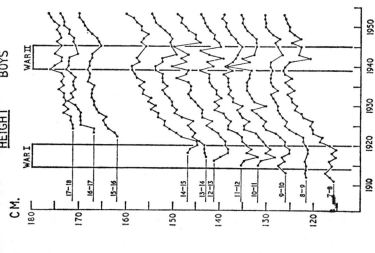

FIG. 5. Absence of acceleration of growth in height of German boys (Volkschule; ages 7–8 to 14–15) during World War I and World War II.[7] (By courtesy of Blackwell Scientific Publications, Oxford.)

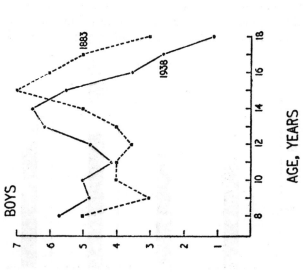

FIG. 4. Growth rate (height gain in cm per year)[7] in Swedish boys. (From Tanner, 1961, by courtesy of Blackwell Scientific Publications, Oxford.)

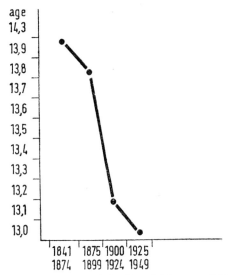

FIG. 6. Age of onset of menarche in Italian girls between 1842 and 1949.[2]

rate of sexual maturation is of special interest since it is known that the onset of menarche is determined mainly by genetic factors[6]: the average difference in age at menarche between identical twins is only 2·9 months, compared to 12·0 months for non-identical twins, 12·9 months for sisters and 18·6 months for unrelated women. However, many factors affect the way in which an individual's genetic endowment is expressed in the course of development: these range from nutrition and exposure to infection, to such things as the standards of hygiene and medicine in the

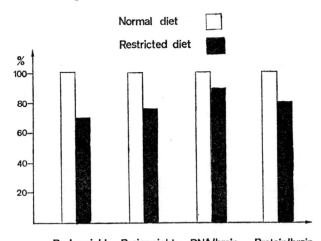

FIG. 7. Weight and DNA content of organs from foetuses of rats underfed during pregnancy.[10]

society in which that person lives. I shall discuss one of these factors, nutrition, in more detail, since its influence on development has been studied in some detail, in both animals and man.

INFLUENCE OF NUTRITION AND DEVELOPMENT

If pregnant rats are underfed their offspring have lower body weights and brain weights than normal, and the amounts of DNA (the genetic material) and protein in their brains (Fig. 7) are reduced.[10] Malnutrition in rats during growth also influences the activity of many enzymes. One enzyme of special interest is sulphotransferase, because it is responsible for the last step in the synthesis of sulphatide, a fatty substance present in the myelin which makes up the sheaths surrounding nerve fibres.[3] The presence of adequate amounts of myelin is essential for the functioning of nerve fibres. The activity of this enzyme varies with age (Fig. 8). No activity is detectable in rats immediately after birth, but it is normally measurable at the eighth day and reaches a peak at about the seventeenth day. Myelin can be detected under the microscope at the same time as the

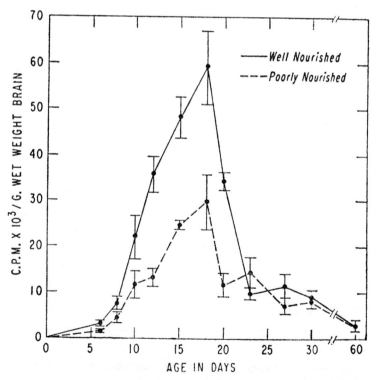

FIG. 8. Activity of sulphotransferase in the brains of well fed and poorly fed rats.[3] The bars represent the range of values. (By courtesy of *Pediatrics*.)

onset of enzyme activity. In underfed rats enzyme activity still increases with age but the level of activity reached is significantly lower. If undernourished newborn rats are given normal amounts of food from before the eighth day of postnatal life, the peak of enzyme activity will be seen at the normal time, but if undernutrition continues after this point, enzyme activity never becomes normal. Undernourished animals also have decreased amounts of other fatty substances (lipids) which make up myelin, again suggesting that undernutrition decreases the myelination of nerve fibres and that if this malnutrition goes on beyond a critical period, no further recovery is possible.

The influence of nutrition on development is more difficult to study in man, because of the enormous complexity of the factors affecting development and the impossibility of separating them. Some milestones in normal human brain development are, however, known.[5] From conception until the seventh month of gestation, the brain cells divide rapidly and the number of cells almost reaches that found in the adult (Fig. 9). From the seventh month until birth, the brain cells increase in size and fine processes (the axons and dendrites) grow out rapidly from the cells

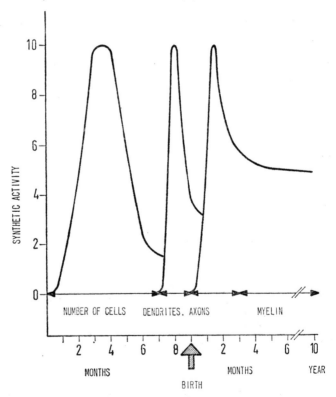

FIG. 9. Schematic representation of brain development in man.[5]

to form the nerve fibres. From birth until the third postnatal month the fibres are rapidly covered with myelin; a slow period of further myelination follows which ends between five and ten years of age.

The time at which the developing individual is undernourished determines which system of the body will be most affected, since the effects are greatest on systems which are rapidly developing. Undernutrition before birth will interfere mainly with the development of the dendrites and axons of the nerve cells; undernutrition after birth, however, will affect myelination of the nerve fibres. Undernutrition before birth and during the first two years of life can decrease the total number of brain cells in man and therefore the head circumference, which is easily measurable[9] (Fig. 10). It can also decrease the weight of the brain and its content of lipids.

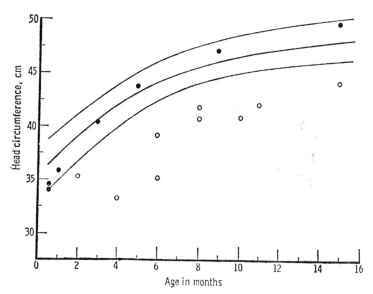

FIG. 10. Changes in head circumference with postnatal age in normal infants (●) and marasmic (underfed) infants (○).[9] (From Winick and Rosso, 1969, by courtesy of *Journal of Pediatrics*.)

There are indications that even if nutrition becomes normal after the second year of life, the abnormal brain development cannot be completely corrected and the observed retardation is irreversible. Impaired brain development will lead to disturbances in mental functioning. It is, however, very difficult and almost impossible to separate the genetic and other factors which may contribute to subnormal intelligence.

In this area the future will certainly bring great changes. Bioengineering will correct defects in the genetic code directly. Molecular biology will learn more about the regulation of genetic expression and metabolism, and this knowledge will be applied to the treatment of as yet untreatable disorders. The intensive work now going on in cell biology will bring knowledge about complex mechanisms of integration. Neurobiology will allow insight into the processing of information in the brain and will thereby improve our knowledge of the mechanisms of learning.

DISCUSSION

Fox: Could you say a little more about the exact function of myelin and the effects of a restriction in its production at this early stage?

Rossi: Undernourishment in the pregnant mother affects DNA (deoxyribonucleic acid) production in the embryo and will lead to a first stage of mental retardation in the child. If malnutrition continues after birth, it influences myelin formation and that will lead to changes in physiological and neurological functions and possible mental retardation.

Pirie: We all have a tendency to assume that bigger means better. I read somewhere that Anatole France had an unusually small brain. Are there any trustworthy figures showing that the brains of intelligent adults differ from the average size?

Rossi: As in so many biological problems, objective criteria are missing. The estimation of the IQ is an example. Poorly nourished children have smaller head-sizes, due to a smaller brain. Another question is whether bigger children are more resistant to infection. Our present impression is that they are not more resistant to infection, but this new point of view requires a follow-up study over many years, with statistical evaluation.

Pirie: My question was specifically about the final performance of an adult. I see the difficulty in measuring or interpreting IQ's for children, but would adults who have achieved something—measured for example by Francis Galton's crude standard,[2] which was roughly equivalent to getting into *Who's Who*—on average have bigger brains?

Comfort: Surely there is a difference between a brain which is inherently large and has been well fed and a brain that might have been large and which has been partially demyelinated. Dr Rossi, do you know of any evidence that a brain which has a low myelin content correlates with a low IQ?

Rossi: In animal studies, those with brains containing less myelin than the control animals have lower scores in learning experiments.

Comfort: It has been argued that early menarche is a reversion to the normal human rhythm rather than an acceleration in our own age. It represents only the age of menarche in Roman and Jewish law. Then there is the question of psychological maturation. We are judging this by quite a number of different standards; obviously you may acquire less experience in a period of 15 years than in a period of 18, but the period of attaining the adult IQ is going to be influenced very much by the age at which the acceleration of growth reaches a peak, isn't it?

Rossi: That is true, but it is very difficult to give an answer about psychological maturation because we have not sufficient material to make an objective judgement.

Abercrombie: Some quite old evidence shows a correlation between height and IQ.[7] If brain size is correlated with height, IQ would be correlated with brain size. There is a tremendous amount of evidence that malnutrition is a bad thing from every point of view.

Comfort: Except longevity!

Abercrombie: Yes, but we are not clear about whether overnutrition is a good thing either, and in particular whether the rapid onset of sexual maturity is a good thing from the point of view of social and intellectual development. Presumably in Freudian terms the development of many human attributes is correlated with the delay of satisfaction of biological urges. Desmond Morris's apes that painted salesworthy pictures stopped being interested in painting when they became sexually mature.[4]

Comfort: I think that in cases of constitutional precocious puberty with full sexual maturity at the age of about six years, only the psychological and the dental development keep to their original rhythm. You don't get an abolition of the Freudian latency period as you might have expected, at any rate not in girls.

Rossi: The trouble in precocious sexual maturity is that big children are always considered older because of their height, and not according to their psychological evolution, which is the true age.

Miller: Any statement about what happens psychologically to either very early developers or very later developers is suspect, because their peer group relationships and the adult expectations are so hopelessly fouled up that the child is under stress all the time. The problem of the IQ is also very difficult because we really do not know how to measure IQ reliably at all. One can see a change of 30 points in the same individual with repeated IQ testing, especially when there are emotional difficulties.

Rossi: This is why I have talked of height and weight and left open the question of psychological maturity. H. J. Mark has a new system[3] which I think is much more objective but more complicated; I hope it may be more reliable.

Miller: There is also a problem in terms of cross-cultural measurement. Some West Indian medical students in England who were doing extraordinarily well in their medical course turned out when tested to have IQ's of about 80.

Reynolds: It is confusing to use the same word 'maturity' for the measurement of physical and psychic phenomena. Psychological maturity is largely dependent on the attitudes of the older generation, whereas this is not an issue in the case of physical maturity. The 13-year-old girl who reaches menarche nowadays has achieved a certain physiological maturity; she hasn't achieved psychological maturity, largely because of parental and other adult attitudes.

Fletcher: I think Darwin in *The Descent of Man* speaks of the maturation of the human individual as being not much different from that of some anthropoid apes.[1] Could you say more about earlier onset of menstruation? Your date of 1841 obviously places most samples in Western European countries within the industrial period, but was the sample drawn from rural or industrial communities?

Rossi: This is a mixed population. Tanner[6] has done a broad study in different groups: rural, as against cities, and different races. The results were similar.

Comfort: Peak retardation seems to have been reached in about 1801.

Raveau: We have done about 1500 IQ tests on the black African immigrant population in France and about the same number of personality tests. The results have been correlated with clinical examinations. A good state of health (in infancy and at the time of the check-up) is highly correlated with good IQ and good standards in the personality tests. Another interesting fact is that among the group of 1500, we had about 200 young women and the higher the IQ, the earlier was the age of menarche. But there was a possible cultural variable—the group with the higher IQ came originally from urban centres.

Fox: That correlation is true in Western European society, too.

Hendrickse: The whole question of growth and maturation, particularly in relation to malnutrition is receiving much international attention. As experimental evidence comes to light one finds more and more support for clinical judgements. One very important point that Dr Rossi mentioned is that not just malnutrition, but the timing of malnutrition in relation to certain physiological events, is significant. Quite obviously the earlier the pernicious influence, the more devastating the effect is likely to be. Over the last nine years a parallel study has been going on in two groups of children in Ibadan, each sample being about 250 children. One is from a particularly privileged ethnic group and the other from a poor market community. The nutritional and medical histories of the two groups are known from one month of age onwards. The problem has arisen of how to assess intellectual development in these comparable groups. About 18 months ago a simple screening device was used, not based on any conventional intelligence testing, but a simple learning device whereby pressing the right buttons for the right colours brought rewards. The results showed statistically highly significant differences in learning ability between the two groups, with the less well nourished, low-weight group doing much worse than their counterparts who share the same natural total environment but have different home environments. The method of testing did not, as far as we could determine, involve factors in which one group had an advantage because of familiarity with the procedure employed. Stock and Smythe in Cape Town showed some time ago a very distinct correlation between early infantile malnutrition, head circumference and intelligence testing.[5] The evidence is accumulating that pernicious nutritional factors, especially early in life, do tend to limit subsequent human intellectual development and attainment.

An interesting change is happening in the wake of civilization in certain West African countries, where breast feeding for two years used to be traditional. Modern advertising is influencing the behaviour of women who become educated and many women are starting their babies on bottle-feeding earlier and earlier. A direct consequence of this, especially among semi-literates in peri-urban communities, is that we are seeing a very early onset of a different type of malnutrition from that which used to be prevalent. We are now seeing severe marasmus in children at a very early age. In terms of what is known about development of the brain, I think this earlier onset of malnutrition might have considerably more deleterious effects in the long run than the older and more florid forms of kwashiorkor.

I would like to hear some sociological comment on this question of early maturation of children in terms of height, weight attainment, onset of menarche and so on, in our society in which the general pattern of social development is such that the young and growing person is shifted further and further away from the day he can assume responsibility in the community. One wonders what additional conflicts we are engendering in the minds of young people who appear to be achieving maturity at an earlier age while at the same time social pressures are increasingly holding them back from becoming full contributing adults in society.

Fox: That is an important point. We are discussing the future of the family, and we have this situation, particularly in middle-class families, that education is keeping young people dependent for longer and longer periods, while they are maturing earlier and earlier. This might indeed be another of those frustrations that is leading to difficulties.

Newson: I question the notion that young people don't have anything responsible to do. Middle-class young people have the responsibility of getting themselves educated. It is as much a job as anything else these days and what perhaps is wrong is that they are valuing this as something less important.

Tavuchis: A very strong argument could be made that there is a conspiracy to over-educate or temporarily to keep children in school longer than is necessary so that they can acquire the social skills needed for survival in this society. For most occupations in an industrial society a bachelor's degree is not necessary. I suspect that most job requirements are artificially inflated and that we are keeping children in school in very artificial, sometimes sex-segregated, age-segregated hot-houses.

Miller: We have to think about what people are educated for. It is a narrow concept to educate them only for a specific task. Technological societies are certainly going to have a major leisure problem in 25 years' time, if not before. We already seem to be dealing with this by the use of television, which invites people to be passive. The problem is to find ways to educate people for present-day society and the society of the future. The length of time spent in school will increase, and the problem is what should be taught.

Abercrombie: I am very interested in this problem of educating for what, and connecting this with the difficulties that students have in paying attention to their university work, in relation to the general problem of disparate rates of maturing physically, mentally, psychologically and sociologically. It is sometimes thought that students of medicine or architecture, for instance, don't have anything like the problems of those in the humanities, since they know what they are being trained for, but this is by no means the case. We ought to look very hard at the whole problem of full-time education continuing directly from school.

Stone: I think nobody in this room is going to have a leisure problem. Have studies been done on where the great divide occurs between those who are being given more and more leisure and no way to fill it, and those who are having even more to do and even less time in which to do it?

Miller: There is a great deal of evidence in industry that people artificially produce overtime. This is not just an economic problem; most of the work could be done in half the time, but at the moment people are solving the leisure problem by not doing their work as fast as technological advance makes possible.

Comfort: I have been hoping that somebody would mention the fact that we are also, of course, living longer. A very large proportion of people now will reach old age; a very high proportion of people in the family will have a long post-reproductive life, and we have the probability that by the year 2000 we will add about 20 per cent to the period of adult vigour by actual moving of the age of senescence; that is, by delaying the mechanism of the deteriorative clock (see Fig. 1). We have reached the stage of a low infant mortality, and a long period of adult vigour preceding the decline of the survival curve; few people are dead before the age of 70 but nearly all are dead by 100. If our research is successful, we shall also move the curve bodily to the right, in other words, we shall prolong the period of adult vigour. There are of course many complications, such as longer retirement, slower turnover of generations, and exacerbations of our tendency now to have a second identity crisis at 40.

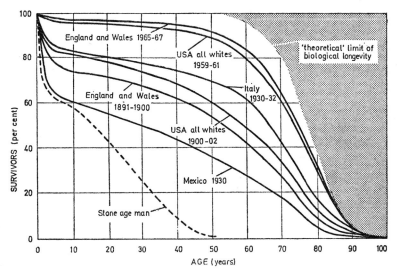

FIG.1 (Comfort). Human survival curves; historical change.

12: The Making of the Modern Family

RONALD FLETCHER

I WANT to argue, in this final paper, that a correct appraisal of the family in modern society can only be achieved by seeing it within a very large perspective—and one which flatly contradicts much that has been said or assumed in the conference so far—though it is in agreement with some ideas put forward earlier[1, 14, 31] to the effect that one of the greatest needs of our time is for a clearly stated reasonable morality.

Earlier Robin Fox adopted a comparative and evolutionary perspective.[9] I want to close the symposium with the same perspective: but with a different emphasis.

We can agree with the evolutionary picture Fox drew of an enormously long period during which human groups were simple hunting and food-gathering communities, followed by the rapid development of complex 'civilization' within the last few seconds (so to speak) of time, and that not too much need be made of the question of how far the 'nuclear' family has been universal among all societies throughout this long period.

He suggested, however, that the modern 'nuclear' family was a 'convenient, compromise arrangement' between the extreme possibilities of the mother–child tie on the one hand, and the total groups of adult males and mothers and dependent children on the other. I want to insist that it is much more than that: that it is a definite social form related not only to the conditions, but also to the moral and political aims of modern industrial societies. It is a social form deliberately created, *not* in the sense that men have sat round a table and constructed the family as a unit in and for itself; but in the sense that it is one unit—appropriate and integral within the whole—in their *entire making of a new society*. Everything that Dr Stone[33] had to say about law reform and the shaping of the family, and the fact that the law and the social services had found no alternative to the family, is of vital importance here. Furthermore, I want to insist that the family—so created—is an excellent social form. We ought to uphold it; to be passionate in its defence as something hardly won from an earlier situation which was in many ways deplorable. Rather than assuming it to be in decline—deficient in many supportive qualities it once possessed—we should be educating people towards its effective fulfilment.[7]

Our greatest need at present is for a *correct perspective of judgement*. Social change is so rapid and complex as to seem a chaos, and it is easy to regard all the ills, fears, dangers, extremities we experience as deteriorations. There are great problems here. No sooner are institutions re-shaped by one generation than they are 'lived in' by the next, who cannot possibly realize the earlier situation out of which they grew. We face real problems here: of communication, of education, and—at the deepest level—of social control. A perspective for judgement is therefore certainly needed: within which action, administration and education can be reliably exercised. The more I study the major sociologists, however, and the more I study history—something which, as social scientists, we still tend to neglect far too much—the more I think that a clear perspective has, in fact, been provided.

THE CRITICAL RECONSTRUCTION OF SOCIETY

The perspective is this: that since about the time of the American and French Revolutions (i.e. a very short time ago) a vast, rapid, and radical transformation of human society has been set afoot, which began in Europe, and is now sweeping over the entire world. The transition is from a condition of relatively simple *Traditional Agrarian Societies* to one of highly complex *Rational Industrial Societies.* Enormous, profound, and subtle differences at every level of human experience—in mythology, religion, art, literature, morality, etc.—are attendant upon this transformation. Within the first condition of society, the over-all 'ethos' was one of 'Man in Nature'—with imponderables larger than man, and going far beyond him, held responsible for his destiny. Within the second condition, the over-all 'ethos' is that of man himself dominating and exploiting his natural resources by knowledge and control. Though revolutionary, this transformation is not so in the sense of historical discontinuity. On the contrary, it is a culmination of man's powers of transformation. Man has always been distinguishable from other species in that he was not bound, like them, to a process of adaptation to his environment, but possessed qualities of mind enabling him to transform his environment. The distinguishing feature of the modern situation is that this power of transformation has assumed an extensiveness and degree amounting to a difference of kind.

At the heart of the transformation is the accumulation of knowledge culminating in critical science, its greater accuracy of prediction, its provision of greater control over nature and society by a mechanized technology, and all the largenesses of scale—in economic productivity, population size, spread and density of urban settlement, etc.—which all this has brought about.

With all these dimensions of transition, the *Ancien Régime*—the traditional order of institutions—collapsed. A new society had to be made. A reconstitution of human institutions in their totality had to be attempted. The same critical condition—of feared collapse and struggle for a reconstituted order of social institutions—occurs, is occurring, and will occur, wherever critical science and industrialization make their impact upon traditional communities.

The actual political situation is that man has had to take upon himself the responsibility for remaking his own society, and, in so doing, for making his own destiny. This transformation is one of the greatest watersheds in human history: the most all-encompassing in that it draws together, for the very first time, literally *all* human societies in the world. And we are now in the midst of it, grappling with its dilemmas. It is therefore of the most fundamental importance for all our judgements, theories, and actions, that we should recognize our position as such.

Within this period, we know that a literature of moral and political philosophy has grown up, and, intimately related to it, a conceptual construction of the social sciences. The significant thing is that all this thought, 'normative' and 'positive' alike, has itself been an engagement in this task of re-making the institutions of society.[7] *The making of the social sciences has been for the re-making of society.*

This is the perspective of social actuality, including social thought and social science, within which, alone, we can properly assess and judge any specific institutional change, and, with the aid of the schema in Fig. 1, I would like to emphasize certain points about it. All the theorists represented here were completely agreed about three basic points.

(1) Rationality and Responsibility

They were agreed, first of all, about their picture of social evolution; about the perspective we have in mind. A relatively long period of 'genetic' development—in which the many traditional orders of societies had taken shape in terms of 'unintended consequences'—had been followed by a condition of increasing rationality and purposive control. Increasing knowledge, increasing control, the necessity of re-assessing and re-making institutions meant that modern society was marked by increasing rationality and responsibility. It is important to see that this rationality applied both to the investigation of facts and to the critical clarification of values, and that it was an outcome of the insufficiency of traditional institutions. A rational critique of institutions, and responsible social action in re-making them, was forced upon men by the dilemmas of social disorder.

(2) Promise and threat: improvement and malaise

Secondly, all were agreed that this new condition of rationality and responsibility carried with it both promise *and* threat. Man's new degrees of knowledge and control, and his deliberate social reconstruction, could bring great improvements but also great disaster. Responsibility was inescapable; but it by no means guaranteed success. Also increasing

FIG. 1. Agreement about the distinguishing features of Traditional Agrarian Societies and Contractual Commercial and Industrial Societies and the modern transition from one to the other.[8]

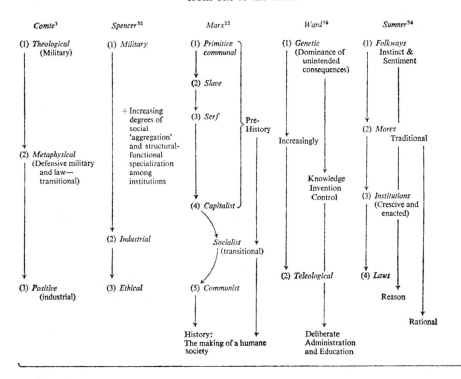

All agreed upon:

(1) The 'net' pattern of social evolution resulting in the contemporary human situation.
(2) The central significance of the transition from a predominantly 'traditional' to a predominantly 'contractual and rational' social order.
(3) The rapid and radical nature of this modern transformation: its promise and threat.

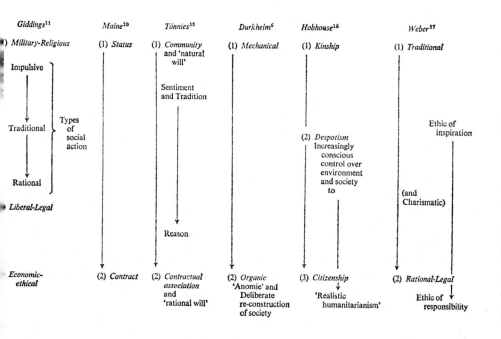

Giddings[11]		Maine[20]	Tönnies[35]	Durkheim[6]	Hobhouse[16]	Weber[37]
(1) Military-Religious		(1) Status	(1) Community and 'natural will'	(1) Mechanical	(1) Kinship	(1) Traditional
Impulsive			Sentiment and Tradition			
Traditional	Types of social action				(2) Despotism Increasingly conscious control over environment and society to	Ethic of inspiration
Rational						
Liberal-Legal			Reason			(and Charismatic)
Economic-ethical		(2) Contract	(2) Contractual association and 'rational will'	(2) Organic 'Anomie' and Deliberate re-construction of society	(3) Citizenship ↓ 'Realistic humanitarianism'	(2) Rational-Legal Ethic of responsibility

(4) The necessity for a deliberate reconstitution of institutions (social reconstruction); the increasing dominance of rational, ethical purpose in the changing nature of institutions.

(5) Human responsibility for the making of society. The necessity for scientific knowledge of man and society and an 'ethics of responsibility'.

rationality and the calculated, contractual basis of an increasing number
of human relationships, led not only to possible improvements but also
to various dimensions of malaise. Two sources of this were clearly distinguished.

One, most clearly analysed by Tönnies,[35] was the spread and dominance of a rationally calculated *contractual* basis for human relationships.
This was primarily the basis of commercial commitments, but its
character spread into all fields of human relationships. It had three
deficiencies. (1) It lacked all those deeper dimensions of 'belonging'
which enriched and sustained the associations of people in simpler
communities. (2) It was limited solely to the terms of the contract; had
no commitment beyond this; and was, at best, a convention insisting
that contracts should be kept, but, at worst, a smooth appearance of
mutual interest veiling a realistic expectation of sharp practice. Under
its conventional politeness—it was ruthless. And (3) it brought the
danger of contractual manipulation. It was, in short, the 'bourgeois'
ethic against which so many fought. Calculated interest was put before
a full humanity. Association resting on contractual definitions replaced
the relationships of whole persons in community.

One corollary of this was that science—itself an analytical, specializ-
ing, supposedly 'value-free' activity—could be utilized in the service of
effective human manipulation. Why not? If science was a matter of 'truth'
independent of other human values, why should it not be used to pursue
self-interest? In short, science itself, which some had hailed as a
liberator of mankind, could become one more servant of de-humaniza-
tion. A moving realization of this is to be found in the *Private Papers of
Henry Ryecroft* by George Gissing.[12] In 1903 he wrote:

"I hate and fear 'science' because of my conviction that, for long to come if not for
ever, it will be the remorseless enemy of mankind. I see it destroying all simplicity
and gentleness of life, all the beauty of the world; I see it restoring barbarism under
a mask of civilization; I see it darkening men's minds and hardening their hearts;
I see it bringing a time of vast conflicts, which will pale into insignificance the thousand wars of old, and, as likely as not, will whelm all the laborious advances of
mankind in blood-drenched chaos.

". . . Oh, the generous hopes and aspirations of forty years ago! Science, then,
was seen as the deliverer; only a few could prophesy its tyranny, could foresee
that it would revive old evils and trample on the promises of its beginning."

A sombre and telling warning indeed!

The second source of malaise was simply that attendant upon rational
choice and responsibility itself. To take traditional values, beliefs and
social procedures for granted on the basis of their unquestioned
authority was easy. To be *responsible* as a personal citizen for knowing,
evaluating, choosing and acting was far from easy. It necessarily entailed
alertness and anxiety. But the anxiety attendant upon responsibility was
held to be good. Max Weber,[37] recognizing modern man's dilemmas,

urged the correctness of an ethics of responsibility, and not an ethics of inspiration, which could no longer be enough.

(3) Moral commitment

The third agreement among all these theorists was their moral commitment to the making of the social sciences for the making of society. This is worth emphasis, because it is sometimes thought that whereas some theorists got their ethics and social science mixed up, and (like Marx[22] or Hobhouse[16]) were quite forthright in advocating political reform in terms of revolutionary change or 'realistic humanitarianism', others (like Durkheim[6] and Weber[37]) were more 'scientifically' correct in studying social facts and social action without moral evaluation. Durkheim's whole plea, however, was for the reconstitution of the economic order of society on the basis of a new ethic, which could no longer be worked out in the philosopher's armchair, but only by the social scientist in the thick of empirical investigations.[6] Weber too, insisting upon the most stringent impartiality of scientific accuracy in the statement and testing of theories, nonetheless argued that sociologists were bound to select their problems in terms of their own evaluations as to what was of cultural significance. In the modern world—in science and political action alike—an ethic of responsibility alone was defensible.[37c]

BASIC UNDERLYING ASSUMPTIONS
Institutions essentially values; institutional change—moral change; social reconstruction in the light of ethical standards

Some of the assumptions underlying these agreements were even more striking in revealing agreed conceptions about the fundamental nature of society. Figure 2 helps to summarize these points.

(i) Man distinctively a moral being

The first basic assumption of the theorists was that man was crucially distinguishable from other animal species by his purposive, moral nature. Men acted deliberately and purposefully in the pursuit of their practical aims. The establishment of values was seen to be the core of both the process of institutionalization and the ordering of the experience and behaviour of the individual. This took the sociopsychological form of 'sentiments'. The 'sentiments' established in society were the values which formed the basis of the social order. They were the constellations of cognition, feeling, evaluation and guidance for action to which people were attached both within themselves and in their social behaviour. Society was essentially a moral matter. *Morals*, in the form of sentiments and sanctions, lay at the heart of social institutions.

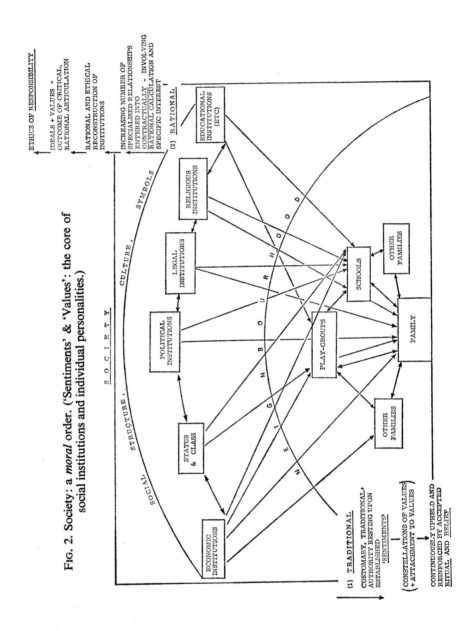

Fig. 2. Society: a *moral* order. ('Sentiments' & 'Values': the core of social institutions and individual personalities.)

Examples of agreement among theorists[8]

Theorists	Contribution		Agreement
Tönnies[35] Westermarck[39] Hobhouse[16]	Large-scale theories of social change, evolution, development.	Major contributions in the making of sociology from (about) 1900 to 1945—from turn of century to Second World War	*All firmly agreed about:*
McDougall[19] Cooley[4,5] Mead[23] Freud[10] Pareto[26]	Theories on the psychological aspects of society. The relations between 'self' and 'society'.		(1) Central importance of *sentiments* in the process of *institutionalization* and *personality and character formation.*
Durkheim[6]	The 'objective' study of social facts.		(2) Basic importance of primary groups, and primary group communications for the formation of 'sentiments' and the 'self'.
Weber[39]	The 'subjective' understanding of social action.		(3) The difficulties and malaise attendant upon the specialized complexity of secondary group networks in modern society.
Malinowksi[21] Radcliffe-Brown[27]	Sociology applied in anthropology		(4) The need for some clarification and simplification of relationships between primary group and secondary group social networks.

It is interesting and important to note how definitely and strongly all the major theorists agreed on this. Many of them have been absurdly separated by caricature. McDougall[19] was dubbed an 'instinct theorist'. Westermarck[39] was labelled an outmoded 'evolutionist', Radcliffe-Brown[27] was a modern 'functionalist'. Freud[10] was distinctively the founder of 'Psycho-Analysis'. Hobhouse[16] was put on the shelf as being really a moral philosopher, whereas Durkheim[6] was a tough minded non-reductionist investigator of 'social facts'. But all these caricatures are nonsensical, and no one could possibly so separate them who had really read their work. All of them placed the same importance upon the sentiments as constellations of values in institutionalization and personality formation alike. This was a perfectly clear agreement.

(ii) *The transformation: From traditional sentiment to rational ideal*

On this basis, therefore, there was also strong agreement about the significance of the modern transformation.

In the 'Traditional Society', the basic sentiments of the social order were not only firmly established and taken for granted, but also continuously reinforced and strengthened by the regular repetition of ritual practice and mythical doctrine. Once this order was disrupted, the values and ideas in the light of which reconstruction was to take place had to be critically clarified. The reason for Weber's insistence upon an ethic of *responsibility* is clear. But one important aspect of this is that in this transformation of social institutions, the struggles to approximate to ethical ideals were increasingly at the heart of the actualities of social change. The empirical facts of social change could not be explained except by reference to the meaningful and ethical purposes of men in their deliberate social action.

Under the differently coloured skin of different concepts, all the major theorists in sociology plainly agreed about these fundamentals. Their central preoccupation was with the vital change from traditional community to complex, contractual society with its rational and ethical critique and the two-sided problem of the responsibility it posed—promise and malaise. For all of them the distinctive changes in the institutions of modern society were largely (and increasingly) rationally, ethically and deliberately *made*. It was not possible, therefore, to explain or to evaluate them, except within this perspective.

(iii) *The error of a scientistic epistemology*

The third point widely agreed upon was that human social and personal action was a category quite distinct from the 'phenomenal events' dealt with by the 'natural sciences'. Institutional change in human society could never be sufficiently explained in terms of physical and biological 'events', or psychological or social 'mechanisms of adjustment'. These elements were certainly present, but an explanation in terms of the imputation of meaning was also necessary.

The other important aspect of this point was that the processes of *knowing* could clarify rational and ethical *ideals* as well as testable theories about *facts*. Indeed they positively had to do both, since, in the human sciences at any rate, the facts could not be understood until the 'idealities', which alone gave them meaning, were clarified. In any satisfactory statement of the nature of the human sciences, and in any satisfactory analysis of the nature of human social life, both were necessary! Explanation was impossible without them.

(iv) *The creation of the modern family: A part of this*

All this may seem remote from a consideration of 'the family in society', but, in fact, it is absolutely vital for the perspective I want to uphold.

The fact is that the modern family has been created as a necessary part of this larger process of approximating to the central ideals of social justice in the entire reconstitution of society. Let us consider a few examples.

During the constitution of modern nation states on the basis of rationally clarified principle, political citizenship for men was established not much more than a hundred years ago. The rights and duties of individuals as responsible members of political society have been clarified and effected in government, law, and social and economic relationships. The same citizenship was extended to women not fifty years ago. With this step has come the effort to obtain equal status for men and women. Sex has been seen to be irrelevant to many of the basic rights and duties of citizenship. In this context the status of women, like that of men, in relation to securing rights and opportunities in the ownership and management of property, in education, in the range of effective occupational choice, and in the entering into and termination of marriage, has been much improved. The status of children and young people has similarly been improved. For women and children alike this was not a deliberate aiming at some ultimate form of the family, but an alleviation of intolerable evils, removing them from the harsh conditions of over-work, ignorance, exploitation and an almost total lack of education which had made life—in conditions of peasant community and domestic industry—a brutal and miserable story. Also, inequalities of income have been reduced by more equitable taxation, minimum standards of income have been established, and many social services have been provided, to approximate as far as possible to the ethical ideal of citizenship in which all are fittingly rewarded for the contribution which they make, and in which civilized standards are maintained for the less fortunate.

The modern family as we now know it—defined by government and law, upheld by morality, and aided by the social services—is the outcome.[7] It is founded on the basis of free personal choice by partners of equal status, and the expected basis of it is that of personal affection (not legal constraint). Responsible, planned parenthood is firmly expected of it: casual and irresponsible parenthood is condemned. Within it children enjoy a high status and much parental and social concern. Dogmatic parental (chiefly paternal) authority has been superseded by reciprocal discussion and sensitivity to the needs of all the members of the family, when decisions are made. We have all come to speak of the 'democratic' family. Physical conditions and neighbourhood services alike have been greatly improved when compared with the distressing nature of earlier industrial and urban growth—which persisted to a chronic extent (as did unemployment) up to 1939. There is a much-improved basis of economic security, and the social and welfare services sympathetically aid families in sustaining the best possible qualities of life. Finally, a *chosen* degree of involvement between the family and its wider kindred has replaced the earlier *necessitous* dependence and constraint.[2, 17]

The making of the modern family has been part of the making of a new society. It is the outcome of efforts to approximate to humane ideals, as well as of some process of adjustment to industrial and urban conditions. On all counts it embodies great improvements. It is not just a convenient arrangement or compromise, but that form of the family which is integrally bound up with (i.e., is an 'institutional entailment' of) the achievement of a new, principled, democratic, industrialized society. It is in itself a great achievement, and is part of the larger achievement of moving more closely than men have ever been before to a just society.

Two points must be briefly emphasized in passing. First: changes in sexual behaviour are not necessarily evidence of the instability of this form of the family as such, or of its unsatisfying nature. On the contrary, the form of the modern family seems a direct entailment of many other aspects of personal status (i.e., with reference to citizenship, property-owning, occupation, education, etc.); and the new emphasis upon personal choice and personal responsibility in sexual behaviour may well be not a breaking away from this form (as is commonly supposed), but actually a concomitant of it. It may reflect no diminution in responsibility with regard to *family* norms at all.*

Secondly, in arguing that the modern family is an 'institutional entailment' of the changes we have considered, we are not, of course, suggesting that it is necessarily in a final or inevitable form. We cannot know

---

* See Geoffrey Gorer's recent survey for *The Sunday Times*.[13] Over 90 per cent of men and women still thought fidelity important in marriage despite the 'safety' of the pill and the increased ease of intercourse outside marriage. Some respondents admitted some premarital and extramarital experience, but regretted it—in the sense that they felt it had a certain spoiling effect on their marital relationship.

what is final here. All we are insisting upon is what the form of the family most definitely is now. But I shall come back to this later. So much for the perspective itself, and for the assumptions which underlie it. I want now to look at the implications of this. What has really emerged as our central theme is how, given the complexities of modern society, nuclear families (and their individual members) can achieve a satisfactory life and a satisfying experience of community. My contention is that the health of the modern family will be better achieved if we look beyond it to the making of a community which engages it more richly with wider social networks, than by any attempt to resuscitate a supposedly secure context of "extended kinship". But first it is worthwhile just to glance at certain implications for the collaboration of the social sciences and for education.

COLLABORATION AMONG THE SOCIAL SCIENCES

Much needs to be said on this topic, but I take it that at this conference we all agree on the basic importance of accomplishing the closest relationship between our various sciences—biology, comparative ethology, psychology, sociology, etc. I shall therefore confine myself to two remarks only.

First, unless the levels and categories of the several approaches are carefully distinguished, close comparisons between sciences can only lead to error. Thus ethological studies certainly have much to offer in comparing the behaviour of other animal species with that of man in society. But the categories of conceptual and ideational meaning in human action must be seen to be distinct from the 'sign stimuli', 'consummatory acts', 'coats of reflexes', etc., of animal behaviour if correct levels of explanation are to be preserved. Human action and the nature of social institutions can never be explained in terms of biological, psychological or sociological 'mechanisms' alone, or in terms of 'phenomenal events'. There is a category of meaning and purpose which goes beyond all these, and which requires not only explanation in terms of the imputation of meaning, but also cultural and historical studies.

Second, one of these category distinctions is the recognition of the *necessity of the associational context for any satisfactory human biology or psychology*. This was insisted upon by all the nineteenth century thinkers like Comte,[3] Marx,[22] Ward,[36] and Giddings,[11] but has been plainly established in the clearest conceptual terms since the work of Durkheim,[6] Cooley[4, 5] and Mead[23]—to mention only the scholars of central importance. Everything Durkheim said to the effect that human association was psychologically creative, everything Cooley and Mead said to the effect that the sharp distinction between the 'self' and 'society' was an error, was true at the most basic level—and established a new perspective of the first importance. There cannot be a satisfactory human psychology except within the associational context. In my experience there are still many people working in the social sciences who have not properly grasped this point and its full dimensions and implications.

The collaboration of all the human sciences is of the greatest importance, then, for the understanding of any one area of social behaviour— but the collaboration needs the utmost care. We must cooperate, but must not end up with the limited picture of a 'human zoo'.

THE IMPORTANCE OF EDUCATION FOR EFFECTIVELY ACHIEVING THE QUALITY OF LIFE IN THE FAMILY WHICH ITS CONTEMPORARY 'FORM' MAKES POSSIBLE

The only point I want to make here is that to have accomplished an institutional 'form' of the family is one thing, but the extent to which families actually appreciate it, and effectively enjoy the qualities of personal life for which it provides, is another. I accept the power of Professor Weiss's argument[38] about the obstacles to stable and fulfilled marriage, the conditions of mobility, isolation, pressures towards a (perhaps falsely conceived) 'self-realization', etc., and I accept their continuity and ubiquity (so to speak) in a complex society like ours. Yet I cannot accept that nothing can be done. The malaise can be countered, but only by education, and it is here again that our perspective is important.

Clearly, people should be educated for the freedom and responsibility which our new institutions require, rather than be offered a backward-looking quest for an extended kinship ethos that they and society are supposed to have lost. Here I agree with Mrs Rogers' emphasis[29] that planning should maximize the range of choice, and that people should be educated towards responsibility and creative choice in their living. Community must be of their own making. Thinking of Professor Weiss's remarks concerning marriage, too, I would want to argue that the 'co-ordinative' and 'complementary' aspects of a relationship are not *polarities*, and that in Britain, at any rate, we have gone a good way towards blending both in what we consider to be a good marriage between equal partners.

At any rate, the reconstitution of the institutions of a society clearly requires a parallel and relevant education. There is a large task before us here, and the perspective I am suggesting has clear implications for it.

But I turn now to what is perhaps our chief concern.

THE FAMILY AND THE MAKING OF COMMUNITY

I have argued that the modern family is good, valuable, to be upheld, as part of a greatly improved society. Even so, we all agree that in the context of modern complexities families can suffer isolation, and that we need to prevent this. Here again the implications of this perspective are, clearly, that it is a mistake to try to reconstitute an extended kinship network, which probably never had the qualities with which we tend to invest it[2, 17] and that we should attempt a forward-looking *making of community* in such a way as to preserve the qualities of family life and freedom which have been achieved. The modern family has assumed its present form within the wider social networks of changed institutions. This has been a decided improvement in almost every way. The further improvement of the family can best be achieved not by dwelling upon anachronistic 'extended kinship networks', but by improving the primary group and secondary group social networks which surround it, and by linking it effectively with those networks. These wider social networks are of vital importance for the qualities of living which are possible, and actually achieved, within the family unit. The making of the modern family, the making of community, must still be within the clear context of improving the institutional fabric of society as a whole.

(a) *Primary group networks*

All our theory suggests a concentration of attention upon the *primary group networks within the neighbourhood*. Within that specific area in Fig. 2 I have deliberately included only other families, play-groups and schools, because these seem to be the vital groupings (though other groups—such as church groups—are no doubt important for some). All psychological theories about the growth of personality emphasize the importance of the early years of infancy and the processes of growth up to and including adolescence; and throughout these years it is experience and behaviour within these relatively small, face-to-face groups of the neighbourhood which are dominant. But two other points are more important.

One is that Cooley[4, 5] and Mead[23] have emphasized that the constraints, expectations, reciprocal judgements and adjustments experienced by children in play-groups are, parallel with experience in the family, of the most fundamental importance for the growth of the 'self' in 'society'.

Their treatment of experience in primary groups, and of primary group communications, for the establishment of sentiments and values both in the 'self' and in the emergence of regulated patterns of conduct ('institutionalized' behaviour) is too well known for me to reiterate; but it seems to me vitally at the heart of this task of the making of community. It is in the widening experience beyond and among families in neighbourhood play-groups that the earliest basis of community experience can be laid, and in which the self can grow in society.

The second emphasis is upon the school—and picks up Professor

Himmelweit's earlier insistence[15] that it is a mistake to take definite personality formation in pre-school years, and definite social factors (such as 'social class'), as being given elements that can be weighted, so to speak, in some kind of amalgamated 'explanation'. School experience is another area of exploratory, primary group experience and behaviour which is a context in its own right for new levels, extensions, and changes of sentiment, value, and attitude-formation (for children, parents, and no doubt teachers alike). It is another important field of conduct and experience within which the self grows within the context of 'association'.

(b) *Secondary group networks in the institutional structure of society*

Primary groups and adolescence, however, are not an end of this matter of 'self' and 'community' experience; neither can they be separated (conceptually or actually) from the networks of secondary groups in the wider institutional framework. The occupations of the parents (and therefore the entire structure of industrial organization and industrial relations), their political affiliations and responsibilities, and so on, will be a part of the quality of their family and primary group networks. Mass communications are nowadays bound to enter into primary group communications, and themselves enlarge the boundaries of experienced 'community'. And so on. Secondary group relationships and the structure of all the major institutions of society must therefore always receive the fullest possible attention.

Even so, this entire area of primary group networks between, among and beyond families, in play-groups and schools, seems clearly to be that manageable area of research and creative social action in which the making of community could be most effective.

I have in mind, too, in these emphases, the many concerns which have been voiced. Mrs Rogers, again, in her architectural design for creative choice,[29] could clearly find much scope in providing design options for such play-group and community-making. Dr Newson's expressed concern[25] about the family as a source of primary group values clearly leans towards such a creative making of community among primary groups. Professor Miller in his concern[24] that children should have wider opportunities for identification with members of their peer-groups, and with adults other than those found in the family, also seems to support the strong need for some community-making. And we have already noted Professor Himmelweit's emphasis upon the school.[15]

The final—and important—point here is that this kind of community-making would retain all the qualities of independent family life which have been achieved, but would *add* something to them. It would not go back on the modern family. It would make possible a *chosen* degree of privacy and a *chosen* degree of group participation: which is what people want.

This perspective on the making of the modern family and on the related task of community-making in the social networks beyond the family seems to me also to carry an extremely interesting perspective for comparative research.

On the one hand, it constitutes a universal hypothesis: that a multiplicity of family forms in traditional societies will approximate towards the modern nuclear family 'type' as industrialization, urbanization, and the connected issues of moral principle and political policy spread. This in itself is a hypothetical guide to theoretical understanding, and to expectations of problems and appropriate policies, But on the other hand, within the context of this 'universal' tendency we know that the actuality is much more complex, and especially that it is the *differences* which are important. Here I especially have in mind Dr Rapoport's earlier comments[28]; and two points seem quite clear.

(i) *Families in their environments: Differences of community-making needed*

The first is that each society has different types of families within different kinds of community conditions. Though there is one institutional form of the family in Britain, there are important variations of the form. Family *types* probably exist which still differ according to occupation almost as strongly as Le Play[18] maintained. A coal-miner's family may have distinctively different community needs from a trawler-man's family and from the families of agricultural workers, steel-workers, school-teachers, medical doctors, and so on. Occupation may well be one central factor, but, as Dr Rapoport suggested,[28] the criteria of difference may be more numerous and more unexpected than we suppose. Systematic research on families in their environments, with special reference to their context of community and community needs, would clearly be worth while.

Again, such research clearly would and could be closely related to social action—and social action already afoot. The Seebohm Report,[30] for example, envisaged a kind of unification of all the welfare services in 'family' social services. The research we are proposing would provide detailed knowledge of a regional and local (community) kind on which such family services could reliably rest. The same kind of desire has emerged quite strongly in the law—though because of cost its realization is still far distant. But all the reforms mentioned by Dr Stone[33]—divorce law reform, the changes in financial provisions following upon divorce, etc.—have been paralleled by a proposal for family courts rather than ordinary courts for matrimonial and family proceedings, so that the unfortunate 'adversary' atmosphere attending such proceedings could be still further reduced. We are still a long way from these things—but the link between research and already-envisaged social action is plain to be seen.

(ii) *Universality and differences among all societies*

The same blend of universal tendency with difference of detail is of course true *among* all societies as well as *within* each of them. Wherever industrialization spreads, the tendency towards the nuclear family type is likely to be experienced. Yet we know well enough that the approximation towards this will be different in terms of the initial kinship systems and the previous and changing socio-economic patterns. But here again internationally linked collaborative research could provide very useful and necessary knowledge for constructive community-making in all these areas in the context of what is, very frequently, *disruptive* social change.

Within each society, and among all societies, such research could provide a blend of helpful knowledge and a basis for the better exercise of that greater responsibility which social change has brought in its train. The making of the modern family and the making of community—within a complexity of change—could at least be made as effective as possible.

URGENCY

My final observation is that this perspective carries with it a great degree of urgency. There are large and difficult obstacles in the way of all that has been suggested. The population explosion *is* an explosion, and is *upon* us. The pollution and massive deterioration of our environment is a real and imminent danger. The contractual manipulation of man by man—and of *masses* of men by a *few*—is a reality, and a grave continual threat. And even within our own subjects the increasing specialization makes us trivial where we should be most profound, and carries that danger of the dehumanization of science itself which Gissing so feared.[12] Some perspective for our time, and I believe it is *this* perspective, is sorely needed, and one great virtue of a conference like this is that it enables us to expose our differing views and so move towards more considered positions which are likely to be more satisfactory.

The making of the social sciences has been for the making of a new society—and this it still is. The making of the modern family has been part of this larger transformation, and we should value and uphold it while moving beyond it to new kinds of community-making. This community-making, if it is to be soundly and wisely based, must not see the family and its kinship relationships in isolation, or in a form appropriate to simpler societies of the past, but in the context of deliberately improved primary group and secondary group networks in the wider social environment. The making of the family must be within the remaking of society as a whole, and the making of community must be such as to preserve the great gains and improvements which have been so painstakingly achieved. Mankind is now involved in a creative struggle. The problems seem well-nigh insurmountable. It is not too dramatic to see it as a life-and-death struggle, which means: we have no time to lose.

DISCUSSION

Weiss: Are you proposing that social forms arise in good part as a development of human rationality because they represent what people want? I think a more dominant view in social science today sees social forms as expressing the forces of irrationality, or at least as resulting from a blind social process. A closely related question is, what is the value of sociology? If social forms arise as a response to human rationality then sociology gives us the basis for developing the world the way we want it. If the social forms arise on their own, as it were independent of human reasons, then sociology is at best an early-warning system, readable only by few. I myself believe in the irrational blind social process although I really hope that the first will turn out to be true.

Fletcher: I emphatically believe in the first—but without denying the power of irrationality in human behaviour. Under the skin of the work of all the major sociologists, one sees that man's 'practical activities' even at the most 'primitive' level are marked by a quality that distinguishes man from the other species: the ability to apprehend ends and to calculate and employ means for their attainment. This is not rationality in a high-flown philosophical sense but in the ordinary sense of purposive, inventive, cooperative activity in relation to practical jobs. I agree that non-rational and irrational elements enter into human conduct in society, and sometimes play a dominant part, but I would flatly deny that there is any evidence of social forms coming into being on their own, independent of human volition and reason. I think this is where Durkheim goes too far and becomes a metaphysician.

Reynolds: In more advanced industrial society there is a trend towards self-seeking, towards the limited interests of oneself or one's immediate family, and no wider perspective. This seems to me to be what one would call rational development; it makes sense given the system we have got. Where is the irrational force in industrial capitalism which provides you with a non-egocentric approach to some of the problems?

Fletcher: This is too big a question for me to answer. I do not think it is true that rationality is limited to contractual calculations. Tönnies[7] and Marx are right in saying that in an industrial-capitalist (bourgeois) society, the contractual relationships that develop in commerce and industry tend to spill over into the treatment of men by men in all their relationships. This danger certainly exists but human rationality always goes beyond that to consider larger ethical principles and ideals. As soon as industrial capitalism raised its head, Tom Paine[5,6] was insisting on human rights and Edmund Burke[1] was denouncing them. Reason is thoroughly engaged in ethical and political questions. It is only the rationality that we have applied to the reconstitution of human relationships in terms of equality of consideration which has brought us a long way towards the chosen, sensitive and mutually considered relationships between man and woman of the kind that Mrs Ali Baig was upholding earlier. Without the criticisms of reason, women would still be in subjection.

Ali Baig: In this age of technology, with social changes ahead more dramatic than any we have yet had, I am dismayed that so little real understanding is even now apparent between one part of the globe and another. Most of you here represent the rational mind of one society, yet you talk in terms of the whole world. I am part of another society and I am also a non-specialist in a group of specialists; my only specialization perhaps being as a wife and mother, which is clearly held at a very low order of rating! The child however is still our concern and we haven't given the child much attention. No security is going to be possible for the child unless the family is itself secure. The family is an indispensible matrix in which the adolescent must grow. The family also has to accommodate to the pressures of technology that face not just some societies, but the whole world. There must be a reasonable moral basis to family life, with an ethic in which the ego has been transcended as part of the disciplines governing each member of a family. This is more important than ever in the new technological era.

Henriques: Professor Fletcher's optimism rather overwhelms me and I can't say I agree with his historical analysis. It sounded as if he was saying that after we have crossed this watershed he so vividly presented to us, we shall have a monopoly of rationality. One or two people like Plato had this kind of dimension and I noticed Professor Fletcher didn't quote any living sociologists to agree with his analysis. We seem to be preoccupied with moral values and maybe this is a very good thing in one sense, but the sort of estimate one can use in society today is surely one based on clinical studies. Do studies of the family in Western society, including the United States, made during the last 20 years bear out in their conclusions your general thesis of this kind of progression? Is the family today exhibiting a greater resilience and making a vital contribution to society? In my own small way, from the inquiries I have made, I have come to the opposite conclusion.

Fletcher: Books like Goode's *World Revolution and Family Patterns*[3] with very wide comparative studies of contemporary family changes in simple societies, in large historical civilizations like India and China as well as in Western societies, do bear out the perspective I have suggested. Nothing I have said implies inevitable progress, but a culmination has been reached in human civilization where the *scale* of change and the *scale* of human control has forced a rational reappraisal of institutions upon us, and this, incidentally, is what distinguishes our time from that of Plato. We all know that Cleisthenes and Solon reconstituted Athenian institutions rationally to take into account changes, and I certainly would not want to claim we have a monopoly of rationality. But the scale of human control is now moving literally towards a *global* situation with an urgency which forces us to take these ethical factors into account. Reading through the abstracts for this conference, I found in every single one not only scientific and empirical references to the family, but also ethical evaluations of it, and if we are going to make these evaluations we must be rational and critical in classifying their basis. Human reason can be as articulate and impartial, in clarifying the presuppositions of our values as it is in establishing knowledge about empirical matters of fact.

Himmelweit: Because I am a psychologist I find this idea of a division between rational and irrational not terribly helpful. We have not the skills to envisage what a changed situation would be like and what would be the cost of this change. As societies we have very little training in charting the costs and the benefits of any situation. We move away from something because it becomes intolerable. In spite of two world wars this century, I still share your optimism that something will happen. But now we also have decisions of a technological nature being made by a very small group, and the results are only seen many years later when they are irreversible. Really two things are happening alongside each other: one, the longer-term significance of the decisions that are made—for example, whether we build high blocks of flats or low housing; and two, the increased concern and readiness to become involved, with rising expectations and a much more acute awareness by people of their own position compared with others—that is, of their relative deprivation. This strengthens the need for community participation in the problems of the neighbourhood.

Adams: We should note that Max Weber saw rationality as a characteristic feature of modern society and yet as having fragmented this society and as having made modern man lose a sense of embracing vision.[8] Rationality has been closely tied up with specialization, leaving us (Weber says) imprisoned in iron cages, a highly organized form of fragmentation.[9] This sort of outcome of rationality gives rise in times of crisis to blatant irrationality. Dr Himmelweit has suggested that solutions to problems like housing can be attacked in the neighbourhood, provided people are not closeted in a narrow way. People can be brought out of this closeting, through rationally devised organizational co-operation for the achievement of a consensus.

There is a fundamental difference among people, and also among religious mentalities, in attitudes to such cooperative efforts. On one side is the cultivation of the self or the concern primarily for privacy (which may lead to political apathy); on the other side is the positive, creative involvement in the community.

Here one can make a rough distinction between what in the phenomenology of religion is called pietism and prophetic religion. A characteristic feature of both religion and secularism in the West (stemming from Greek as well as from Judeo–Christian prophetic thought and practice) is the view that man is capable of changing the environment, whereas the tendency of pietism in the West and of Oriental religions in general has been to disregard the environment with its problems of institutional social change and to cultivate the inner life and in this way make life tolerable. Here the assumption often is that if the individual achieves inner peace or maturity he will be able to cope with institutional problems —indeed that institutional problems will take care of themselves. This is the Billy Graham approach, whether it appears in religious or in secular circles. In 'scientific', psychological circles this view appears in the assumption that somehow the laws of group (or institutional) dynamics are similar to the laws governing individual dynamics. (This is the opposite of the Marxist assumption that everything is to be understood in terms of social, institutional forces[2].) I take it that the recent interest in general systems theory, in communications, in ecology, in techniques of intervention, and in community psychiatry bespeaks scepticism about the assumptions and therapies of individualistic psychology and psychotherapy (especially evident in traditional child psychiatry).

Let us return to the question of neighbourhood groups that fail even to attempt to cope with the environmental problems. Mirra Komarovsky's studies are dismal indeed in their outcome.[4] She has found that on average the people who live on Manhattan (New York City) belong, apart from the church, to less than one association per person. Many of these people are 'educated' and professional people, as well as the lower class. She suggests that one could scarcely find a better definition of the 'mass man' than one who is not involved in these middle associations concerned with public policy. This situation offers the ideal milieu for Big Brother to gain and maintain control. Again, the problem is to be seen as at least in part that of 'excessive familism'.

Miller: I would like to put in a plea for irrationality. As Professor Fletcher showed, he knows people are irrational, but he was obviously putting a very high value on rationality. I suggest that one of the tasks of the family, which is crucial if we are to survive, is somehow to free the imaginativeness and the creativity of people, both of which are highly irrational. However, the implication of what has been said is that to be rational is fine, to be irrational is not fine; and I don't think this is true. We can be destructively irrational, but we can also be most constructively irrational in the process of change and in the process of life. It isn't enough to draw a diagram with which everybody essentially agrees about the neighbourhood, the play group and schools and families and so on. If human beings are to abandon their biological creativity, and they have to do this, how then are they to replace the making of babies with a different sort of creativity?

Reynolds: Psychologists talk about the family in terms of individual development—in terms of basic developmental norms, pathological aberrations and so on. This is not the same as the frame of reference used by sociologists, who are interested in the family as a cultural or structural unit and in its potentialities for effecting social change. Our first task is to find the common language which we can use to talk about the very real problems in psychology, psychiatry and sociology. Once we have a common language, a second problem will arise, which is how to relate our research findings to the practical problem which people all seem to face in rearing their children: how not to lose communication with them, and how to maintain a dialogue between parents and children about social issues. I am thinking now of Dr Spock. As a psychologist he taught America and the world how to rear children developmentally and then he suddenly became aware of what they were being reared for and said "Right, all these wonderful children we have produced must now try and dodge the draft". He very dramatically showed how there may be total conflict between psychology and sociology. I would like to see a situation in which parents are able to rear happy healthy children and talk to them about the major sociological issues which their society faces.

Comfort: It's arguable, I think, whether talking to them about the sociological issues will keep them out of Vietnam.

Adams: We have not yet mentioned the importance of ritualization in the family. Ritual is one of the major means of transmitting a sense of values and of involving the different age groups. As examples, punishment in the family or the celebration of family events cannot be effectively carried through in a casual way. The ritualization of these aspects of family life is a way of underlining their significance. Is ritualization completely gone in the contemporary family, and if so, is this not something to be taken into account when we think of the family of the future?

Comfort: I was hoping somebody would raise this point. It seems to me that our 'primitives' are immensely sophisticated in emotional technology, which takes a large part of their time. We have an equally sophisticated physical technology without an emotional counterpart.

I am not going to attempt to suggest what forms emotional technology should take, but perhaps the family is one of its instruments.

Miller: It would indeed be alarming if the family lost the ritual structure. For example, every family idiosyncratically develops its own controlling techniques. These partly depend on unconscious factors worked out between the family members, as well as on cultural patterns. Changing fathers or mothers may destroy these. This is one reason for the disruption which occurs when a mother figure is replaced; it is not just that the new mother 'smell' is different, but she brings a new set of rituals.

Hendrickse: A term used frequently throughout this meeting and which is at the back of everybody's mind, engendering anxieties, is population pressure. We have come to accept that this term corresponds to something finite, but is this really true? Certain countries in Europe 20 or 30 years ago were extremely anxious about their falling birth rates. Prosperity didn't bring them a population explosion. Even now there are countries, Czechoslovakia for instance, where parenthood is actively encouraged because governments are worried about the decline in national birthrates. When we talk about population pressure, we are really talking in terms of anxiety about world food supplies in relation to the projected growth of population. Technologically advanced countries have achieved a considerable measure of population control already. The concern is that the vast exploding populations in Africa, Asia and elsewhere will bring about unbalance. I have already expressed my views about where one starts on this problem, and that is not in terms of birth control, but in terms of ensuring survival. I have no doubt, and I am not alone in this view, that given two things—the increased chance of survival of children and a reasonable expectation of advancement for these children—people will limit their family size to that which gives optimal advantage to their offspring. We have begun to see this already in West Africa. The main issue about developing countries, population explosions and so forth, is the need for concerted and positive international effort for *genuine* development to be centred in these countries. So far, so-called development programmes have actually been deleterious in many 'developing' situations, although advantageous elsewhere. This is a crucial consideration if we think of the problem globally. A meeting such as this, which is essentially oriented towards Western industrial technological society, is not necessarily applicable to the rest of the world, and is liable to be misinterpreted.

Finally, our concern with the effects of the breakdown of the family has centred mainly on the future role of women, but how does this reflect on man? It is biologically feasible to have a woman's world, in which a small bank of men is retained only as a fertilizing agency. Women could run the world. It is not biologically possible, however, to have a male world. I think there is a deep secret worry in the minds of many men about their role in future society. What started off as the emancipation of women could conceivably end in the elimination of men. If men feel sterilized by the pill; if the new morality says, because the world population is increasing, "Thou shalt not procreate", this must have profound psychological effects. We seem to be moving towards a world in which it would seem that everybody would be happier with a neuter gender, and with a machine that could produce a baby without involving people in the event.

Fairbrother: It is very sad that Dr Hendrickse is so worried about the future role of men, because their role has always been to improve the standard of living of mothers and children and I don't see why it should change.

Miller: There is individual male anxiety about a man's role, but also as a group men suffer from an institutionalized helplessness. Society has become highly bureaucratized and this has produced a return to decision making as in a feudal society. Decisions are made in which no cognizance is taken of the needs of members of the society. Individuals in most social groups have to deal with helplessness in a unique way. Behind each family now there is the blast of Hiroshima. Apart from the time of the Black Death, when families felt that they could be casually obliterated, I don't think families have experienced such a feeling before and this must influence the state of the family, its status and its future.

Comfort: I think that we are already moving perhaps towards ways in which the citizen, by his recalcitrance, can make himself felt. The prospect of being hanged wonderfully concentrates the mind.

13: Chairman's Closing Remarks

ALEX COMFORT

I wondered when we came here what the function of this conference was. One function was clearly communication between ourselves and with the people who are going to read this discussion. The other function, I suppose, is one of prediction and this we haven't been able entirely to discharge, although we have perhaps made some steps in that direction. We have outlined a number of processes and factors which bear or are likely to bear on the future pattern of the family: demography, architecture, control of fertility; also greater longevity, which I tried several times to inject into the discussion, because it involves the survival of relatives and so affects family structure very markedly. This trend is going to be accompanied by smaller families leading to a shortage of relatives. We have talked about the likely increase of adult survival into post-reproductive life and the prospect perhaps of two sequential life-spans and life styles.

Apart from these individual points, the discussion has turned on our own self-estimates, both as intellectuals of various kinds and as individuals. A lot has been said on the role of women. Indeed, one proposal was to make this the subject of the conference in the first place and if we had, I think we would have covered very much the same ground. The role of the mother is well defined, and there has never been much argument about who is who's physical mother. There has been discussion of the possible uniqueness of the mother and baby relationship, and we have been left with the impression that the role of the father is variable. Rather than defining the role of woman, we may need to think of what is the future role of man.

We may have underestimated how far the biological role of woman is being fundamentally altered by control over fertility and by the new cultural options for women to adopt another role, and one which is not so strictly biologically patterned. We said that women are approaching the option of divorcing erotic and reproductive relationships completely, throughout either the whole or part of the lifespan. We suggested that this has large gains and possibly also unforeseen emotional effects. We have not really delimited these; I don't know if we can do so at the moment, but we should go on to try to do so in future work, in so far as the consequences can be foreseen.

The role of woman and the role of man always has been, and is being, programmed quite largely by expectations, but in present society, expectations are increasingly diverse. There is not only diversity between East and West, but actual diversity within Western cultures. I am not an anthropologist, but I have the impression that far from being treatable as a single society showing a regular Gaussian distribution of personality, our society is much more like a mixture of tribes jumbled together, showing great disparities in patterns of rearing, within an overall culture which is none the less identifiable. What man or woman expects of society, of the family and of themselves depends clearly on what they biologically and personally are; also on what they have been led to expect by their particular upbringing. A great many of our problems seem to me to arise when the expectation is unrealistic, either because the social fiction we acquire is unrealistic in the first place, or because in a time of rapid change, of the order of less than one generation, the reality of behaviour in society is changing relative to the pattern we have learned. Thus the woman who has been led by education and observation either to expect or to rebel against conventionally patterned marriage, may be quite unprepared for the actuality when it arises. I would agree with several speakers who have pointed out that sociology has a sizeable responsibility in this respect, merely through the propaganda it conducts in society.

I think we can agree that the family pattern will probably change, but the question arises whether it is feasible and desirable to change it purposively. I am a pessimist and I hesitate even on the considerations we have heard to do more than predict. I don't think at the moment that we have the levers with which to change the family, and I certainly would not wish that it should be changed even by the present expert company without references to the changees! Since prediction is itself a form of intervention, if we predict that polygamy will become universal, we are taking a step in that direction.

Institutions grow like Topsy, and are not easily plannable, which may be a very good thing because our bloodymindedness is perhaps our most valuable adaptive character *vis-à-vis* Popes, professors, pundits and the proletariat. Institutions are unplannable if only because unconscious factors are involved; the steam locomotive was designed to pull trains, but it emerged as a very numinous ancestor figure, almost a religious object, which differs quite markedly from its electrical and diesel successors. The space programme which was in other aspects the apogee of rational technology is in fact a practical re-enactment of the archetypal exploits of a Stone Age wizard. The only prediction I am willing to make here is that the family *will* change, but I think it will change towards a more widely acceptable diversity of patterns and towards a greater degree of personal choice, and this we are already seeing.

There are individual future factors. We have talked about the effect of infertility, first on female roles and secondly in limiting the size of family units by limiting the number of available relatives. This is now both culturally and demographically inevitable and we have to allow for it. I mentioned longevity as leading to a potential duality of the lifespan—the possibility of a reproductive followed by a companionate relationship and even, in the absence of any further control over ageing, a potential second identity crisis in middle life in both men and women. It is harder, things being as they are, for women than for men to form a second identity when their period of child rearing has passed, and this is a problem which is with us already. Shortage of kin is certainly a problem for the young but it is also very markedly a problem for the old. I notice a very striking orientation towards youth in all our discussions and nobody here has behaved as if people age or said much about the fact that when old they continue to have needs. I think this neglect tells us something about our own preconceptions—preconceptions that will have to change.

Another topic we discussed in some depth was the rate of development, both in relation to biological factors and also in response to peer group expectation. Then there is the question of the feedback from the increasing and often highly selective input of stimulation from society, much of which is non-verbal. In contrast to the rural environment, the stimuli we are subjected to are discursive stimuli. But they are mediated very largely by things and not by people. Modern media in one sense enable people to relate to people—the telephone and the motor car are means to keep the family together over long distances. Mass media also produce a category of 'relations' which are artificial and a substitute for family relations; relations with figures such as the Dales and the Archers and the semi-mythological beings that we identify as pop stars, who can be compared historically with Hercules and Venus. These trends to artificial person-substitutes may increase or may be wholly rejected, as the young are tending to reject them.

We come here to Professor Fletcher's malaise; the cause of it is perhaps a problem of feedback from our environment, and it extends not only to human relations but to ecology and to pollution. Primitive man, if you think of the Australian aborigine, has very little control over his environment, but much feedback from it. Even the English countryman as opposed to the English townsman has a lot of feedback from non-man-made objects. The primitive has a way of treating things and animals as if they were people. By contrast, scientific industrial man obtained vast control over his environment with virtually no feedback from it. The ideology that tends to go with this involves treating people as things or animals, where the aboriginal treats things or animals as people. I think we are on our way towards a post-scientific man for whom the artist perhaps is a model; modern sculpture is now perhaps more aware than any time since the primitive past of the materials being used. Henry Moore is much more concerned with the numinousness and *haeceitas* of things and the numinousness of structures as seen in their nature. Biologists in a sense go along with him. I feel that the family and the individual in the post-scientific world have to find ways of reconciling control with feedback. This will be feedback both from people and from things and we might on occasion do worse than treat things as if they were people. It might be a healthier orientation than our present one of treating people as things. Here I would reiterate what Dr Miller said about the creative aspects of irrationality. Technology is going the same way. The step between mechanization, in which there is no feedback from machine to man, and automation, in which there is a dialogue with a machine, seems highly important as a model of what I mean. We are even planning to computerize medicine—an idea which makes the divergence between reductionist medicine, with the doctor as detached observer, and existentialist medicine, where the dialogue is between doctor, patient and society, a lot more acute. We shall actually, I think, be within reach eventually of experimentation with a computerized psychiatry: by this I mean the possibility of a machine with which the patient can conduct a dialogue, using it as a mirror, in that the person with whom he has conducted the dialogue is himself. There might be uses for such a system. It is interesting that some autistic children can relate more easily to a machine system than they can to a human therapist.

It is not the duty of the Chairman to inject concerns of his own, however, that have not been discussed in the course of the meeting. We have ended up with ethics, and I think rightly. If I can summarize any sort of ethical trend (though here I think one is on dangerous ground and risks injecting a personal opinion), it is likely to be a tendency towards greater personalism: by that I mean a greater sense of discrete identity, greater fortification of the boundaries of the self as against the environment and as against others. There may be greater isolation, which may be a loss, but also greater individual responsibility as against directed behaviour, or other-directed behaviour, and greater rejection of explicit direction. We have talked about responsibility towards the child, which is the easiest part of sexual responsibility for the community to legislate; there is also responsibility towards the emotional need of partners, sometimes more than one partner, which we haven't tried to define. Quite clearly if sexual freedom becomes greater we are going to escape altogether from the context which we now know as 'family', into this much more general field of human relations. I think that in general we shall see kinship, both cognate and agnate kinship, which is an exclusive mechanism, getting more and more blurred. On one hand we may see a greater communication, a thing which the hippies are striving towards;

we may in fact through numerical lack of relatives be coming to act out literally the ethical view that all men are brothers. I think we shall find a far greater variety of institutional forms of living. Not that we shall move towards monogamy, polygamy, or whatever other sort of ogamy, but all of these will coexist, and will be tolerated. Whether we individually regard them as ideal solutions or not perhaps should not compromise our willingness to accept people who find them more helpful than we do.

I think I also see a greater acceptance of restraint in giving-behaviour, the antithesis of what Mrs Ali Baig described—a greater restraint in involvement. I think we shall develop the idea that it is not only a right but a duty to hold back some part of oneself in the interest of identity. What will be the consequences I wouldn't presume to state. Whether this is, as Dr Weiss suggested, an extended Protestant ethic, I don't know, but it seems to go with the kind of responsibility we shall acquire. I don't think our satisfactions are going to be increasingly career-centred; they are going to depend at least as much on *being* as on *doing*. We are rather in the same position as a meeting in 1780 trying to predict the consequences of the Romantic movement. These ranged from Napoleon to Blake and from large orchestras to republicanism and nationalism, and no 18th-century man could possibly have hoped to predict them. I think we all experience, and the young experience very strongly, that living is coming to feel different and that we have passed some kind of watershed in human sensibility. And it might be a good thing if we could hold more conferences like this one and explore some of the ways which the sensibility is changing in order to reduce the number of Napoleons and increase the number of Blakes.

In all this the State and the community as abstractions really play very little part, and in fact they have played no part in our own thinking here. The young tend to see them as wholly other, wholly alien forces beyond their control; their view may offend people who think they should be more fully participant in a democracy when we have one, but they are only verbalizing what the majority of people now feel, that the institutional structure, like the emperor, has no clothes, and that a reconstruction from below is necessary before any sort of participation or dialogue or reform can become practicable. You may feel that as a known anarchist, I should not bias the summing up in this way. I wouldn't do it if I thought I *was* biasing it. What the ethical side in the meeting has suggested to me is that not only adolescents but cultures pass through a crisis of becoming self-directed. Whether they do it once or many times, whether there is in fact a directional historical process, I don't want to argue. We may be passing into that crisis as a culture with the same risks and the same rewards for the individual. I won't pursue this, because time will tell, but I have said already and I would repeat here that I think it depends on our ability to develop a flexible emotional technology—and by 'technology' I mean not a manipulative but an associative one, to match our capacity for physical technology. This will demand a capacity to reconcile the ability to feel with the ability to think, the imagination with the intellect. If this is a problem for the family of the future I don't know how it will be resolved, but it is just possible that the family, as a microcosm of political institutions, will have the task of resolving it.

Bibliography

1: COMPARATIVE FAMILY PATTERNS
ROBIN FOX

BOWLBY, J. (1969). *Attachment and Loss.* Vol. 1: *Attachment.* London: Hogarth Press and Institute of Psychoanalysis.
FOX, R. (1967). *Kinship and Marriage.* Harmondsworth: Penguin Books.

Discussion

1. BOWLBY, J. (1969). *Attachment and Loss.* Vol. 1: *Attachment.* London: Hogarth Press and Institute of Psychoanalysis.
2. MURDOCK, G. P. (1949). *Social Structure.* New York: Macmillan.

2: THE ANALYSIS OF FAMILY ROLES
NICHOLAS TAVUCHIS

1. BELL, C. R. (1969). *Middle Class Families.* London: Routledge & Kegan Paul.
2. BLOOD, R. O., and WOLFE, D. M. (1960). *Husbands and Wives: The Dynamics of Married Living*, p. 6. New York: Free Press (Macmillan Co.).
3. BOTT, E. (1957). *Family and Social Network.* London: Tavistock Publications.
4. CARDEN, M. L. (1969). *Oneida: Community to Modern Corporation.* Baltimore: Johns Hopkins Press.
5. EDWARDS, J. N. (ed.) (1969). *The Family and Social Change.* New York: Knopf.
6. EISENSTADT, S. N. (1956). *From Generation to Generation: Age Groups and Social Structure.* Glencoe, Illinois: Free Press.
7. FIRTH, R. (ed.) (1956). *Two Studies of Kinship in London.* London: Athlone Press.
8. GEIGER, H. K. (1968). *The Family in Soviet Russia.* Cambridge, Mass.: Harvard University Press.
9. GLICK, P. C. (1957). *American Families.* New York: Wiley.
10. GOFFMAN, E. (1959). *The Presentation of Self to Everyday Life.* New York: Anchor.
11. GOODE, W. J. (1963). *World Revolution and Family Patterns.* New York: Free Press (Macmillan Co.).
12. GOODE, W. J. (1965). *Women in Divorce.* New York: Free Press (Macmillan Co.).
13. GOODE, W. J. (1968). The theory and measurement of family change. In *Indicators of Social Change: Concepts and Measurements*, p. 313, ed. Sheldon, E. B. and Moore, W. E. New York: Russell Sage Foundation.
14. HAAVIO-MANNILA, E. (1969). Some consequences of women's emancipation. *Journal of Marriage and the Family*, **31**, 123–134.
15. HAAVIO-MANNILA, E. (1969). The position of Finnish women: regional and cross-national comparisons. *Journal of Marriage and the Family*, **31**, 339–347.
16. HANNERZ, U. (1969). *Soul Side: Inquiries Into Ghetto Culture and Community.* New York: Columbia University Press.

17. KIRKPATRICK, C. (1968). *The Family: As Process and Institution*, 2nd edn, pp. 325–407. New York: Ronald Press.
18. KOMAROVSKY, M. (1962). *Blue-collar Marriage*. New York: Random House.
19. LEMASTERS, E. E. (1970). *Parents in Modern America*. Homewood, Ill.: Dorsey Press.
20. LIEBOW, E. (1967). *Tally's Corner: A Study of Negro Streetcorner Men*. Boston: Little, Brown.
21. MACCOBY, E. E. (ed.) (1966). *The Development of Sex Differences*. Stanford, Cal.: Stanford University Press.
22. MANNHEIM, K. (1952). The problem of generations. In *Essays in the Sociology of Knowledge*, pp. 276–322, ed. Keskemeti, P. New York: Oxford University Press.
23. MILLER, D. R., and SWANSON, G. M. (1958). *The Changing American Parent*. New York: Wiley.
24. NEUBECK, G. (ed.) (1969). *Extra-Marital Relations*. Englewood Cliffs, N.J.: Prentice-Hall.
25. ORDEN, S. R., and BRADBURN, N. M. (1969). Working wives and marriage happiness. *American Journal of Sociology*, **74**, 393–407.
26. PAULME, D. (ed.) (1963). *Women of Tropical Africa*, p. 1. London: Routledge & Kegan Paul.
27. PETERSEN, K. K. (1969). Kin network research: a plea for comparability. *Journal of Marriage and the Family*, **31**, 271–280.
28. REISS, P. J. (1963). The extended kinship system: correlates of and attitudes on frequency of interaction. *Journal of Marriage and the Family*, **24**, 333–339.
29. ROBINS, L. N., and TOMANEC, M. (1962). Closeness to blood relatives outside the immediate family. *Journal of Marriage and the Family*, **24**, 340–346.
30. ROSSI, A. S. (1964). Equality between the sexes: an immodest proposal. *Daedalus* [*The Woman in America*], **93**, 607–652.
31. ROSSI, A. S. (1965). Naming children in middle-class families. *American Sociological Review*, **30**, 499–513.
32. SAFILIOS-ROTHSCHILD, C. (1969). Family sociology or wives' family sociology? A cross-cultural examination of decision-making. *Journal of Marriage and the Family*, **31**, 290–301.
33. SCHULZ, D. A. (1969). *Coming Up Black: Patterns of Ghetto Socialization*. Englewood Cliffs, N.J.: Prentice-Hall.
34. SEARS, R. R., MACCOBY, E. E., and LEVIN, H. (1957). *Patterns of Child Rearing*. Evanston, Ill.: Row, Peterson.
35. SEELEY, J. R., SIM, R. A., and LOOSLEY, E. W. (1956). *Crestwood Heights*. New York: Basic Books.
36. SPIRO, M. E. (1956). *Kibbutz: Venture in Utopia*. New York: Schocken.
37. STREIB, G. F., and ORBACH, H. L. (1967). Aging. In *The Uses of Sociology*, p. 628, ed. Lazarsfeld, P. F., Sewell, W. H., and Wilensky, H. L. New York: Basic Books.
38. TAVUCHIS, N. (1968). *An Exploratory Study of Kinship and Mobility Among Second Generation Greek-Americans*. Ph.D. Dissertation, Columbia University.
39. TAVUCHIS, N. (1970). Mobility and family: problems and prospects. In *Clara Brown Arny Symposium on Family Values*, Minneapolis, 1970. Minneapolis: University of Minnesota Press. In press.
40. VINCENT, C. (1961). *Unmarried Mothers*, pp. 3–5. New York: Free Press (Macmillan Co.).
41. WILLMOTT, P., and YOUNG, M. (1960). *Family and Class in a London Suburb*. London: Routledge & Kegan Paul.

Discussion
1. SINGTON, D. (ed.) (1965). *Psychosocial Aspects of Adolescent Drug-taking.* Oxford: Pergamon.
2. WEISS, R. S. (1970). *The Contributions of an Organization of Single Parents to the Well-being of its Members.* Working paper, Laboratory of Community Psychiatry, Harvard Medical School.
3. WEISS, R. S. (1971). *Social Ties: the relationships of female heads of household in low-income circumstances.* In preparation.

3: PARENTAL RESPONSIBILITY FOR ADOLESCENT MATURITY
DEREK MILLER

1. BETTELHEIM, B. (1969). *Children of the Dream.* New York: Norton.
2. BOWLBY, J. (1969). *Attachment and Loss.* Vol. 1: *Attachment.* London: Hogarth Press and The Institute of Psychoanalysis.
3. ERIKSON, E. H. (1968). *Identity: Youth and Crime,* New York: Norton.
4. FOX, R. (1967). *Kinship and Marriage.* Harmondsworth: Penguin Books.
5. GOODALL, J. (1965). Chimpanzees of the Gombe Stream Reserve. In *Primate Behaviour,* pp. 425–473, ed, DeVore, I. New York: Holt, Rinehart & Winston.
6. MILLER, D. (1969). *The Age Between.* London: Cornmarket-Hutchinson.
7. PINCHBECK, J., and HEWITT, M. (1970). *Children in English Society,* Vol. 1. London: Routledge & Kegan Paul.
8. TREVELYAN, G. M. (1967). *English Social History.* Harmondsworth: Penguin Books.
9. YOUNG, M., and WILLMOTT, P. (1957). *Family and Kinship in East London.* London: Routledge & Kegan Paul.

Discussion
1. BELL, C. (1969). *Middle Class Families.* London: Routledge & Kegan Paul.
2. GANS, H. (1967). *Levittowners.* New York: Random House.
3. JUROVSKY, A. (1968). At the *International Conference on Social Psychology,* Prague, 1968. (Unpublished paper).
4. KANDEL, D., LESSER, G., ROBERTS, G. C., and WEISS, R. S. (1968). *Adolescents in Two Societies.* Harvard University: Laboratory of Human Development.
5. YOUNG, M., and WILLMOTT, P. (1957). *Family and Kinship in East London.* London: Routledge & Kegan Paul.
6. WILLMOTT, P., and YOUNG, M. (1960). *Family and Class in a London Suburb.* London: Routledge & Kegan Paul.

4: FUTURE FAMILY PATTERNS AND SOCIETY
F. H. M. RAVEAU

1. BASTIDE, R. (1960). *Les religions africaines au Bresil: vers une sociologie des interpénétrations de civilisations.* Paris: Presses Universitaires de France.
2. KLINEBERG, O., and ZAVALLONI, M. T. (1969). *Nationalism and Tribalism among African Students.* Paris: Mouton.
3. LANTERNARI, V. (1962). *Religions des peuples opprimés.* Paris: Maspero.
8*

4. LAUWE, P. H. CHOMBART DE (1965). *Essais de sociologie*, 1952–1964. [*L'évolution de la vie sociale*]. Paris: Ouvrières.
5. MORIN, F. (1970). *Les Shipibos: trois siècles d'ethnocide.* Colloque international sur l'ethnocide. Paris: C.N.R.S.
6. RAVEAU, F. H. M. (1966, 1968, 1969). *Les Africains en France.* Paris: Ecole Pratique des Hautes Etudes.

Discussion

1. BABCHUCK, N., and BATES, A. P. (1963). The primary relations of middle-class couples. *American Sociological Reviews*, **28**, 377–384.
2. BRILL, A. A. (1932). *Psychoanalytic Quarterly*, **1**, 7.
3. DEAG, J. (1971). In preparation.
4. FOGARTY, M., RAPOPORT, R., and RAPOPORT, R. N. (1970). *Careers, Families and Roles.* London: Allen & Unwin. In press.
5. HUXLEY, A. L. (1955). *Brave New World.* Harmondsworth: Penguin Books. [First published with foreword 1950.]
6. ITANI, J. (1959). Paternal care in the wild Japanese monkey. *Primates*, **4** (2), 11–66.
7. KALOGERAKIS, M. G. (1963). The role of olfaction in sexual development: *Psychosomatic Medicine*, **25**, 420–432.
8. KUMMER, H. (1968). *Social Organization of Hamadryas Baboons.* Basle: Karger.
9. MEAD, M. (1939). *From the South Seas.* New York: Morrow.
10. MEAD, M., and WOLFENSTEIN, M. (1955). *Childhood in Contemporary Cultures.* Chicago, Ill.: University of Chicago Press.

5: MARRIAGE AND THE FAMILY

R. WEISS

1. ADAMS, B. N. (1968). *Kinship in an Urban Setting.* Chicago: Markham.
2. BURGESS, W., and LOCKE, H. J. (1945). *The Family.* New York: American Book Company.
3. DUNCAN, O. D. (1969). Social forecasting, the state of the art. *The Public Interest*, No. 17, 88–118.
4. FOSTER, H. H. (1969). The future of family law. *Annals of The American Academy of Political and Social Science*, **383**, 129–144.
5. FREED, D. J., and FOSTER, H. H., JR. (1969). Divorce American style. *Annals of The American Academy of Political and Social Science*, **383**, 71–88.
6. FREEDMAN, R., and COOMBS, L. (1966). Child spacing and family economic position. *American Sociological Review*, **31**, 631–648.
7. HOLLINGSHEAD, B. (1950). Class differences in family stability. *Annals of the American Academy of Political and Social Science*, **162**, 39–46.
8. KEPHART, W. A. (1955). Occupational level and marital disruption. *American Sociological Review*, **20**, 456–465.
9. LINDSEY, B. B., and EVANS, W. (1927). *The Companionate Marriage.* New York: Boni and Liveright.
10. PARKE, R., JR. (1969). *The Bureau's Role in Social Indicators.* Springfield, Va.: U.S. Department of Commerce.
11. PARKE, R., JR., and GLICK, P. C. (1967). Prospective changes in the marriage and the family. *Journal of Marriage and the Family*, **29**, 249–256.
12. RAPOPORT, R., and RAPOPORT, R. N. (1969). The dual career family. *Human Relations*, **22**, 3–30.

13. SUSSMAN, M. B. (1965). Empirical studies in the United States: relationships of adult children with their parents in the United States. [In *Social Structure and the Family: Generational Relations*, part III, ed. Shanas, E., and Streib, G. F. Englewood Cliffs, N.J.: Prentice-Hall.
14. U.S. BUREAU OF THE CENSUS (89th Edition, 1968). *Statistical Abstract of the United States*. Washington, D.C.
15. WEISS, R. S., and SAMELSON, N. M. (1958). Social roles of American women: their contribution to a sense of usefulness and importance. *Marriage and Family Living*, **20**, 358–366.

Discussion

1. GANDHI, MAHATMA (1927, 1929). *My Experiments with Truth*, 2 vols. Ahmadabad: Navjivan Press.
2. HUNT, N. (1961). *Two Early Political Associations*. London: Oxford University Press.
3. NADLER, E. B. (1968). Social therapy of a Civil Rights organization. *Journal of Applied Behavioural Science*, **4**, 281–298.
4. ROBERTSON, D. B. (ed.) (1968). *Voluntary Association*. Richmond Va.: John Knox Press.
5. SMITH, M. G. (1962). *West Indian Family Structure*. St. Louis, Mo.: Washington University Press.
6. WEBER, M. (1958). *The Protestant Ethic and the Spirit of Capitalism*. New York: Scribner.

6: ENVIRONMENTAL PLANNING AND ITS INFLUENCE ON THE FAMILY

SU ROGERS

1. THE CENTRE FOR LAND USE AND BUILT FORM STUDIES, UNIVERSITY OF CAMBRIDGE. [For preliminary studies see, MARCH, L. (1967). *RIBA Journal*, **74**, 334–337.]
2. CHERMAYEFF, S., and ALEXANDER, C. (1963). *Community and Privacy*. New York: Doubleday.
3. FANNING, D. M. (1967). Families in Flats. *British Medical Journal*, **4**, 382–386.
4. HOWARD, E. (1898). *Tomorrow a Peaceful Path to Real Reform*. [Now as: (1902). *Garden Cities of Tomorrow*, ed. Osborn, F. J. London: Faber.]
5. PARKER MORRIS REPORT (1961). *Homes for Today and Tomorrow*. Ministry of Housing and Local Government. London: H.M.S.O.
6. YOUNG, M., and WILLMOTT, P. (1957). *Family and Kinship in East London*. London: Routledge & Kegan Paul.

Discussion

1. BANFIELD, E. C., and BANFIELD, L. F. (1958). *The Moral Basis of Backward Society*. Chicago: Free Press of Glencoe.
2. BRADBURN, N. M., and CAPLOVITZ, D. (1965). *Reports on Happiness*. Chicago: Aldine.
3. CALHOUN, J. B. (1962). Population Density and Social Pathology. *Scientific American*, **206**, 139–148.
4. DURKHEIM, E. (1952). *Suicide*. London: Routledge & Kegan Paul.

5. GURN, G., VEROFF, J., and FELD, S. (1960). *Americans View their Mental Health.*
   New York: Basic Books.
6. HALL, E. T. (1966). *The Hidden Dimension.* New York: Doubleday.
7. LASLETT, P. (1965). *The World we have Lost.* London: Methuen.
8. TURNBULL, C. (1966). *Wayward Servants.* London: Eyre & Spottiswoode.

7: THE FAMILY AND THE LAW IN 1970
O. M. STONE

1. BAXTER V. BAXTER [1948] A.C. 274.
2. Cmd. 9248 (1954). Report of the departmental (Hurst) committee on the
   Adoption of Children. London: H.M.S.O.
3. Cmd. 9678 (1956). Report of the Royal Commission on Marriage and
   Divorce. London: H.M.S.O.
4. Cmnd. 2742 (1965). The Child, the Family and the Young Offender. London:
   H.M.S.O.
5. Cmnd. 3051 (1966). Report of the (Russell) Committee on the Law of Succession in relation to illegitimate persons. London: H.M.S.O.
6. Cmnd. 3065 (1966). Social Work and the Community (Scotland). London:
   H.M.S.O.
7. Cmnd. 3342 (1967). Report of the (Latey) Committee on the Age of Majority.
   London: H.M.S.O.
8. Cmnd. 3448 (1967). Report of the (Perks) Departmental Committee on Criminal
   Statistics. London: H.M.S.O.
9. Cmnd. 3601 (1968). Children in Trouble. London: H.M.S.O.
10. Cmnd. 3684 (1968). Report of the (Adams) Committee on Civil Judicial Sta-
    tistics.
11. Cmnd. 3703 (1968). Report of the (Seebohm) Committee on Local Authority
    and Allied Personal Services. London: H.M.S.O.
12. Cmnd. 4112 (1968). Civil Judicial Statistics for the year 1968. London:
    H.M.S.O.
13. GARDINER, BARON OF KITTISFORD (1966–67). House of Lords Debates vol. 280,
    col. 774.

Discussion

1. ASPINALL V. ASPINALL (1967). London: *The Times,* 23 February.
2. FORTES, M. (1949). *The Web of Kinship among the Tallensi,* p. 101. London:
   Oxford University Press.
3. Law Commission (1965). Blood Tests and the Proof of Paternity in Civil Proceedings. Law Comm. No. 16, para. 5. London: H.M.S.O.
4. Law Commission (1968). The Interpretation of the Statutes. Law Comm. No. 21.
   London: H.M.S.O.
5. SOWA V. SOWA [1961] P. 70.

8: BIOLOGICAL REGULATION OF REPRODUCTION
ANNE McLAREN

1. AUSTIN, C. R. (1969). Variations and anomalies in fertilization. In *Fertilization:
   Comparative Morphology, Biochemistry and Immunology,* Vol. 2, ed. Metz, C. B.,
   and Monroy, A. New York: Academic Press.

2. CHANG, M. C. (1968). *In vitro* fertilization of mammalian eggs. *Journal of Animal Science*, **27**, suppl. 1, 15–22.
3. COMFORT, A. (1961). *Come Out to Play*. London: Eyre & Spottiswoode.
4. EDITORIAL (1969). Cloning and the Jockey Club. *Nature, London*, **222**, 210.
5. EDWARDS, R. G., BAVISTER, B. D., and STEPTOE, P. C. (1969). Early stages of fertilization *in vitro* of human oocytes matured *in vitro*. *Nature, London*, **221**, 632–635.
6. GERMAN, J. (1968). Mongolism, delayed fertilization and human sexual behaviour. *Nature, London*, **217**, 516–518.
7. GRAHAM, C. F. (1970). Parthenogenetic mouse blastocysts. *Nature, London*, **226**, 165–167.
8. KERR, M. G., and McLAREN, A. (1970). Egg transfer. *Science Journal*, **6**, 51–56.
9. LAWICK-GOODALL, J. VAN (1968). The behaviour of free-living chimpanzees in the Gombe Stream Reserve. *Animal Behaviour Monographs*, **1**, 161–311.
10. McLAREN, A., and BOWMAN, P. (1969). Mouse chimaeras derived from fusion of embryos differing by nine genetic factors. *Nature, London*, **224**, 238–240.
11. MICHAEL, R. P., and ZUMPE, D. (1970). Rhythmic changes in the copulatory frequency of rhesus monkeys (*Macaca mulatta*) in relation to the menstrual cycle and a comparison with the human cycle. *Journal of Reproduction and Fertility*, **21**, 199–201.
12. MILLER, D. (1970). This volume, pp. 25–32.
13. SCHELLEN, A. M. C. M. (1957). *Artificial Insemination in the Human*. Amsterdam: Elsevier.
14. SMITH, T. B. (1961). Et dona ferentes. *Juridical Review*, **6**, 179–183.
15. SWYER, G. I. M. (ed.) (1970). Control of human fertility. *British Medical Bulletin*, **26**, 1–91.
16. TARKOWSKI, A. K., WITKOWSKA, A., and NOWICKA, J. (1970). Experimental parthenogenesis in the mouse. *Nature, London*, **226**, 162–165.
17. UDRY, J. R., and MORRIS, N. M. (1968). Distribution of coitus in the menstrual cycle. *Nature, London*, **220**, 593–596.
18. WEISMAN, A. I. (1947). Studies on human artificial insemination. *Western Journal of Surgery, Obstetrics and Gynecology*, **55**, 348–51.

Discussion

1. SNYDER, R. G. (1961). The sex ratio of offspring of pilots of high performance military aircraft. *Human Biology*, **33**, 1–10.
2. WESTOFF, C. F., ROBERT, G., POTTER, J. M., PHILIP, C. S., and ELIOT, G. M. (1961). *Family Growth in Metropolitan America*. Princeton, N.J.: Princeton University Press.

9: THE DEVELOPMENT OF CONTRACEPTION: PSYCHODYNAMIC CONSIDERATIONS

T. SJÖVALL

1. ELLIS, A., and ABARBANEL, A. (1961). *The Encyclopaedia of Sexual Behaviour*, p. 406. New York: Hawthorne Books.
2. HIMES, N. E. (1963). *Medical History of Contraception*. New York: Gamut Press.
3. MEAD, M. (1969). At *VII Nobel Symposium*, Saltsjöbaden, Stockholm. In *Dagens Nyheter*, 16th October.

4. MILLER, P. R. (1970). Social activists and social change: the Chicago demonstrations. *Am. J. Psychiat.*, **126**, 1752–1759.
5. WRIGHT, H. (1968). *Sex and Society*, p. 91. London: Allen & Unwin.
6. ZETTERBERG, H. (1969). *Om sexuallivet i Sverige* (On Sex Life in Sweden). Stockholm: Statens Offentliga Utredningar.

Discussion
1. CARTER, C. O. (1969). An ABC of Medical Genetics, *Lancet*, **1**, 1203–1206.
2. DAVIS, K. (1967). Population policy: will current programs succeed? *Science*, **158**, 730–739.
3. HUXLEY, A. L. (1955). *Brave New World*. Harmondsworth: Penguin Books. [First published with foreword, 1950.]
4. KIRK, R. (1964). *Shared Fate*. New York: Free Press (Macmillan Co.).
5. KITTSON, R. H. (pseudonym) (1968). *Orphan Voyage*. New York: Vantage Press.
6. LAING, R. D. (1967). *The Politics of Experience*, p. 64. New York: Ballantine.
7. MARCUSE, H. (1964). *One-Dimensional Man*, p. 14. Boston: Beacon Press.
8. ROPER, M. (1969). In *China Profile*, pp. 113–135, ed. Terrill, R. G. New York: Friendship Press.
9. WRIGHT, H. (1968). *Sex and Society*. London: Allen & Unwin.

10: CHANGES IN CONCEPTS OF PARENTHOOD
JOHN AND ELIZABETH NEWSON

1. BERNSTEIN, B. (1970). Education cannot compensate for society. *New Society*, **15**, no. 387, 344–347. [Published in shorter form in Rubinstein, D., and Stoneman, C. (ed.) (1970). *Education and Democracy*. Harmondsworth: Penguin Books.]
2. JACKSON, B. (1968). Going through the mill. Manchester: *The Guardian*, 20th December.
3. NEWSON, J., and NEWSON, E. (1963). *Infant Care in an Urban Community*. London: George Allen & Unwin: Chicago: Aldine.
4. NEWSON, J., and NEWSON, E. (1967). The pattern of the family in modern society. *Public Health*, **81**, 176–190.
5. NEWSON, J., and NEWSON, E. (1968). *Four Years Old in an Urban Community*. London: Allen & Unwin; Chicago: Aldine.

Discussion
1. HIMMELWEIT, H. T., and SWIFT, B. (1969). A model for the understanding of school as a socializing agent. In *Trends and Issues in Developmental Psychology*, ed. Mussen, P., Langer, J., and Covington, M. New York: Holt, Rinehart & Winston.
2. IMANISHI, K. (1957). Social behaviour in Japanese monkeys. *Psychologia*, **1**, 47–54.

11: CHANGING TRENDS IN CHILD DEVELOPMENT
E. ROSSI, AND N. HERSCHKOWITZ

1. AICARDI, G., and RUGIATI, S. (1965). Osservazioni sul peso di neonati a Sassari dal 1933 al 1963. *Minerva paediatrica*, **17**, 936–942.

2. BENASSI GRAFFI, E. (1965). Ricerche sull'età media di comparsa della puberta negli ultimi 100 anni. *Minerva paediatrica*, **17**, 1136–1140.
3. CHASE, H. P., DORSEY, J., and McKHANN, G. M. (1967). The effect of malnutrition on the synthesis of a myelin lipid. *Pediatrics*, **40**, 551–559.
4. DUBOS, R., SAVAGE, D., and SCHAEDLER, R. (1966). Biological freudianism. *Pediatrics*, **38**, 789–800.
5. MCILWAIN, H. (ed.) (1955). In *Biochemistry and the Central Nervous System*, p. 179. London: Churchill.
6. PETRI, E. (1935). Untersuchungen zur erbbedingtheit der menarche. *Zeitschrift für Morphologie und Anthropologie*, **33**, 43–48.
7. TANNER, J. M. (1962). *Growth at Adolescence*, 2nd edn. Oxford: Blackwell Scientific Publications.
8. DE TONI, E., and AICARDI, G. (1965). L'incremento staturale della popolazione maschile in Provincia di Sassari. *Minerva paediatrica*, **17**, 1857–1863.
9. WINICK, M., and ROSSO, P. (1969). Head circumference and cellular growth of the brain in normal and marasmic children. *Journal of Pediatrics*, **74**, 774–778.
10. ZEMAN, F. J., and STANBROUGH, E. C. (1969). Effect of maternal protein deficiency on cellular development in the fetal rat. *Journal of Nutrition*, **99**, 274–282.

Discussion

1. DARWIN, C. (1946). *The Descent of Man.* Thinker's Library Edition. London: Watts. [First published 1871.]
2. GALTON, F. (1963). *Hereditary Genius: An inquiry into its laws and consequences.* Meridian Books. Gloucester, Mass.: Smith. [First published 1869.]
3. MARK, H. J. (1962). Elementary thinking and the classification of behaviour. *Science*, **135**, 75–87.
4. MORRIS, D. (1962). *The Biology of Art.* London: Methuen.
5. STOCK, M. B., and SMYTHE, P. M. (1963). Does undernutrition during infancy inhibit brain growth and subsequent intellectual development? *Archives of Disease in Childhood*, **38**, 546.
6. TANNER, J. M. (1962). *Growth at Adolescence*, 2nd edn. Oxford: Blackwell Scientific Publications.
7. TERMAN, L. M. (1925). Mental and physical traits of a thousand gifted children. In *Genetic Studies of Genius*, Vol. 1. Stanford. Cal.: Stanford University Press.

12: THE MAKING OF THE MODERN FAMILY

RONALD FLETCHER

1. ADAMS, J. L. (1970). This volume, pp. 135–136.
2. BLYTHE, R. (1969). *Akenfield: Portrait of an English Village.* London: Allen Lane, The Penguin Press.
3. COMTE, A. (1852). *System of Positive Polity.* Vol. 2: *Social Statics,* chap. 3. London: Longmans Green.
4. COOLEY, C. H. (1964). *Human Nature and the Social Order.* New York: Schocken. [First published 1902.]
5. COOLEY, C. H. (1962). *Social Organization.* New York: Schocken. [First published 1909.]
6. DURKHEIM, E. (1933). *The Division of Labour in Society.* New York: Macmillan. [First published 1893.]

7. FLETCHER, R. (1966). *The Family and Marriage in Britain.* Harmondsworth: Penguin Books.
8. FLETCHER, R. (1971). *The Making of Sociology.* London: Michael Joseph.
9. FOX, R. (1970). This volume, pp. 1–8.
10. FREUD, S. (1922). *Group Psychology and the Analysis of the Ego.* London: Hogarth Press. [First published 1921.]
11. GIDDINGS, F. H. (1898). *The Elements of Sociology.* New York: Macmillan.
12. GISSING, G. (1903). *The Private Papers of Henry Ryecroft.* London: Constable.
13. GORER, G. (1970). Survey on sex and marriage. London: *The Sunday Times*, 15th, 22nd and 29th March.
14. HENDRICKSE, R. (1970). This volume, pp. 133–134, 137.
15. HIMMELWEIT, H. (1970). This volume, pp. 151–153, 155–156.
16. HOBHOUSE, L. T. (1951). *Morals in Evolution*, chaps. 4–5. London: Chapman & Hall. [First published 1906.]
17. LASLETT, P. (1965). *The World We Have Lost.* London: Methuen.
18. LE PLAY, F. (1855). *Les Ouvriers Européens.*
19. MCDOUGALL, W. (1948). *An Introduction to Social Psychology.* London: Methuen. [First published 1908.]
20. MAINE, H. (1913). *Ancient Law.* London: Routledge. [First published 1861.] See also: (1874). *The Early History of Institutions*, and (1871). *Village Communities.*
21. MALINOWSKI, B. (1944). *A Scientific Theory of Culture*, chap. 10. Chapel Hill: University of North Carolina Press.
22. MARX, K. (1961). *Economic and Philosophic Manuscripts of* 1844, pp. 100–101. London: Lawrence & Wishart.
23. MEAD, G. H. (1965). In *George Herbert Mead on Social Psychology*, pp. 5–7, ed. Strauss, A. Chicago: University of Chicago Press.
24. MILLER, D. H. (1970). This volume, pp. 25–32.
25. NEWSON, J. (1970). This volume, pp. 139–151.
26. PARETO, V. (1966). *Vilfredo Pareto: Sociological Writings.* London: Pall Mall Press.
27. RADCLIFFE-BROWN, A. R. (1952). *Structure and Function in Primitive Society.* London: Cohen & West. See also: (1964). *A Natural Science of Society.* New York: Free Press (Macmillan Co.).
28. RAPOPORT, R. (1970). This volume, pp. 45–46, 48–49.
29. ROGERS, S. (1970). This volume, pp. 69–74.
30. SEEBOHM REPORT (1968). Report of the Committee on Local Authority and Allied Personal Social Services. London: H.M.S.O. [Cmnd. 3703].
31. SJÖVALL, T. (1970). This volume, pp. 117–127.
32. SPENCER, H. (1876). *Principles of Sociology*, vol. 1, pt. 2. London: Williams & Norgate.
33. STONE, O. (1970). This volume, pp. 87–95.
34. SUMNER, W. G. (1959). *Folkways*, chaps. 9–12. New York: Dover Publications. [First published 1906.]
35. TÖNNIES, F. (1955). *Community and Association.* London: Routledge & Kegan Paul. [First published as *Gemeinschaft und Gesellschaft*, 1887.] See also: (1961). *Custom: An Essay in Social Codes.* New York: Free Press. (Macmillan Co.).
36. WARD, L. (1902). *Dynamic Sociology.* New York: Appleton. See also: (1903). *Pure Sociology.* New York: Macmillan.
37. WEBER, M. (*a*) (1947). *The Theory of Social and Economic Organization.* Chicago: The Free Press of Glencoe. See also: (*b*) (1949). *The Methodology of the Social*

Sciences. Chicago: Free Press of Glencoe, and (*c*) (1932). *From Max Weber*. London: Routledge.
38. WEISS, P. (1970). This volume, pp. 51–61.
39. WESTERMARCK, E. (1921). *The History of Human Marriage*. London: Macmillan. [First published 1891.] See also: (1906). *The Origin and Development of the Moral Ideas*. London: Macmillan, and (1936). *The Future of Marriage in Western Civilization*. London: Macmillan.

Discussion

1. BURKE, E. (1969). *Reflections on the Revolution in France*. Harmondsworth: Penguin Books. [First published 1790.]
2. FROMM, E. (1970). *The Crisis of Psychoanalysis*. New York: Holt, Rinehart & Winston.
3. GOODE, W. J. (1963). *World Revolution and Family Patterns*. New York: Free Press.
4. KOMAROVSKY, M. (1946). The voluntary association of urban dwellers. *American Sociological Review*, **11**, 686–698.
5. PAINE, T. (1970). *The Rights of Man*. Harmondsworth: Penguin Books. [First published 1791–1792.]
6. PAINE, T. (1956). *The Age of Reason*. Baltimore: Ottenheimer. [First published 1794–1796.]
7. TÖNNIES, F. (1955). *Community and Association*. London: Routledge & Kegan Paul.
8. WEBER, M. (1947). *The Theory of Social and Economic Organization*. London: Oxford University Press.
9. WEBER, M. (1958). *The Protestant Ethic and the Spirit of Capitalism*, pp. 181–182. New York: Scribner.

Members of the Symposium

M. L. JANE ABERCROMBIE

Reader in Architectural Education, and Director of the Architectural Education Research Project, Bartlett School of Architecture, University College London. Taught Zoology at Birmingham University; researched for 10 years on selection and training of medical students in Anatomy Department, University College London; Paediatric Research Unit, Guy's Hospital. Main interest in perception, communication and group interaction, and in finding ways of making information about human behaviour available to students so that they see and think more clearly, and act more effectively.

Publications include: Penguin Dictionary of Biology (with M. Abercrombie and D. J. Hickman); Penguin New Biology, 32 vols. (founded and edited); The Anatomy of Judgement, 1960; Visual, Perceptual and Visuomotor Disorders in Cerebral Palsy, 1964.

Married with one son.

J. L. ADAMS

Distinguished Professor of Social Ethics, Andover Newton Theological School, Massachusetts; Chairman, Committee on International Organizations, American Acadamy of Arts and Sciences; Professor Emeritus of Christian Ethics, University of Harvard.

President, American Society of Christian Ethics; Chairman, Committee on Church and State, Civil Liberties Union of Massachusetts; Member, International Council, La Société Européenne de Culture; Member, Massachusetts State Board, American Civil Liberties Union; Member, Massachusetts State Board, Americans for Democratic Action; Fellow and member of Board of Directors, Society for the Arts, Religion and Contemporary Culture.

1936–38, spent over a year in Germany observing underground movements and interviewing Nazi and anti-Nazi leaders and was at one time a prisoner of the Gestapo. Fulbright research scholar, Germany 1962–63; Guest Professor, Marburg University, 1962–63; Observer, Vatican II Council, Rome, 1962; Hibbert Lecturer in British Universities (Oxford, Manchester, Liverpool), 1963. Special interests lie in the fields of application of religion to social life and religion and the arts. In 1969, his former students at Harvard Divinity School formed FREE (Fellowship for Racial and Economic Equality) to combat white racism in the southern region of USA.

Publications include: The Changing Reputation of Human Nature, 1943; Paul Tillich's Philosophy of Culture, Science and Religion, 1965 (now in paperback edition); translations of: The Protestant Era (Paul Tillich, 1948), What is Religion? (Paul Tillich, 1969) and The Dogma of Christ (Erich Fromm, 1965); and numerous articles and translations of articles on social ethics, race relations, the church and society.

Married with three daughters.

TARA ALI BAIG

Vice-President, International Union for Child Welfare, Geneva, since 1966, and of Indian Council for Child Welfare, New Delhi; Chairman, SOS Children's Villages

International (India); Chairman, National Family Planning Awards Committee. Educated University of Dacca. Member of Nehru's Planning Committee, 1938–44; founder Civil Hospitals Emergency Committee; Famine Relief; founder Women's Organization, Pondicherry, 1950; General Secretary National Council of Women and Fundamental Rights Committee, 1958; General Secretary, Indian Council for Child Welfare under Presidentship of Indira Gandhi, 1958–61; Chairman, Child Welfare Plan (3rd); Member, Central Social Welfare Board; Vice-President, International Women's Club, Iran, 1962–65; Director (Social), UNCTAD Conference, New Delhi, 1968; Hon. Chairman, World Congress of Child Welfare, Stockholm, 1969.

Publications include: Articles, radio talks and T.V.; children's books; Moon in Rahu (novel); Women of India (chief editor); and Iran's first Social Welfare Directory.

Married with three sons and a daughter.

M. BORRELLI

Largo San Gennaro a Materdei, Naples; Oratory of St. Philip, Via Duomo 142, Naples.

Ecclesiastic. Educated Major Archdiocesan Seminary, Naples. One of the founders of ONARMO, Naples, 1946; founder of first JOC in Naples, 1947, of IRP, Naples, 1948, of 'The House of the Urchins', Naples, 1950.

Publications include: La Relazione tra il Conservatorio dei Poveri di Gesù Cristo e l'Oratorio di Napoli, 1961; A Streetlamp and the Stars, 1963; I Documenti dell'Oratorio Napoletano, 1964; Lo Scugnizzo (monthly magazine) since 1950.

A. COMFORT

Department of Zoology, University College London; Director, MRC Group on Ageing since 1962.

Lecturer in Physiology, The London Hospital, 1948–51; Nuffield Research Assistant, University College London, 1951–54; Nuffield Research Fellow in the biology of Senescence, University College London, 1954–62. Member of Ciba Foundation symposium on Man and his Future (1963).

Publications include: The Pattern of the Future; Sexual Behaviour in Society; Authority and Delinquency in the Modern State; The Biology of Senescence.

Married with one son.

NAN FAIRBROTHER

27 Weymouth Mews, London W1.

Educated University of London. Writer and lecturer on landscape and land use; is associated with a new international centre for environmental studies now being founded at Beatenberg in Switzerland. Member of the Institute of Landscape Artists.

Publications include: Children in the House, 1954; Men and Gardens, 1956; The Cheerful Day, 1960; The House, 1965; New Lives, New Landscapes, 1970; and numerous articles and book reviews.

Married with two sons.

R. FLETCHER

Formerly Professor and Head of Department of Sociology, University of York, 1964–68, and Visiting Professor, University of Essex, 1968–1969; studied philosophy and economics at Bristol, 1948–51 and sociology at the London School of Economics, 1951–53; Lecturer in Sociology at Bedford College and Birkbeck

College, University of London, 1953–63. Auguste Comte Memorial Lectures, LSE, 1966.

Publications include: Instinct in Man, 1957; Issues in Education, 1960; Human Needs and Social Order, 1965; The Family and Marriage in Britain, 1962 and revised editions; Auguste Comte and the Making of Sociology, 1966. Has now left university life to devote himself to study and writing. 'The Making of Sociology' a large-scale study of sociological theory is to appear in the autumn of 1970.

Married with two sons.

R. Fox

Department of Anthropology, Rutgers University, New Brunswick, since 1967. Graduated in Sociology, London School of Economics; Harvard University, 1957–59; studied Pueblo Indians in New Mexico; taught at University of Exeter and London School of Economics. Fellow: Royal Anthropological Institute, Zoological Society of London, American Anthropological Association. Current interests are largely centred on the implications of research in animal—particularly primate—behaviour for an understanding of human evolution and behaviour.

Publications include: The Keresan Bridge: A Problem in Pueblo Ethnology; Kinship and Marriage: an Anthropological Perspective; contributions to New Society; and various papers on Incest, Witchcraft and curing, and other anthropological topics; television work and broadcasting.

Married with three daughters.

HILDE HIMMELWEIT

Professor of Social Psychology at London School of Economics and Political Science since 1964; and Chairman of the Academic Advisory Council, Open University since 1969.

Graduated in psychology and modern languages, University of Cambridge. Clinical psychologist, Maudsley Hospital; Reader in Psychology, LSE, 1953–64; Director, Nuffield Television Enquiry, 1954–58; Visiting Professor, Department of Psychology, University of California, Berkeley, 1959; Research Consultant, Israeli Instructional Television Trust, 1965–68; Chairman of Research Committee, Open University, on preparatory courses and Member of Planning Committee, 1967–69; Fellow, Centre for the Advanced Study of the Behavioural Sciences, Stanford, 1967; Research Consultant. Inner London Education Authority, 1968.

Publications include: Television and the Child (jointly), 1958; numerous articles and chapters on: television, personality theory and measurement, attitude development and change, socialization, social mobility, school and higher education.

Married with one daughter.

E. R. LEACH

Provost of King's College, Cambridge, since 1966; University Reader in Social Anthropology, since 1957.

Lecturer, later Reader, in Social Anthropology, London School of Economics, 1947–53; Lecturer, Cambridge, 1953–57; Anthropological Field Research, Formosa, 1937; Kurdistan, 1938; Burma, 1939–45; Borneo, 1947; Ceylon, 1954, 1956. Fellow of King's College, Cambridge, 1960–66; Fellow, Center for Advanced Study in Behavioral Sciences, Stanford, 1961. Member, Social Science Research Council, since 1968. Vice-President, Royal Anthropological Institute, 1964–66; B.B.C. Reith Lecturer, 1967. President, British Humanist Association, 1970. Member of Ciba Foundation symposium on Caste and Race (1966).

Publications include: Rethinking Anthropology, 1961; A Runaway World?, 1968; Genesis as a Myth, 1970; Lévi-Strauss, 1970; editor and contributor to various anthropological symposia, and numerous papers in Man, Journal of the Royal Anthropological Institute, New Society, Current Anthropology, etc.

Married with a son and a daughter.

R. G. HENDRICKSE

Senior Lecturer, School of Tropical Medicine and Department of Child Health, University of Liverpool, since 1969. (Special appointment to develop postgraduate courses in tropical paediatrics.)

Staff member McCord Zulu Hospital, Durban, 1949–54; Postgraduate training in Glasgow and Edinburgh, 1955; Senior Registrar, University College Hospital, Ibadan, 1955–57; Lecturer in Paediatrics, University of Ibadan, 1957–62; Professor and Head, Department of Paediatrics, University of Ibadan, 1962–69; Director, Institute of Child Health, University of Ibadan, 1964. Awarded Heinz Fellowship of the British Paediatric Association; and Rockefeller Foundation Fellowship. Special appointments include: Member of Council, University of Ibadan; Advisor of Federal Nigerian Government on various child health problems; Vice-President, Paediatric Association of Nigeria; Member of Advisory and Executive Committees of Institute of African Studies, University of Ibadan; Advisor on African Region to International Foundation for Child Health (New York Inc.). Consultant Editor of Clinical Paediatrics; member of Ciba Foundation study group on Nutrition and Infection (1967).

Married with one son and four daughters.

F. HENRIQUES

Professorial Fellow and Director, Centre for Multi-Racial Studies, University of Sussex, since 1964; and Director, Joint University of the West Indies and University of Sussex Research Centre, Barbados.

Educated London School of Economics and Brasenose College, Oxford. Lecturer in Social Anthropology, University of Leeds, 1948–64. Member of Ciba Foundation symposium on Caste and Race (1966).

Publications include: Family and Colour in Jamaica, 1953, rev. edn. 1968; Jamaica, Land of Wood and Water, 1957; Coal is Our Life (with N. Dennis and C. Slaughter), 1956; Love in Action, 1959; Prostitution and Society, Vol. I, 1962, Vol. II, 1963, Vol. III, 1967. Contributions to: Handbook of Latin-American Studies, 1966; Ciba Foundation Report on Immigration, 1966; Encyclopaedia Britannica, 1966; and various papers in sociological journals.

Married with three sons.

ANNE MCLAREN

Senior Principal Scientific Officer, Agricultural Research Council Unit of Animal Genetics, University of Edinburgh.

University of London, financed by research grants from Agricultural Research Council, 1952–59; Agricultural Research Council Unit of Animal Genetics, University of Edinburgh, since 1959. Special interests: genetics, embryology, reproductive physiology, biochemistry and immunology of the mouse, especially that aspect of the embryonic environment represented by the mother. Until recently, edited Advances in Reproductive Physiology. Member of Ciba Foundation symposia on Congenital Malformations (1960) and on Preimplantation Stages of Pregnancy (1965).

Married with one son and two daughters.

D. H. MILLER

Professor of Psychiatry, University of Michigan, Ann Arbor, since 1969.
Graduate of Leeds University Medical School and of the Menninger School of Psychiatry, Topeka, Kansas, USA: formerly Chairman, Adolescent Unit, Tavistock Clinic, London, 1965; Consultant Psychiatrist, Herts Training School for delinquent boys, Ware; and Consultant Psychotherapist, Broadmoor Hospital. Lectured at the Institute of Criminology and the Institute of Architecture in Cambridge and at universities of London and Sussex. Member: Royal Medico-Psychological Association, American Psychiatric Association and Detroit Psychoanalytic Society; Associate member of the British Psycho-analytic Society.

Publications include: Growth to Freedom, 1966, in USA, 1965; a chapter on The Adolescent in the Family in 'The Dilemma of the Family', Lomas, 1967. The Age Between, Adolescents in a Disturbed Society,1969; and many articles and scientific papers on adolescence, delinquency, and the family.

Married with one son and two daughters.

J. NEWSON

Reader in Child Development, University of Nottingham, where he and his wife, Elizabeth, have founded and now jointly direct their Child Development Research Unit. In 1958, they began a long-term survey to investigate how parents in an urban community feel and behave towards their children, and the different strategies which they adopt in dealing with the many issues which arise in practice as children grow up. The sample comprises some 700 children living in the City of Nottingham and representative of the whole social spectrum.

Publications include: Infant Care in an Urban Community, 1963; Four Years Old in an Urban Community, 1968; The Family and the Handicapped Child (with Sheila Hewett), 1970

Married with one son and two daughters.

N. W. PIRIE

Head of Biochemistry Department, Rothamsted Experimental Station, Harpenden, since 1947.
Demonstrator in Biochemical Laboratory, Cambridge, 1932–40; Virus Physiologist, Rothamsted Experimental Station, 1940–46. Member of Ciba Foundation symposium on Man and his Future (1963).

Publications include: Scientific papers on various aspects of biochemistry, but especially on separation and properties of macromolecules; articles on viruses, the origins of life, biochemical engineering, and the need for greatly extended research on food production and contraception.

Married with one son.

RHONA RAPOPORT

Senior Social Scientist, Tavistock Institute of Human Relations, since 1969; and Consultant Social Scientist, Political and Economic Planning, since 1967.
Colonial Social Science Research Fellow and Sociologist, East African Institute of Social Research, 1950–52; Assistant Psychologist, Tavistock Clinic, 1952–53; Research Fellow, Radcliffe College, Harvard, 1953–54; Senior Sociologist studying families of psychiatric patients at Belmont Social Rehabilitation Unit, 1954–57; Research Associate, Joint Commission for the Study of Mental Illness and Health, USA, 1957–59; Lecturer on Mental Health, Harvard University School of Public

Health and Medical School, and director of Family Research in the Community Mental Health Programme, 1959–66. Member: Executive Committee of International Scientific Commission on the Family; and Cross-National Family Research Consortium.

Publications include: Jinja Transformed (with C. Sofer); Women and Top Jobs (with Michael Fogarty and Robert Rapoport); and various papers in social science journals on the family. In press: two books on the family, one on family and career and on on the dual career family (with Robert Rapoport).

Married with a son and a daughter.

F. H. M. RAVEAU

Professor in the Faculty of Medicine and Deputy Director of the Charles Richet Centre at the École Pratique des Hautes Études, University of the Sorbonne, Paris.

Qualified in both medicine and anthropology and trained as a psychoanalyst in France and Switzerland. Especial interest is in problems of colour in interethnic relations. Is currently taking part in a joint project with the Centre for Multi-Racial Studies at the University of Sussex.

Is engaged on research into *ethnocide* and also questions of the acculturation in France of three different groups: Africans, Haitians and those from Guadeloupe and Martinique. Goes regularly to Peru for field work among Amazonian Indians. Member of Ciba Foundation symposium on Caste and Race (1966).

Publications: books and articles on interethnic relations and various aspects of social morbidity.

V. REYNOLDS

Lecturer in Anthropology, Department of Sociology, University of Bristol.

Doctoral research on social behaviour of rhesus monkeys, 1961; field research on social behaviour of wild chimpanzees, 1962; Fellow, Center for Advanced Study in the Behavioral Sciences, Stanford, California, 1963. Main interest is in the comparative study of man and the non-human primates.

Publications include: Budongo, a forest and its chimpanzees; The Apes; and articles and papers in anthropological journals.

Married with a son and a daughter.

SU ROGERS

Richard and Su Rogers, Architects. Visiting critic Cambridge School of Architecture and the Architectural Association School of Architecture, since 1967.

Graduated in Sociology, London School of Economics. Postgraduate research at Yale University School of City Planning; Consultant to US Federal Government, Urban Land Institute and Federal Housing Association advising on 'subdivisions'. Represented British Architects at Paris Biennale; Prizewinner of the Ideal Home Exhibition, 'House for Today', 1967; RIBA Award for work of outstanding quality, 1969.

Married with three sons.

E. ROSSI

Qualified in medicine at University of Milan. Trained in Switzerland as a paediatrician and held appointments at the Children's Hospital, Zürich, 1942–50. Visiting scholarships to USA, 1951.

Appointed to Faculty of Medicine, University of Zurich, 1952. Since 1956 Professor and Chairman, Department of Paediatrics, University of Berne. Honorary degrees from University of Brazil and University of Clermont-Ferrand, France. Member of Swiss Committee for Nutrition Problems and a Senate member of the Swiss Academy of Medicine and of the Research Committee. President of the Society of Biochemistry, Berne, 1961–65. President of the Swiss Advisory Board for Medical Teaching, 1967. President of the European Society for Paediatric Research, 1968. President of the Scientific Executive Board of the International Cystic Fibrosis Association, 1969.

Publications include: Books on heart disease and carbohydrate metabolism in children and cystic fibrosis. In Press: Diseases of the Heart in Children (with Professor H. Graham). Editor and contributor to many international paediatric publications.

Married. No children.

T. SJÖVALL

Head, Psychiatric Service, Mental Health Bureau, City of Stockholm, since 1968; President, Swedish Association for Sex Education, since 1964; Member of the Swedish State Commission for Sex Education, since 1964; Member of the Governing Body of the International Planned Parenthood Federation (IPPF), since 1963; Vice-President of the Europe and Near East Region of the IPPF, since 1966; Chairman of the Central Medical Committee of the IPPF, since 1969.

Trained in University of Uppsala Medical School, 1933–40; trained in clinical medicine and psychiatry, 1940–47; Inspector for the mental care of children and youth, Swedish National Board of Health, 1947–49; Rockefeller Fellow, Beth Israel Hospital, Boston, and Boston Psychoanalytic Institute, 1949–51; President of the Swedish Psychoanalytic Society, 1963–67; Founder and first President of the Swedish Association for Group Psychotherapy, 1962–66; Training analyst of the Swedish Psychoanalytic Institute, since 1961.

Publications on psychiatry, psychosomatic medicine, social medicine and sexology.

Married with two sons and a daughter.

OLIVE M. STONE

Reader in Law, London School of Economics and Political Science, University of London, since 1964. Of Gray's Inn, Barrister, 1951.

Former Civil Servant. Assistant lecturer in law LSE, 1950; Lecturer 1952; Reader 1964; Fulbright Scholar Columbia Law School New York, 1965–66; Adviser to Family Law Project of Ontario Law Reform Commission, 1966; Hayter travel grant to Moscow and Leningrad, under Universities Exchange Scheme, May–June 1968; Visiting Professor, Law School of University of Virginia, February to June 1969. Member of Council of Fédération Internationale des Femmes des Carrières Juridiques.

Publications include: 'Commonwealth and Dependencies', Halsbury's Laws of England, 3rd Edn. 1953 (joint editor); 'Family Law', Law Reform Now, 1963 (joint author, chap.); Chapter on Family Law in Annual Survey of Commonwealth Law, 1966; Chapter on the World of Wedlock in 'In Her Own Right', 1968; and articles in various English, American, and German legal and other publications.

N. TAVUCHIS

Assistant Professor of Sociology, College of Arts and Sciences, Cornell University, Ithaca, New York.

Graduate Faculties, Columbia University; Affiliations: American Sociological Association; and American Anthropological Association.

Publications include: Pastors and Immigrants: the Role of a Religious Elite in the Absorption of Norwegian Immigrants; An Exploratory Study of Kinship and Mobility Patterns of Second Generation Greek-Americans (un-published PhD dissertation).

Research in progress: A socio-demographic profile of Greek-Americans in the United States; a cross-cultural analysis of naming patterns and patterns of kinship solidarity; and an historical analysis of the American population: 1900–1970 (with Parker G. Marden).

Married with two sons.

R. S. WEISS

Lecturer in Sociology, Department of Psychiatry, Harvard Medical School, Boston, Massachusetts, since 1964; and Lecturer, Department of City Planning, Massachusetts Institute of Technology, since 1968. Visiting Professor, Department of Sociology, Brandeis University, since 1969. Educated University of Buffalo, New York, and University of Michigan, Ann Arbor. Assistant Study Director, Survey Director, Survey Research Centre, University of Michigan 1951–54; Study Director 1954–57; Assistant Professor, University of Chicago, 1957–60; Visiting Lecturer, General Education, Harvard University, 1960–61; Assistant Professor, Department of Sociology, Brandeis University, 1960–62; Associate Professor Department of Sociology, Brandeis University 1963–68; Member of Task Force on Family Law and Policy, Citizen's Advisory Council on the Status of Women, US Department of Labor, 1966–68.

Publications include: 'Social Roles of American Women: Their Contribution to a Feeling of Usefulness and Importance', Marriage and Family Living (with N. C. Samelson); 'Some Issues on the Future of Leisure', Social Problems (with D. Riesman); 'Work and Automation: Problems and Prospects', Contemporary Social Problems (with D. Riesman). Various papers, including 'Social relationships and the crisis of new parenthood'.

Married with two sons.

INDEX OF AUTHORS*

Numbers in bold type indicate a contribution in the form of a paper; numbers in plain type refer to contributions to the discussions.

* Author and Subject Indexes compiled by Mr. William Hill.

INDEX OF SUBJECTS

Printed by William Clowes & Sons Limited, London, Colchester and Beccles

125268